IMAGES
of America

CHESTERFIELD TOWNSHIP

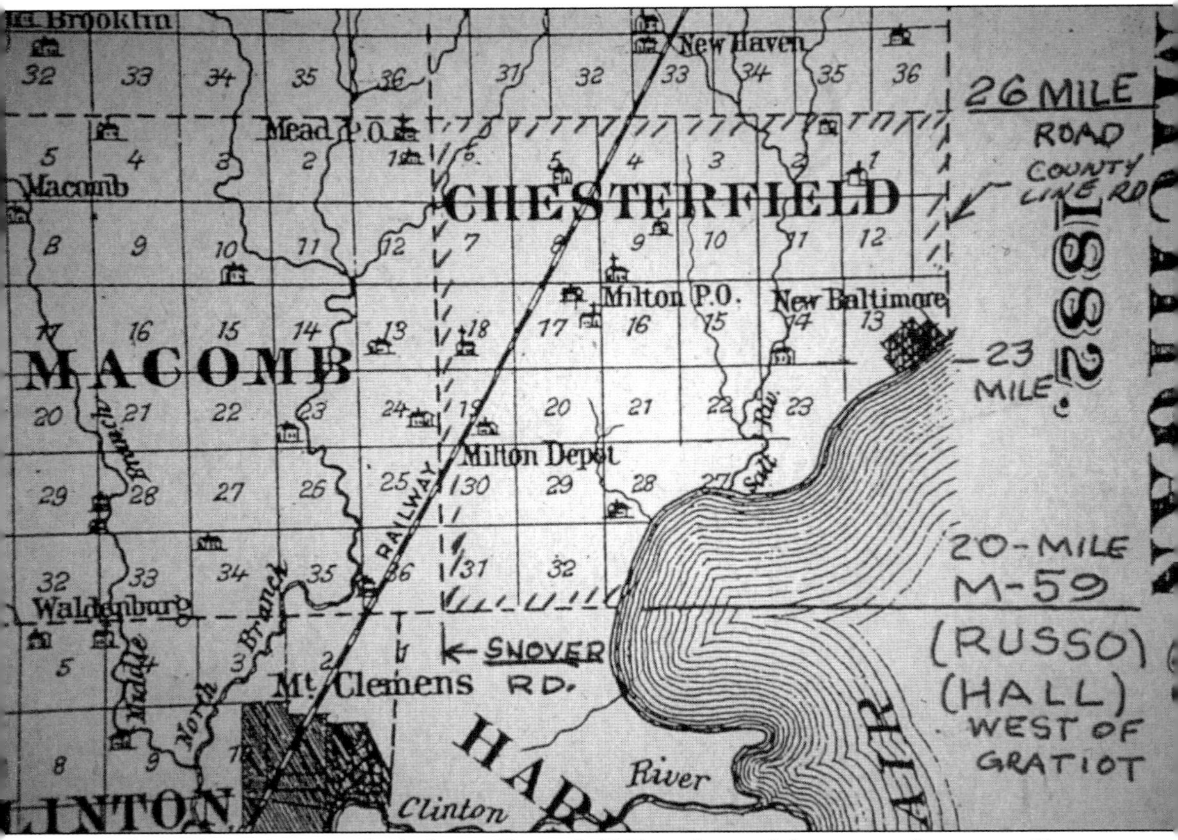

This early-1900s map, which shows Chesterfield Township and the surrounding areas, illustrates that Chesterfield had a few sections swallowed up by Anchor Bay and Lake St. Clair. There are no sections 24, 25, and 26 and also no sections 33–36. (Townships were usually divided into 36 sections.) The map has building icons denoting churches (the crosses) and schools. Many former communities are noted, including Milton at 24 Mile Road.

On the Cover: This is a 1937 photograph taken at Jerome's Corner/Jerry Jo's Restaurant at 23 Mile Road and Gratiot Avenue. Since the 1960s, this intersection has been the busiest corner in the township. The busy crossroads were unfortunately named by State Farm Insurance Company to be one of the 10 most dangerous intersections in the country in the 1990s. This image shows, from left to right, Evelyn, Helen, Jerome A., and Jerome W. Zischerk. (Courtesy of Marie Allemon.)

IMAGES
of America

CHESTERFIELD TOWNSHIP

Alan Naldrett for the
Chesterfield Historical Society

ARCADIA
PUBLISHING

ISBN 978-0-7385-7803-3

Published by Arcadia Publishing
Charleston, South Carolina

Printed in the United States of America

Library of Congress Control Number: 2009943770

For all general information, please contact Arcadia Publishing:
Telephone 843-853-2070
Fax 843-853-0044
E-mail sales@arcadiapublishing.com
For customer service and orders:
Toll-Free 1-888-313-2665

Visit us on the Internet at www.arcadiapublishing.com

This book is dedicated to Bob Mack, for his invaluable assistance, and Geri Mack and Richard Gonyeau, who helped me realize that some of the best stories occurred right down the street!

Contents

ACKNOWLEDGMENTS

I would like to thank Bob Mack, who helped provide the majority of photographs for this book from his vast slide collection. All images, unless otherwise credited, are courtesy of him. I would also like to thank Bob for his assistance in getting the slides scanned and formatted. Also, as far as scanning goes, thanks to Paul Torney for providing essential labor, assistance, and photographs.

For content, there are many predecessors who have provided information about the history of Chesterfield. Foremost among them would be Bernard Trinity, who wrote *Many Yesterdays*, a wonderful history of Chesterfield and its early days. Also instrumental in the gathering of Chesterfield information was Rich Gonyeau and his history columns in the local papers *The Anchor Bay Beacon* and *The Bay Voice*. Karl Mark Pall's research and previous writings were invaluable, and once again thanks must go to Bob Mack, who filled in much of the information for the photographs. George Furton's book *Can't Keep My Feet on the Ground: Life's Memories* provided more information. Also, thanks to Roy and Eileen Rivard of the Chesterfield Township Historical Society for providing early photographs, as well as to Loraine DeMuynck, who bestowed further information and images. Rev. Richard Rickard gave us valuable knowledge on the Weller School, which he attended, as well as general information about the early one-room schoolhouses. Dr. E.J. Rynearson's *The History of the Anchor Bay School System* was a valuable source of information on the early schools of Chesterfield Township.

Thanks to Dolly Allemon, Marion Allemon, Tracy Antrikin, Mary Hortos, Jim Genso, Wilma Henry, the Kraft family, Allie Reynolds, Russell Smith, Tom Pilarowski, Kathy and Duane Vosburg, Deb Walsh, Deanna Kaherl Wolschon, and everybody else who provided information and helped gather photographs.

Finally, I would like to thank my editors, John Pearson and Anna Wilson, and copy editors and proofreaders David A. Castle, Sherrel J. Hissong, and Jessica Mickey for all their efforts on behalf of the book.

The author is donating his royalties from sales of this book to the Chesterfield Township Historical Society.

Introduction

Chesterfield Township, Michigan, came into being in 1842 in a bill passed by the Michigan Legislature called Public Act 57. The area that became Chesterfield Township was carved out of what had been referred to as the lake area of Macomb Township. Although most townships were 32 square miles large, Chesterfield was only given 28; it was said that six of the square miles were underwater. The elders of the township were told to provide a name for the area, and they chose to name it after the very popular noble of England, Philip Dormer Stanhope—a man of great esteem with polished and elegant manners who was also the fourth Lord Chesterfield. Although there were a few Lord Chesterfields, this most famous one lived from 1694 to 1773 and had a number of sayings attributed to him, such as "advice is seldom welcome, and those who need it the most, like it the least," and "an injury is much sooner forgotten than an insult." His quotations were from letters he wrote to his son.

Although named for an Englishman, Chesterfield's earliest inhabitants were the Native Americans, chiefly the Ojibwa/Chippewa tribes. The Native Americans moved into the area 5,000 to 10,000 years ago as the glaciers from the most recent Ice Age receded, forming Lake St. Clair and the many creeks and rivers of the vicinity. An early source stated that the Chesterfield area was not visited much at first except as a burial ground. Many discoveries of large deposits of early Native American mounds containing human remains would appear to support this early legend. Chesterfield is located in Macomb County, which was originally called Pagigendamowinaki (Chippewa for "great burial place of the Indians"). Other early accounts mention the existence of an early Native American village near Lake St. Clair and the Au Vase River.

Around the 1760s, the French began settling in the area. Because they were able to befriend and trade with the Native Americans, the Chesterfield area became the home of many French families who settled in the Salt River area.

The French and Indian War, which ended in 1763, brought English settlers to the Michigan region but did not end the French settlements of the area. The French and Native Americans continued to coexist, as did the British and Native Americans. It was not until Michigan became an official territory in 1805 that the unfortunate actions toward the area's original inhabitants began. In 1807, Native American chiefs were persuaded to relinquish their rights to the area via a treaty they probably did not understand, titled the Treaty of Detroit. This same treaty established two reservations within Chesterfield Township that were used until 1830, when most of the Native Americans were relocated out of the area.

Colorful stories of the early inhabitants remain, including that of Chief Maconce of the Swan Creek Ojibwas convincing the tribe not to follow up with hostilities after the suspicious drunken drowning of their previous chief, Maconce's brother, in nearby Mt. Clemens. The French and English both had their colorful tales, including the moveable schoolhouse of the early French inhabitants and a fabled lost treasure of Englishman Captain Marsac. (It seems he buried it and died before he could retrieve it.)

Chesterfield Township, which survived a massive tornado on May 8, 1964, has had other interesting tales, such as a police chief who was fired for accepting a $10,000 loan from one of the local bars in the 1990s. There are many stories of blind pigs, speakeasies, and rum running during the Prohibition years as well.

Chesterfield Township's present-day role has progressed from its early years as a sparsely settled region to being known at one time as the fastest-growing community in the state of Michigan.

One

The Earliest Inhabitants

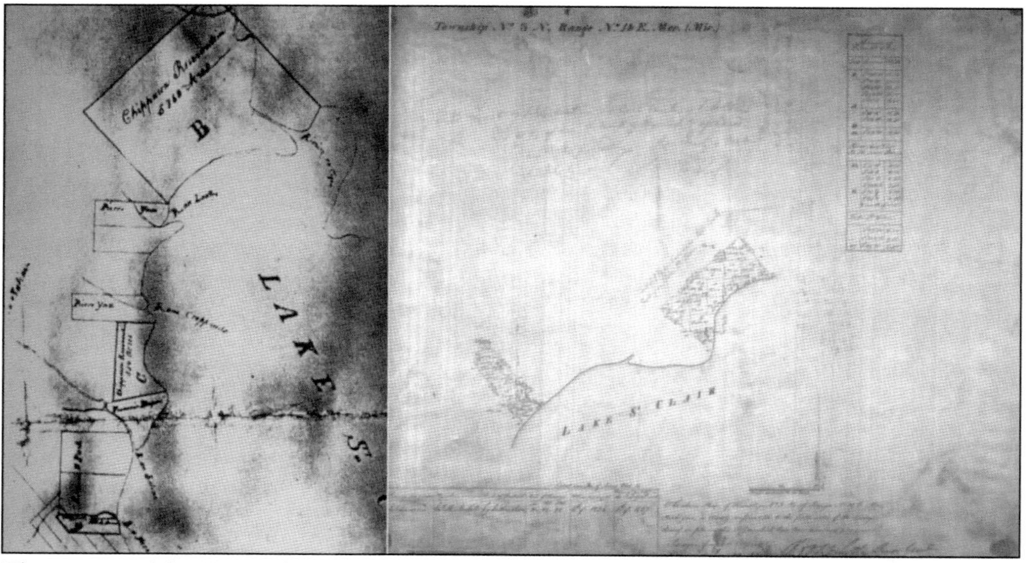

These maps of the Native American reservations in Chesterfield are from the National Archives in Washington. They read, "Plan of the Indian Reservations on Lake St. Clair in the Territory of Michigan. Surveyed in March 1810 . . . Aaron Greely Surveyer [*sic*] of Michigan Territory." The first inhabitants of the Chesterfield Township area were Native American tribes, chiefly the Ojibwas/Chippewa. They mostly lived near the shore of Lake St. Clair and near the banks of the many rivers and streams in the area for over 10,000 years. In 1807, various Native American chiefs surrendered their claims to the lands in southeast Michigan.

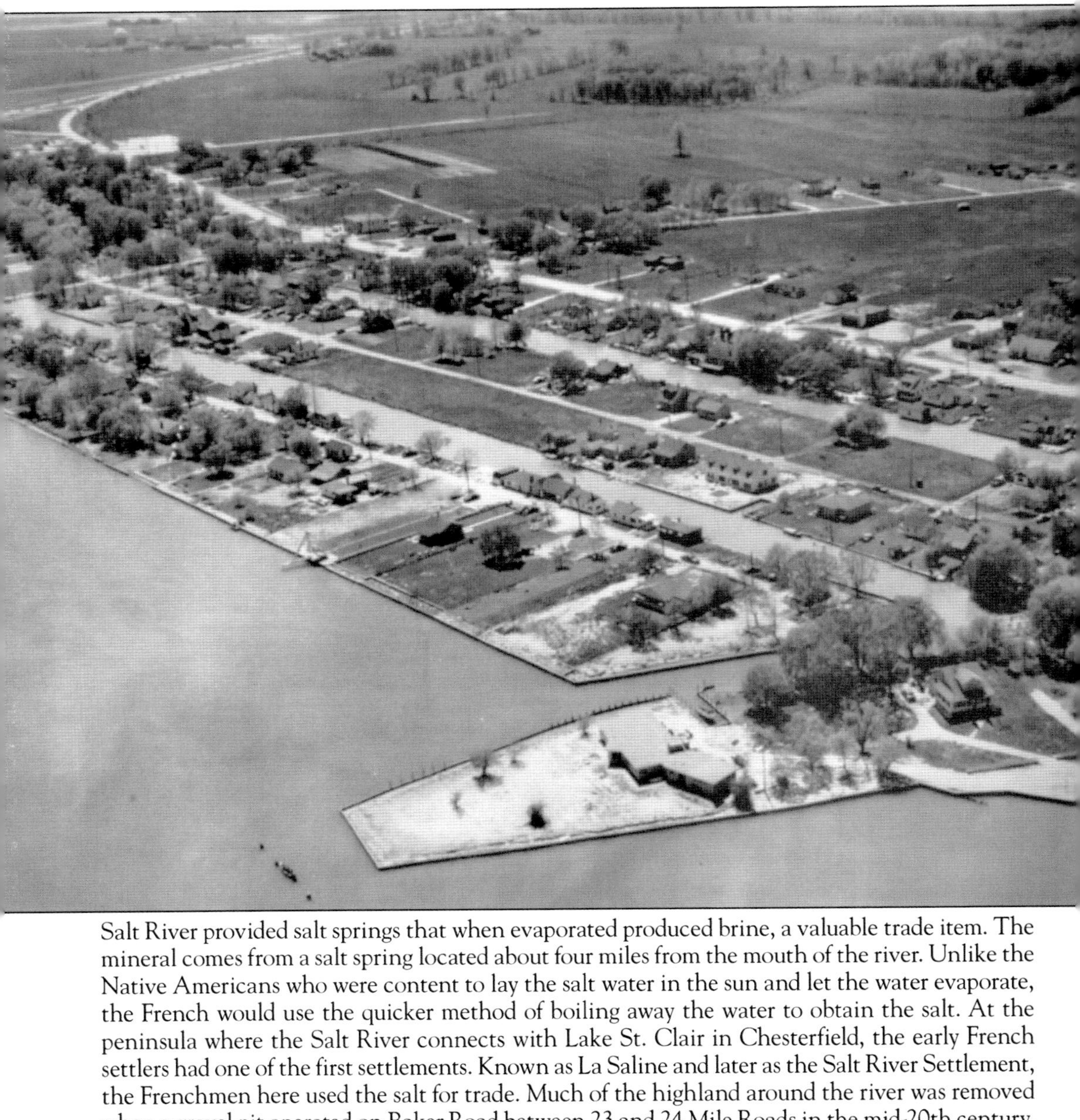

Salt River provided salt springs that when evaporated produced brine, a valuable trade item. The mineral comes from a salt spring located about four miles from the mouth of the river. Unlike the Native Americans who were content to lay the salt water in the sun and let the water evaporate, the French would use the quicker method of boiling away the water to obtain the salt. At the peninsula where the Salt River connects with Lake St. Clair in Chesterfield, the early French settlers had one of the first settlements. Known as La Saline and later as the Salt River Settlement, the Frenchmen here used the salt for trade. Much of the highland around the river was removed when a gravel pit operated on Baker Road between 23 and 24 Mile Roads in the mid-20th century. In the late 1980s, the Salt River Golf Course was built along this area. At one time, around the sixth hole of the course, there was an old house where artifacts such as pottery and an 1840s coin were found. This aerial photograph of the Salt River from the 1950s includes a view of the area that was the original French settlements.

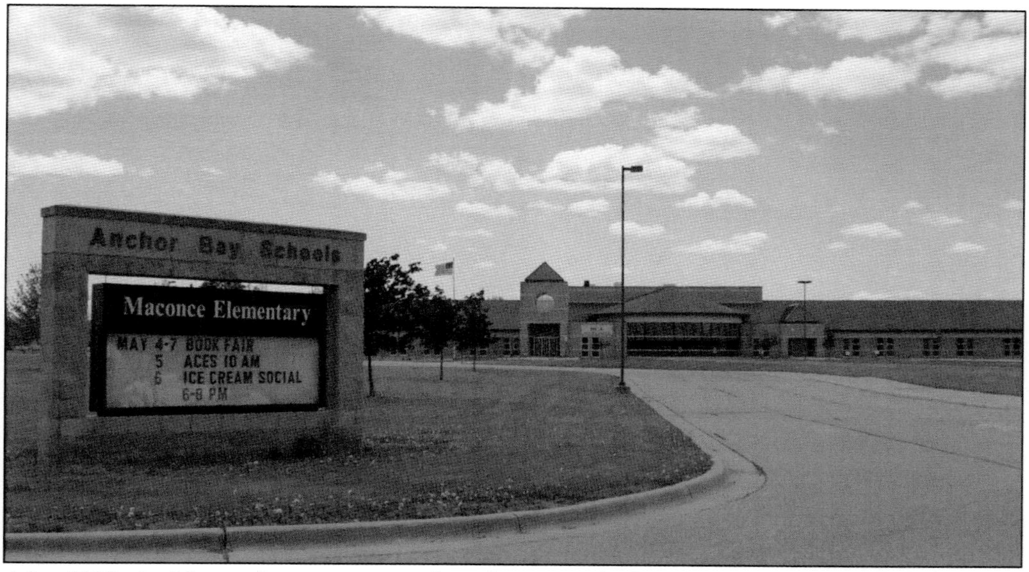

After 1830, the Native Americans were forced to move farther west. Macompte was the chief of the Aux Vase Reservation until succeeded by his son Cum-kum-e-non. When Cum-kum-e-non was given alcohol in Mt. Clemens by the white settlers, he fell in the water and drowned. This almost caused an uprising between the settlers and Native Americans. Cum-kum-e-non's brother Maconce helped ease tensions among the Native Americans and settlers and subsequently became chief. There is now a school in the Anchor Bay School District, pictured above, named for Chief Maconce. The French built earthen huts and developed strip farms, which were long, thin pieces of land with the narrow end near the lake. This allowed access to the available natural waterways for most of the landowners, as pictured by the boundary lines in the plat map below. After the French and Indian War, the English began to control the land until about 1815 when the treaty ending the War of 1812 gave the American colonies control of the area.

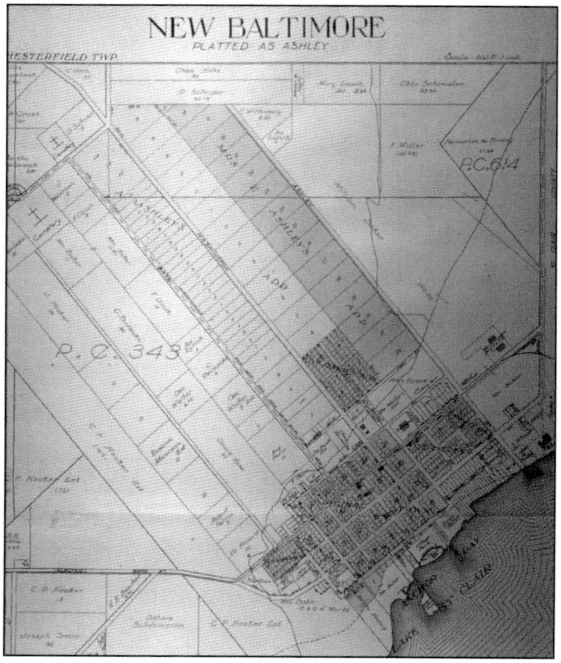

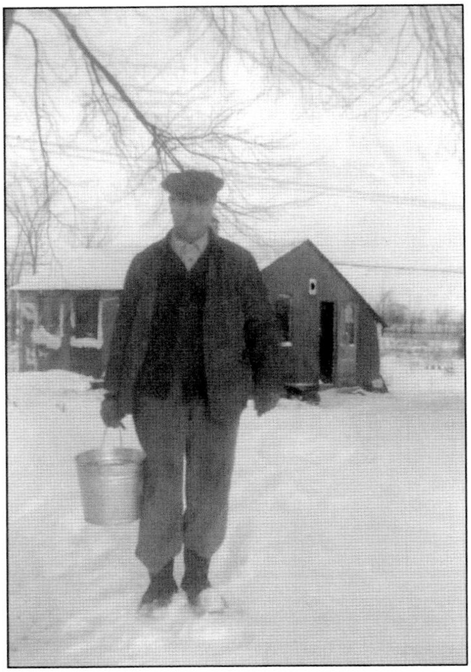

Michigan became a territory in 1805, and larger groups of immigrants began to make their homes in the area. In 1818, Chesterfield was surveyed by William Wampler. New farmers had their land documented, and the first land claims were rerecorded. Side roads off of Gratiot Avenue were constructed. William Allemon, seen here, was an early farmer. (Courtesy of Dolly Allemon.)

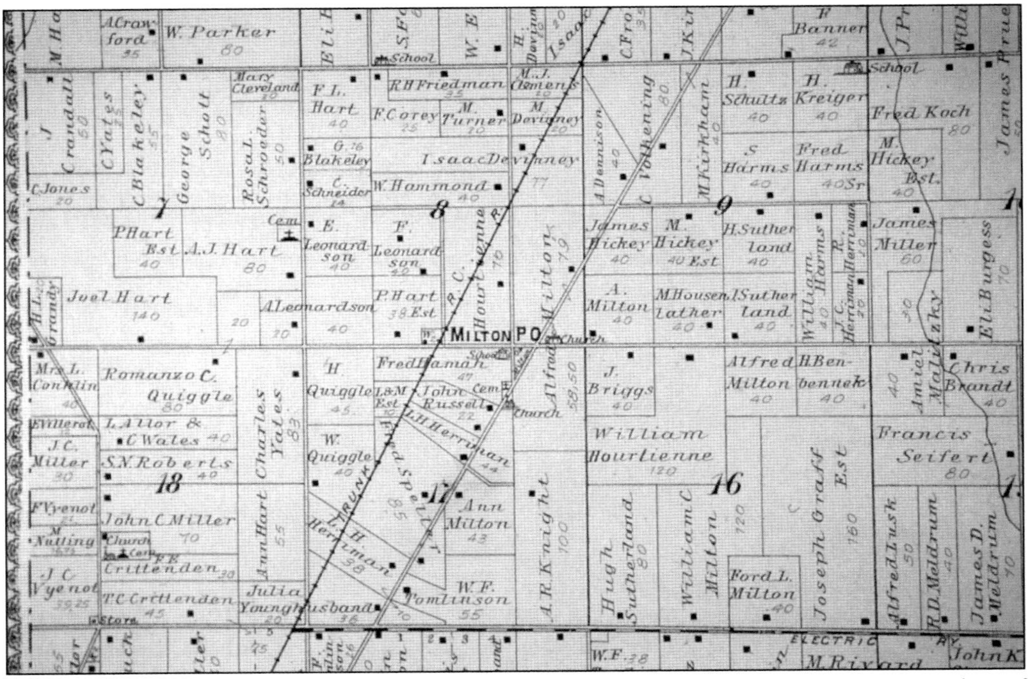

In 1842, via Public Act 57, the Michigan State Legislature officially created the township of Chesterfield. Originally part of Macomb Township, a new township government was formed the same year. Samuel P. Canfield was elected the township supervisor and had an annual salary of $25.62. The first township budget was $75.00. In 1850, Chesterfield's population was 1,002 people, but by 1860 it had more than doubled to 2,157. Log buildings became obsolete as schools, churches, and homes were built out of boards from the new sawmills. Gristmills, also known as corn or flour mills, were erected to grind grain into flour.

Two

Defunct Settlements, Villages, and the Interurban Railroad

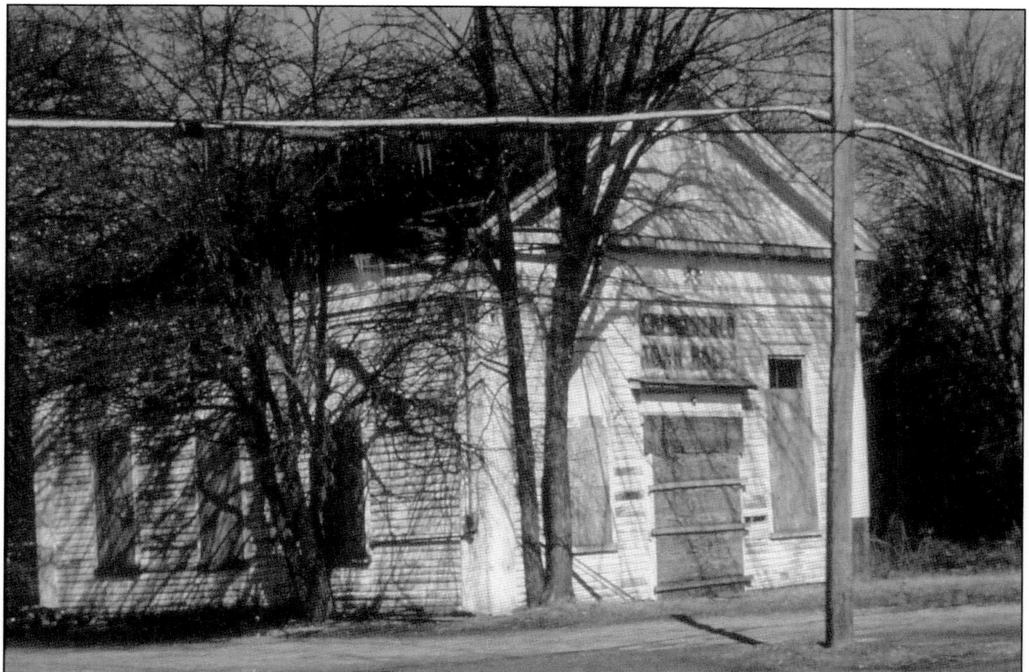

Once the Congregational Church of the village of Milton, this building was sold to Chesterfield Township in 1928 to be used for township purposes and had a sign reading, "Chesterfield Town Hall." It was remodeled in 1930 and used for township business and civic events. Unfortunately, the building burned down, due to arson, a short time before it was scheduled to be moved to the Chesterfield Historic Village in 1992.

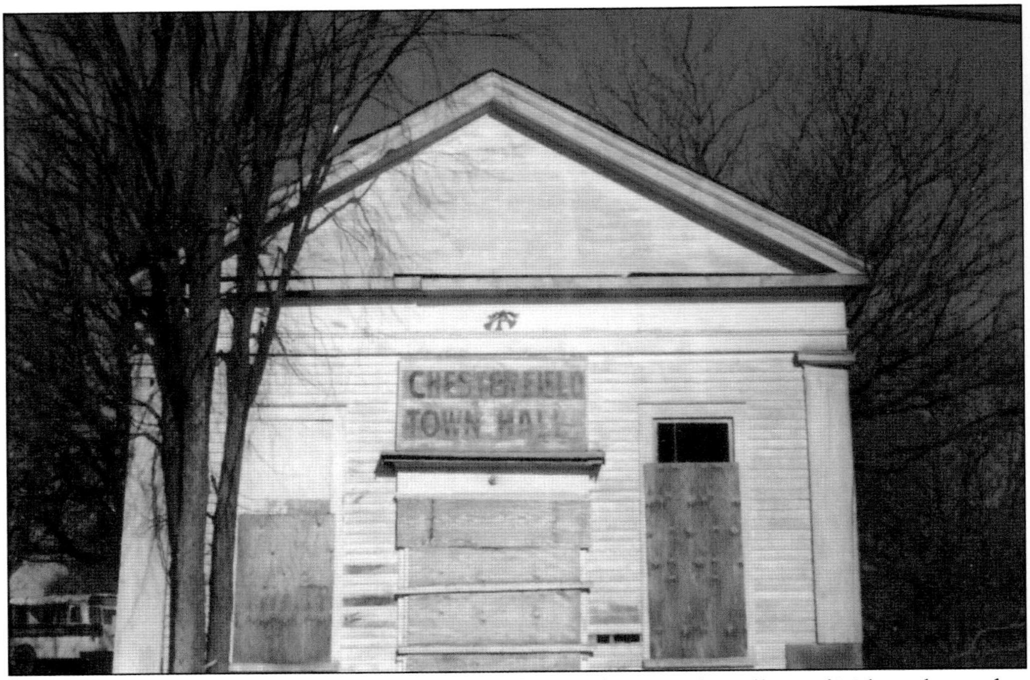

The largest vanished community of Chesterfield Township was the village of Milton, located at Bates Avenue and 24 Mile Road just off Gratiot Avenue, and was a station on the Grand Trunk Railroad. Milton's first post office was started by town namesake Robert O. Milton in 1837, which was located in his house, called the New Haven Post Office. It was moved closer to New Haven with Alfred D. Rice establishing a new Milton post office thereafter. Milton then had another separate post office from January 10, 1856, to July 15, 1904, with Edmund Matthews as the postmaster. The Methodist church went broke, and that building was sold to New Haven to be converted to a grain elevator. The Milton School was at Bates and Gratiot Avenues. The village of Milton also boasted a Baptist church, a physician, a blacksmith, a dry goods and grocery store, a couple of taverns, and more than a dozen homes. At the time, over 200 people lived in Milton.

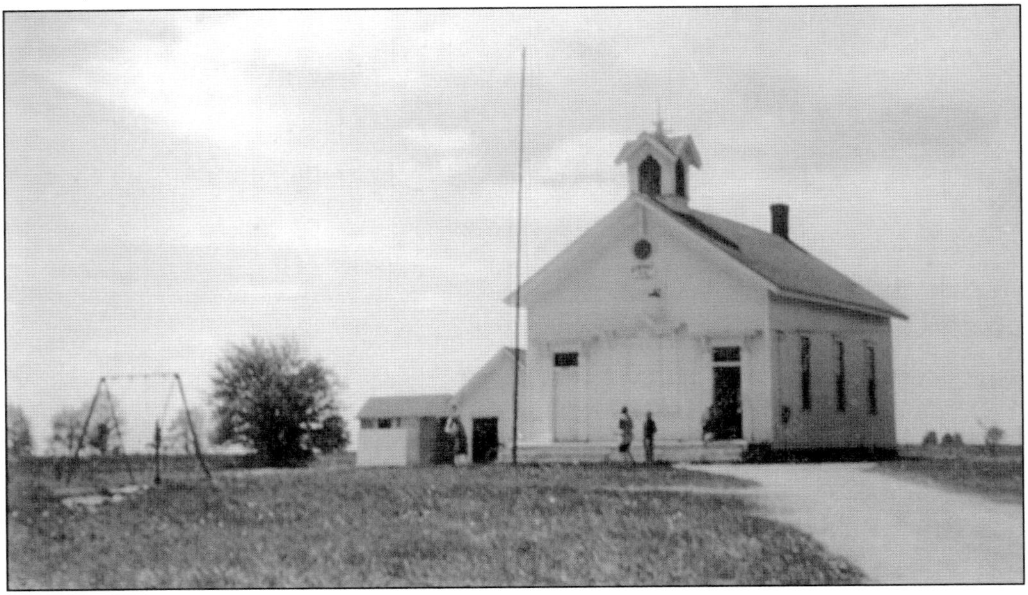

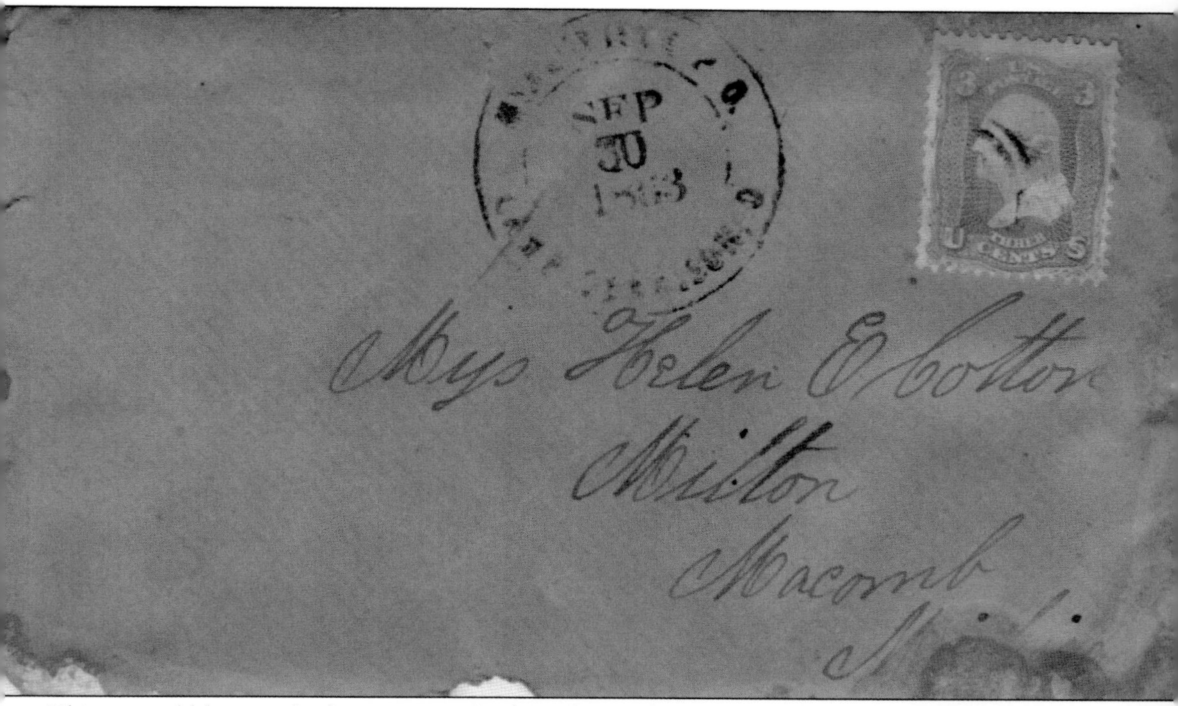

This very old letter, which appears to be from September 30, 1863, bears a postmark that is largely worn away. It is interesting that the address is merely the name and town with no street address needed.

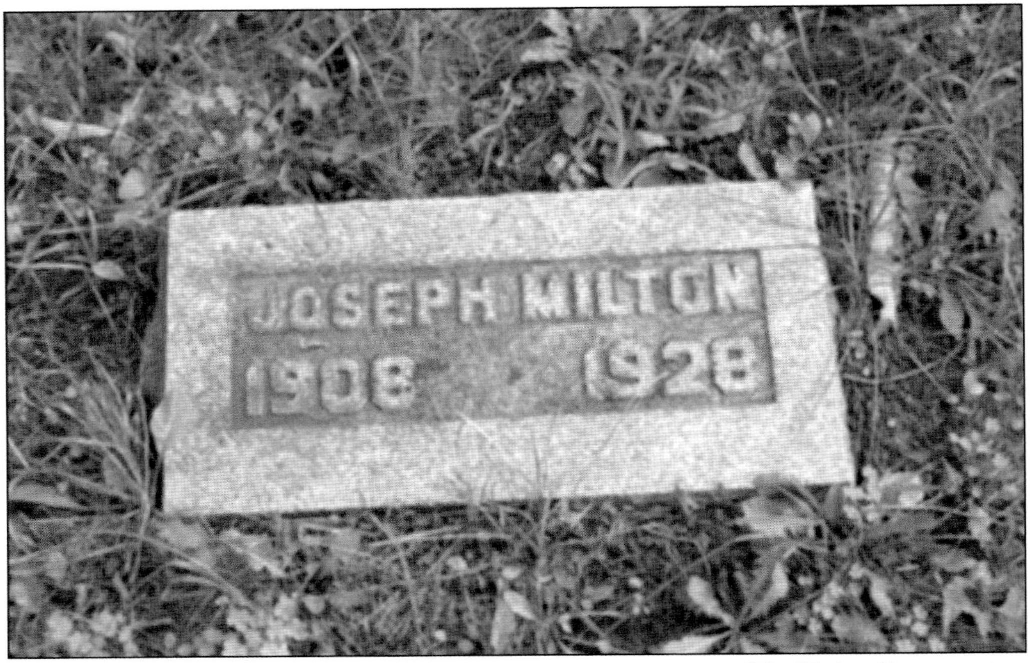

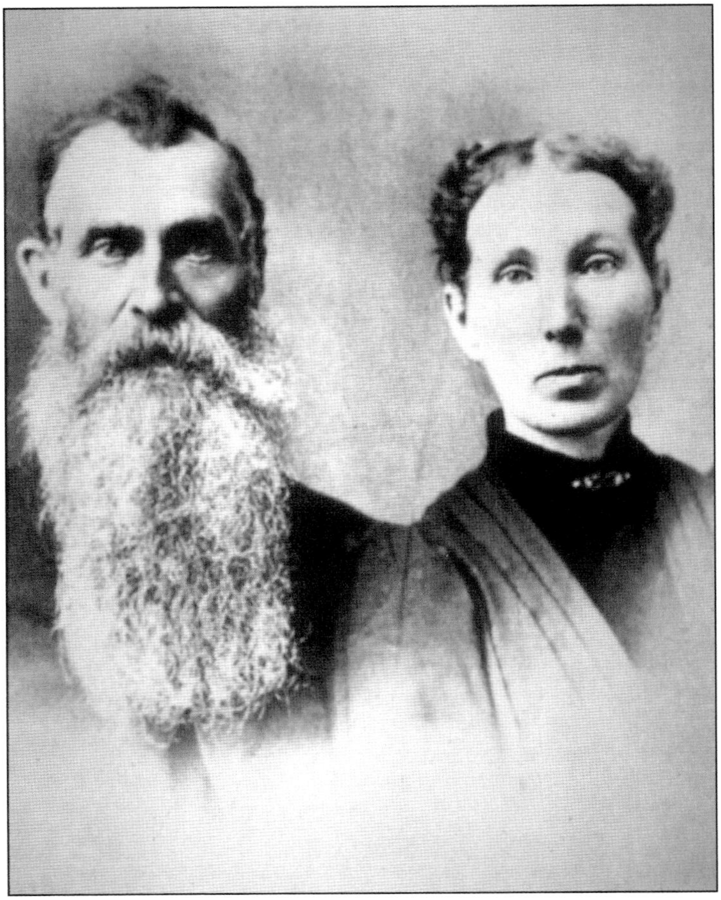

The Union Cemetery is on Fairchild Road near 23 Mile Road. Many members of the Milton family are buried here in what was then the Union Burying Ground, established by the Union Burying Ground Society in 1846. The society was originally formed to buy the land to establish the cemetery. Pictured at left are Ford Milton and his wife.

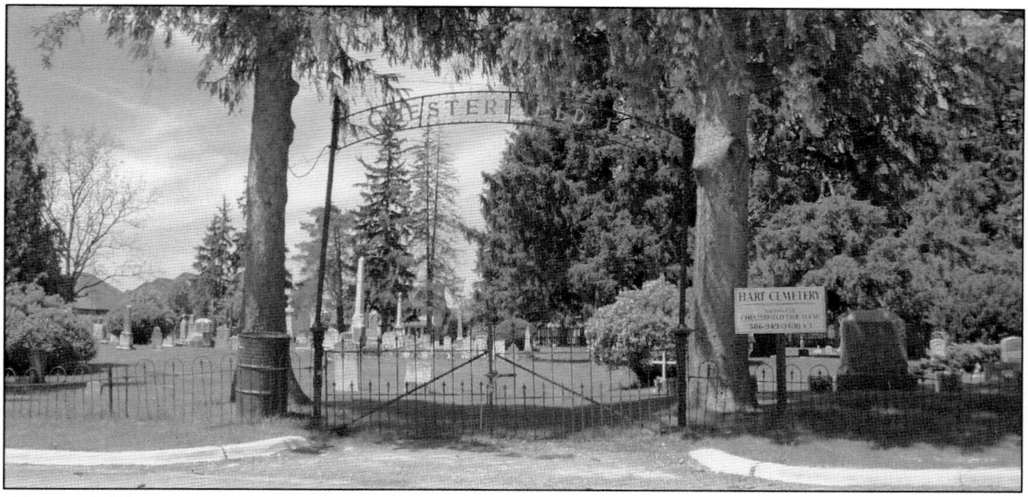

Chesterfield Cemetery on Chesterfield Road was originally known as Hart Cemetery. After La Saline, a French settlement at the mouth of the Salt River, a new settlement grew around the railroad tracks at Chesterfield Road and 25 Mile Road. It came to be known as Hart, probably for settler James Hart. The US post office there in 1837–1838 was called Heart, most likely because there was already a "Hart" in Michigan. There are many Revolutionary War veterans buried here. In 1846, the land for this cemetery was purchased from James Hart for $32.50 by the township group called the Union Burying Ground Society. Chesterfield Road was once called Cemetery Road because of this graveyard. The township purchased 26 lots in this cemetery in 1926 to use as a potter's field, a burial ground where people too poor to purchase a plot were buried. However, there is no record of the township ever using the plots. (Courtesy of Trinity Archives.)

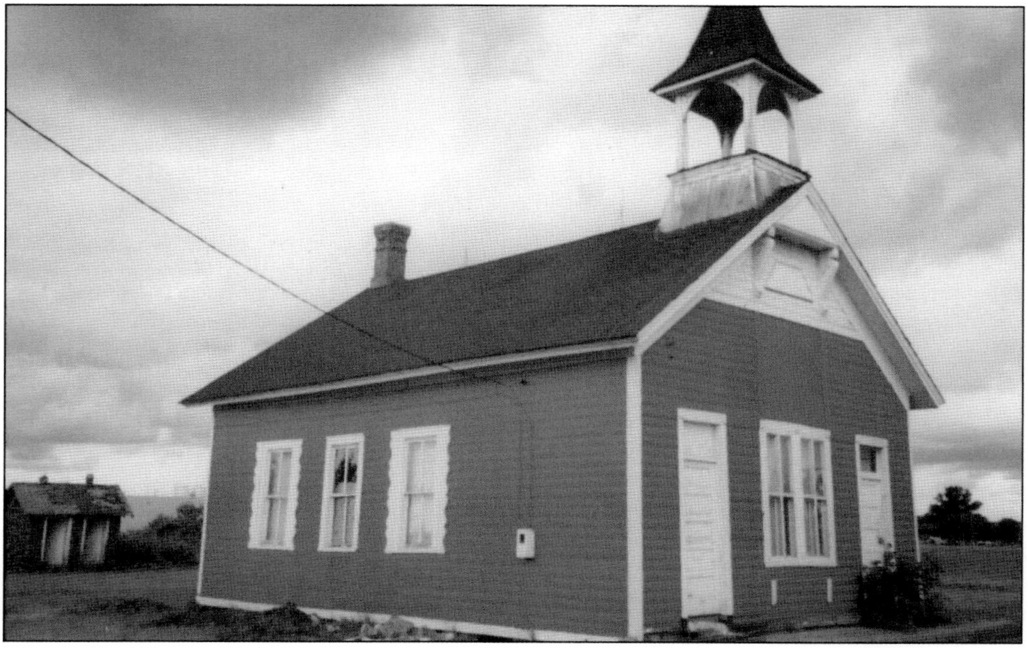

Chesterfield District School No. 1 is pictured here. Better known as the Weller School, it was located on Gratiot Avenue at 22 Mile Road in the village of Chesterfield. It has since been moved to the Historical Village of Chesterfield on Sugarbush Road near Graham Street. (Courtesy of Trinity Archives.)

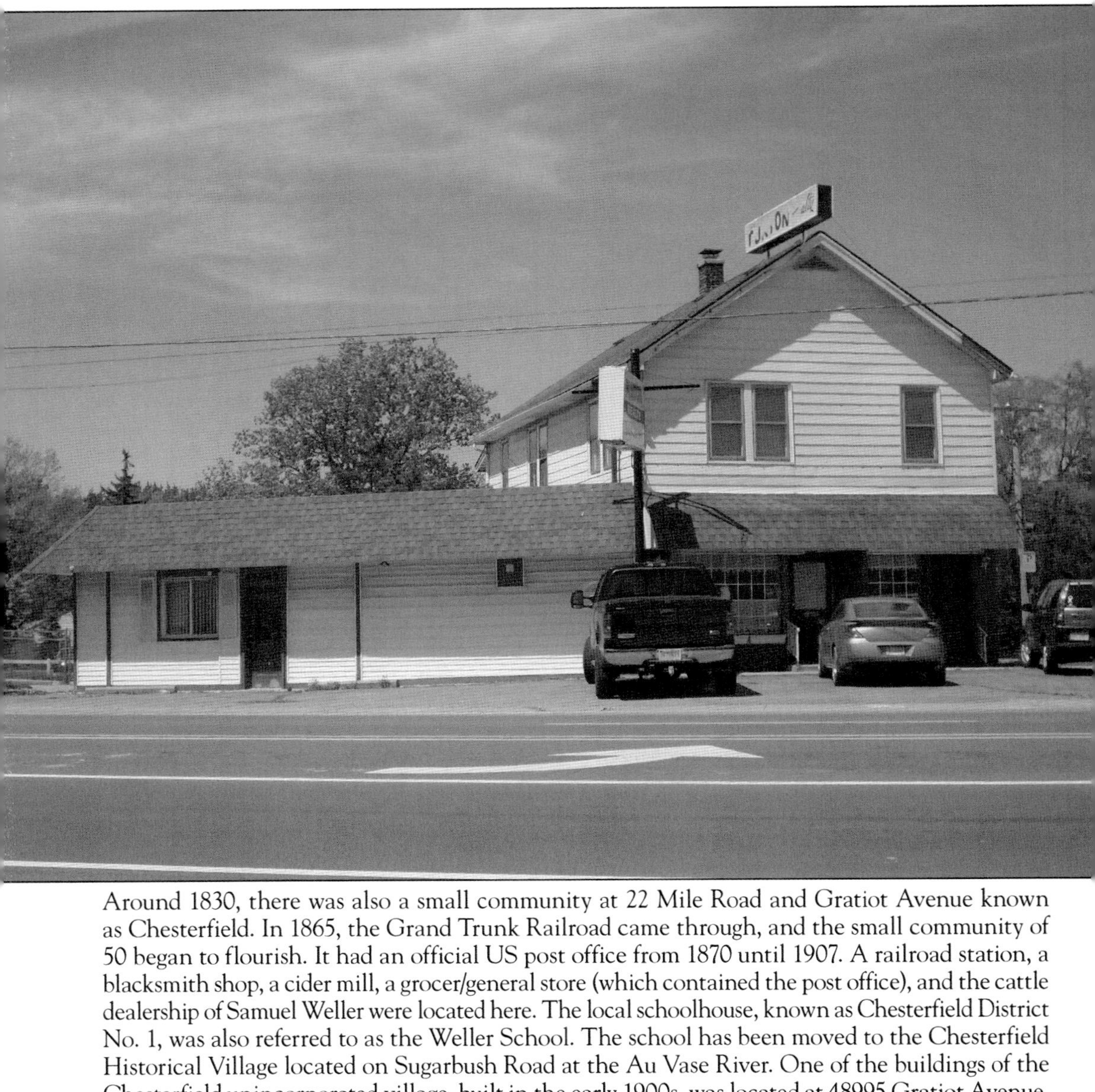

Around 1830, there was also a small community at 22 Mile Road and Gratiot Avenue known as Chesterfield. In 1865, the Grand Trunk Railroad came through, and the small community of 50 began to flourish. It had an official US post office from 1870 until 1907. A railroad station, a blacksmith shop, a cider mill, a grocer/general store (which contained the post office), and the cattle dealership of Samuel Weller were located here. The local schoolhouse, known as Chesterfield District No. 1, was also referred to as the Weller School. The school has been moved to the Chesterfield Historical Village located on Sugarbush Road at the Au Vase River. One of the buildings of the Chesterfield unincorporated village, built in the early 1900s, was located at 48995 Gratiot Avenue. The structure was owned by the Fraser family, who operated it as a gas station and grocery store. It was later repurposed as the Family Tavern and featured a dance floor. In the early 1960s, the bar moved next door. In 1967, the building was purchased by George Furton and used as a real estate office, which it has been for over 40 years. (Courtesy of Trinity Archives.)

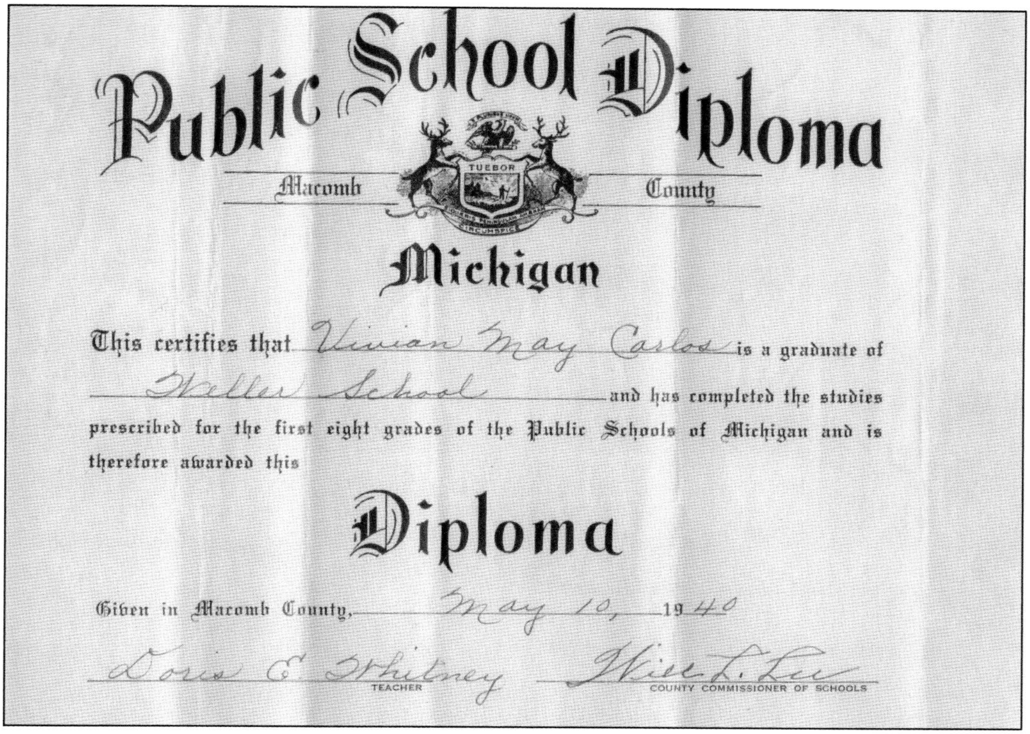

Public School Diploma

Macomb County

TUEBOR

Michigan

This certifies that Vivian May Carlos is a graduate of Weller School and has completed the studies prescribed for the first eight grades of the Public Schools of Michigan and is therefore awarded this

Diploma

Given in Macomb County, May 10, 1940

Doris E. Whitney — TEACHER

Will L. Lee — COUNTY COMMISSIONER OF SCHOOLS

The Weller School, like most one-room schoolhouses of the era, encompassed grades one through eight. After eighth grade, students went to Mt. Clemens or New Baltimore's Hathaway Institute. Upon reaching school each morning, the student would enter on the right if male and on the left if female. The outhouse was also segregated by sex, with two separate entrances. This unique-for-the-time outhouse was moved brick by brick from its original location to the Chesterfield Township Historical Village. Once there, it was reassembled under the direction of George Deeby (the road going through the historical village has been named for the Deeby Family). The Chesterfield Township Historical Society raised money for the move and reconstruction by selling memberships in the Outhouse Club. After the outhouse was reassembled, members were invited to sign the outhouse walls.

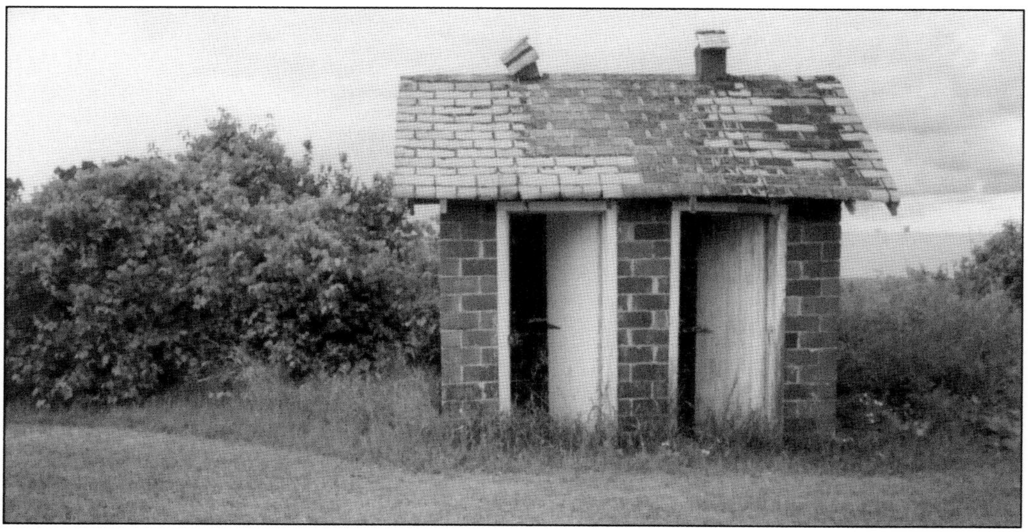

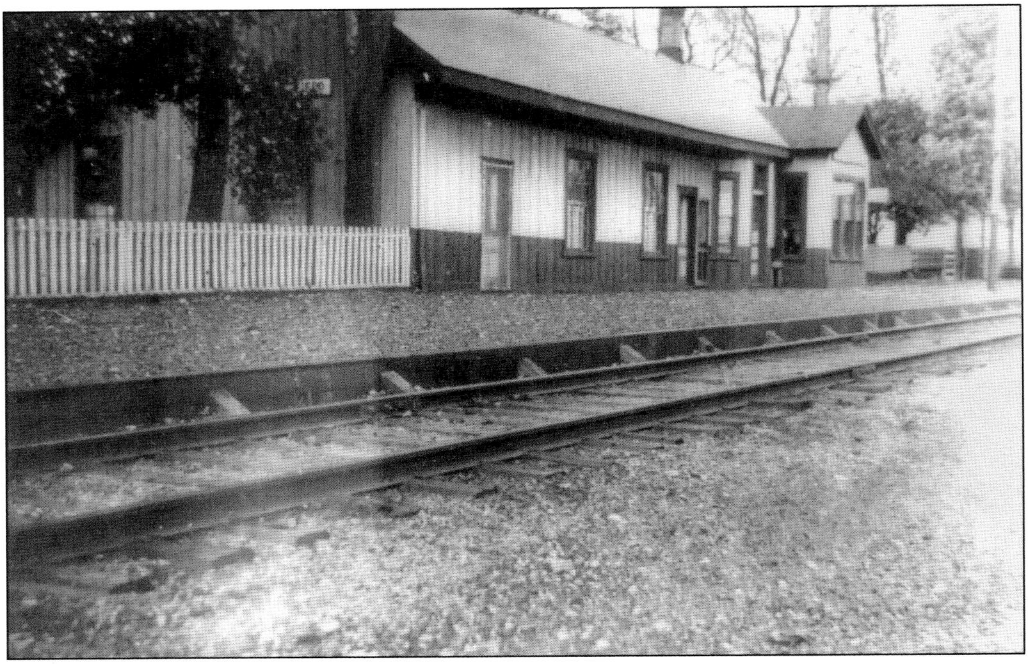

The depot at Gratiot Avenue between 21 and 22 Mile Roads was built in 1898 and was holding together well in 1917, the date of these photographs taken by the Interstate Commerce Commission. (Both, courtesy of Michigan Transit Museum).

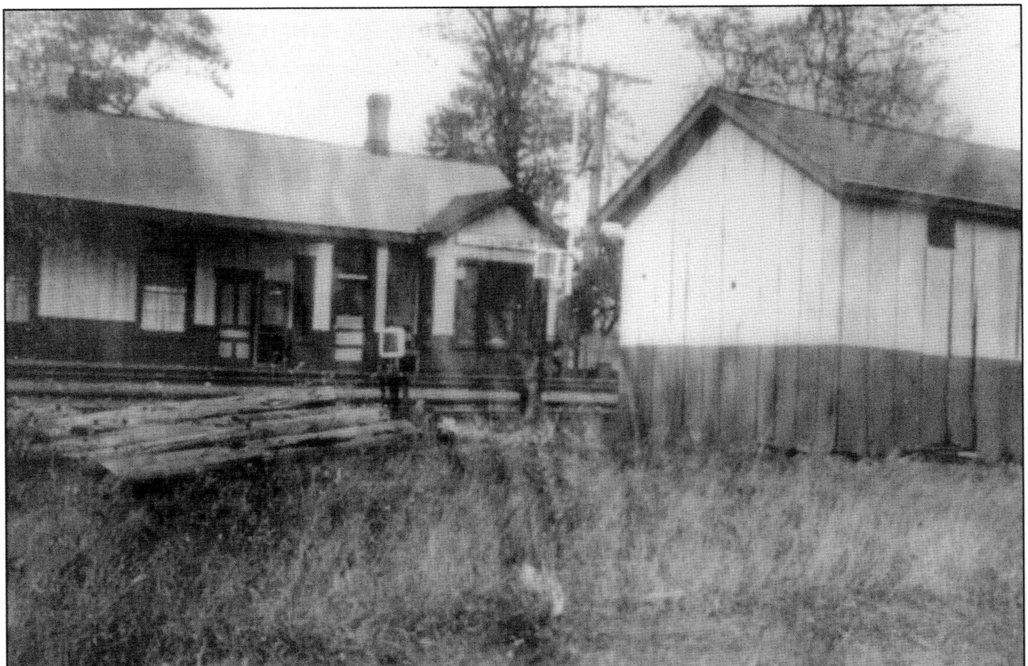

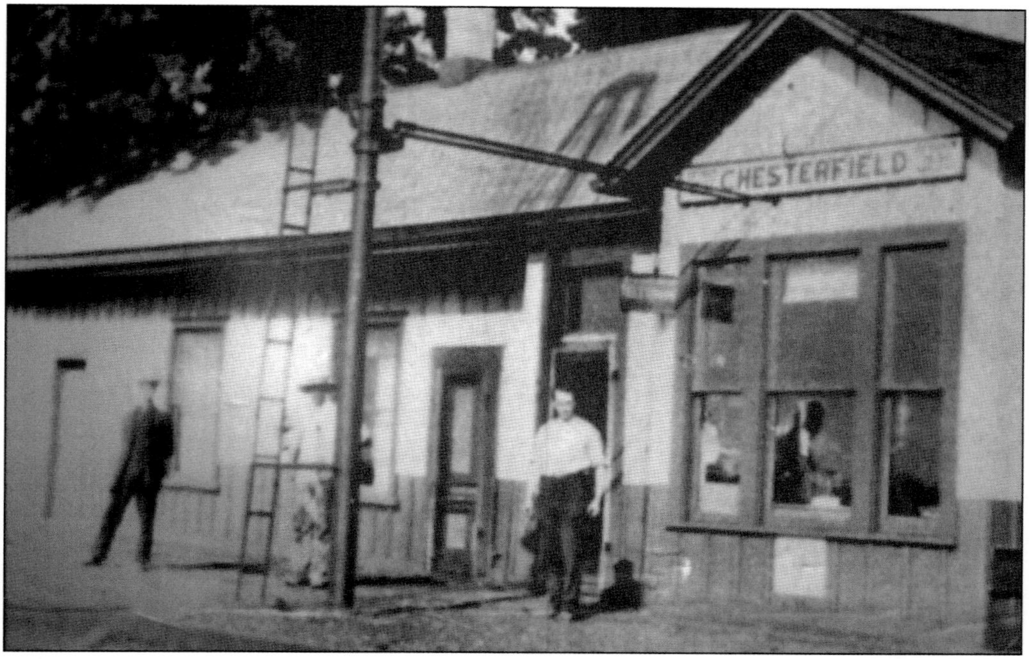

A few other communities also thrived in the 19th century. One settlement, at the corner of Fairchild and 23 Mile Roads, was known as Fairchild or Slippery Corner because an old clay-bottomed road caused buggies to slide into the ditch. In 1906, it had its own post office and acted as a station on the Rapid Railway. The Chesterfield Railroad Depot served this Fairchild area. Also pictured is a long-surviving municipal structure at 49701 Fairchild Road that was part of the community. According to a 1912 newspaper article, around 1836 there was an unnamed village with a frame schoolhouse, hotel, blacksmith shop, ashery, and two dwelling houses by 26 Mile Road and the Fort Gratiot Turnpike. The newspaper also noted that the village was "now extinct." East Union was a settlement that had a post office from January 10, 1856, until November 4, 1864; the postmaster was Daniel Shattuck. The settlement was located in Section 18 of Chesterfield Township, between 23 and 24 Mile Roads, in the west end of Chesterfield. (Both, courtesy of Trinity Archives.)

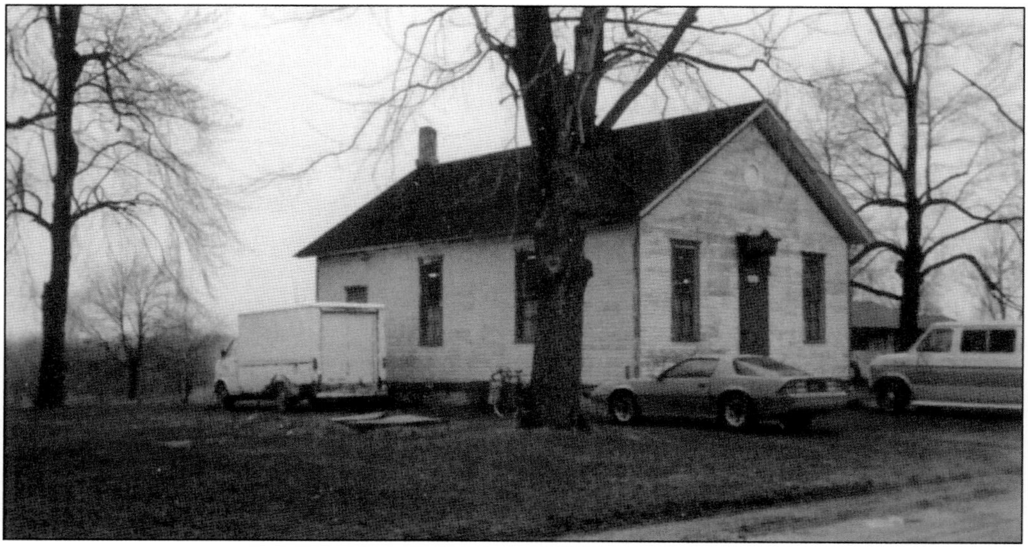

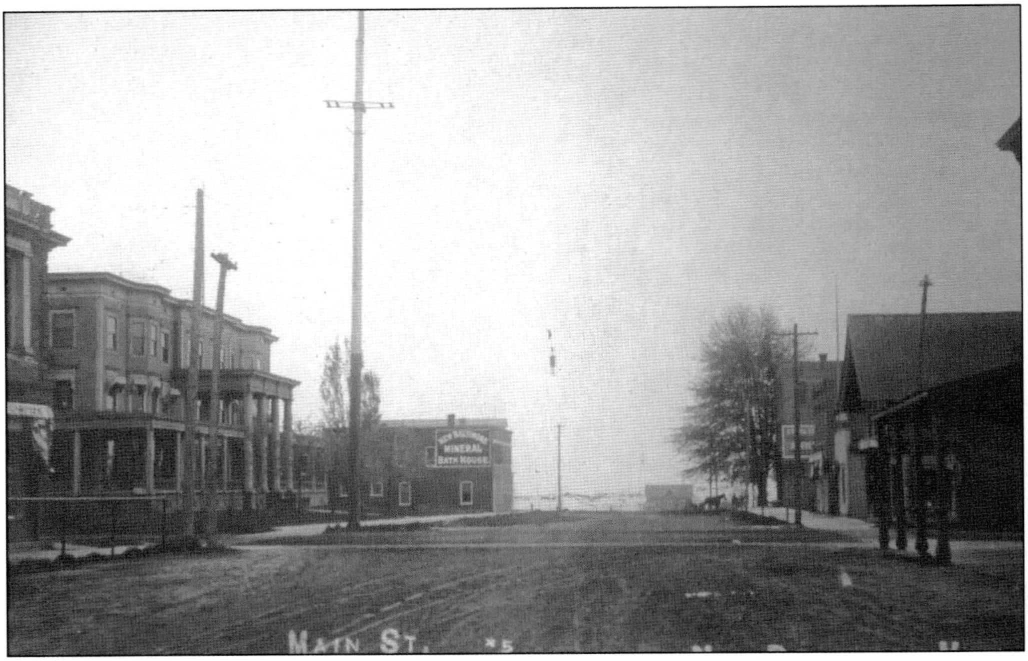

This is a view of the crossroads in downtown New Baltimore of Washington Street near Main Street, facing toward Anchor Bay, about 1909. The Chesterfield Hotel in New Baltimore, around the early 1900s, was located at the end of Washington Street, near Anchor Bay. New Baltimore survived a major fire in 1870 and rebuilt its downtown.

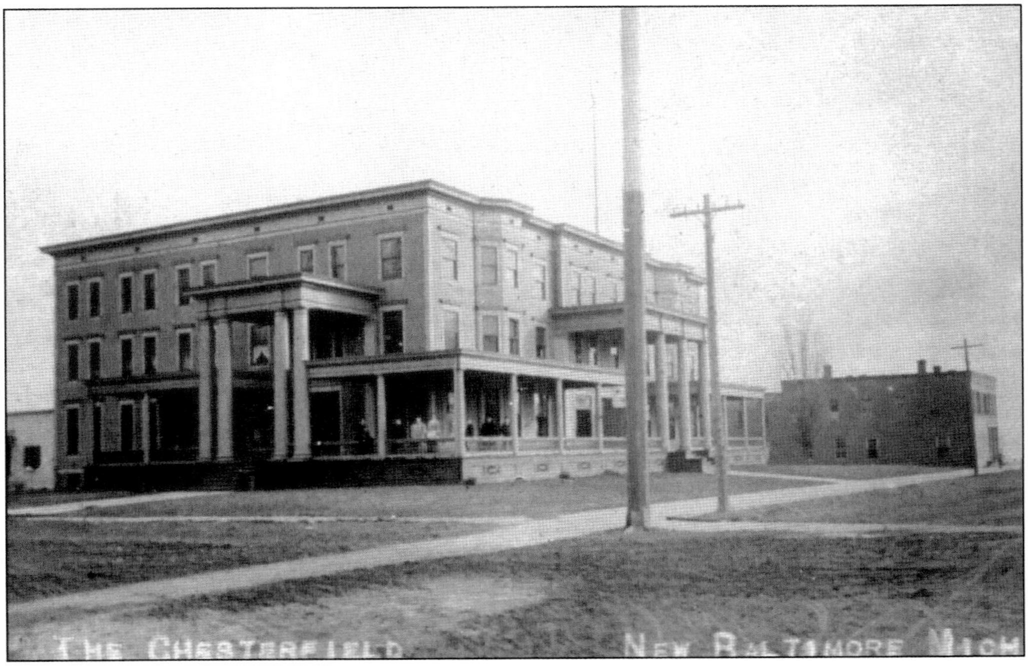

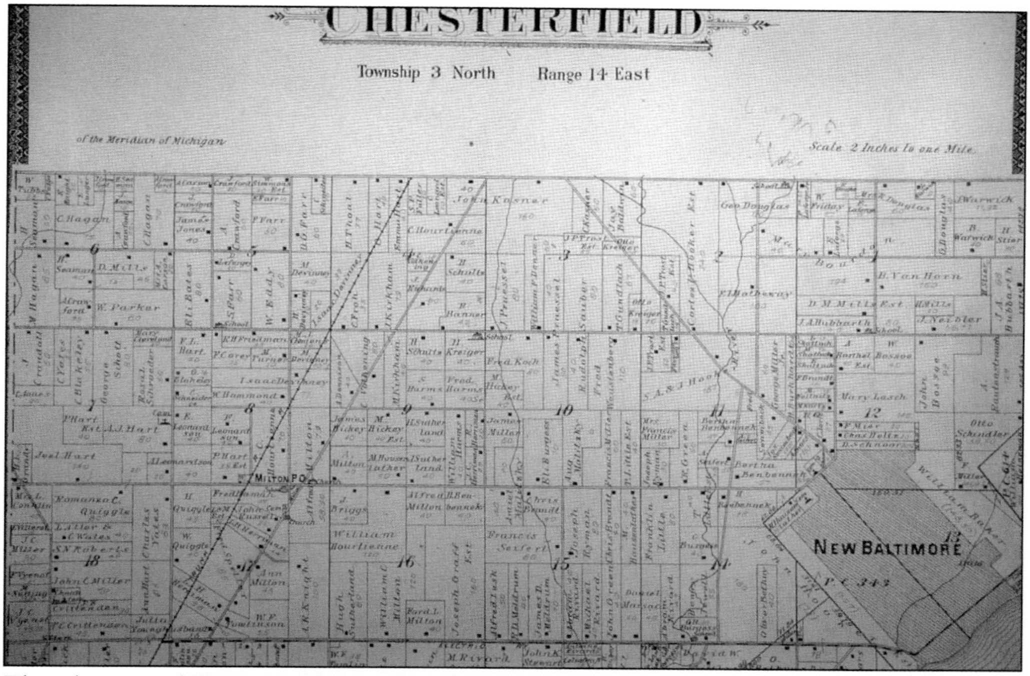

This plat map of Chesterfield Township shows many names familiar in the history of the area, including Baker, Bates, Bethuy, Donner, Friedman, Hart, Hathaway, Hooker, Koch, Kosner, La Forge, Maliskey, Marsac, Meldrum, Miller, Milton, Rivard, Siefert, Sutherland, and Yates.

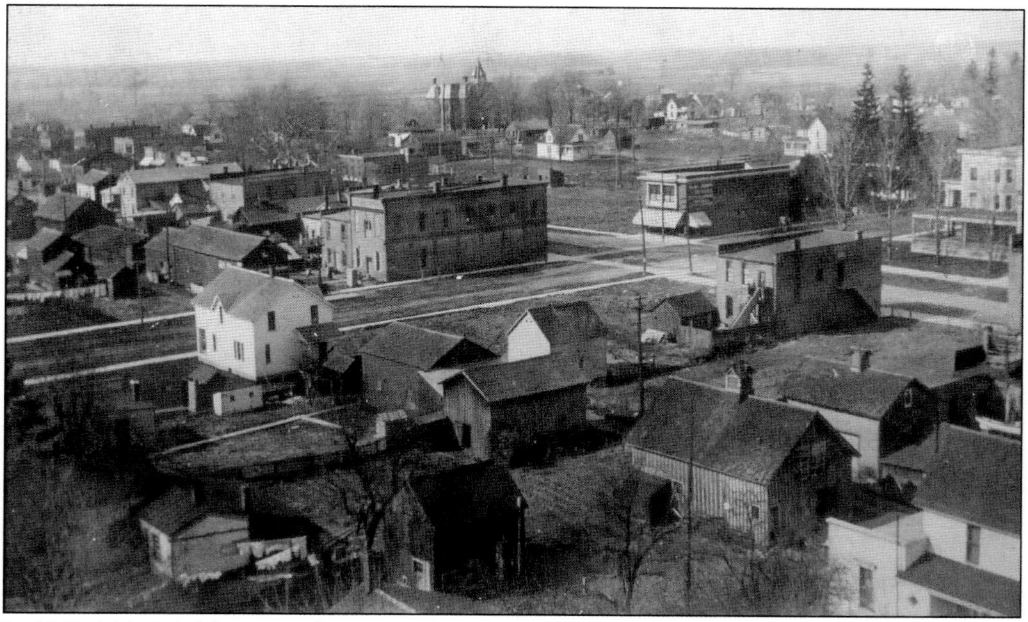

In 1845, Alfred Ashley came from Mt. Clemens, erected a dock, and built a sawmill in an eastern area of Chesterfield. In 1851, he platted the village that was at first known as Ashley. When it was given its first post office with Alfred Ashley as the postmaster, it was called Ashleyville. There were a few other towns named Ashley in Michigan, so it was renamed New Baltimore on March 7, 1855, and incorporated as a village in 1867. In 1931, it was incorporated as a city. As of the 2010 census, the population is over 7,000.

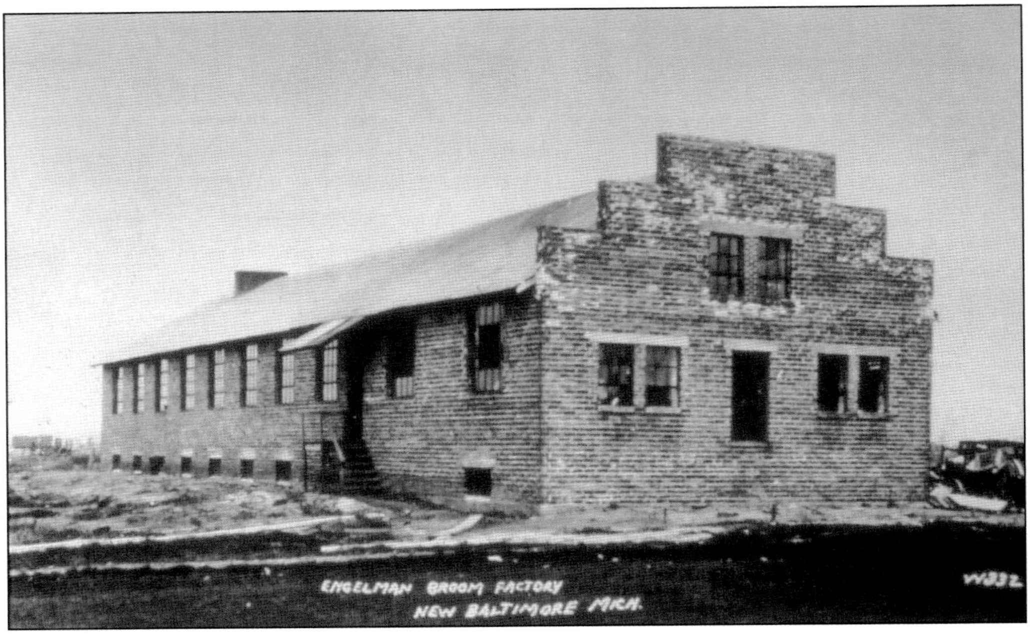

The city boasted various industries, including three stave mills producing the parts for barrels used all over Michigan. Pictured above is Englemans Broom Factory. Pictured below is one of the oldest surviving business buildings in New Baltimore, Schlosser's Block, across the street from the location of the Chesterfield Hotel. This building at various times has been a hardware store, candy store, IGA grocery store, and a soap business.

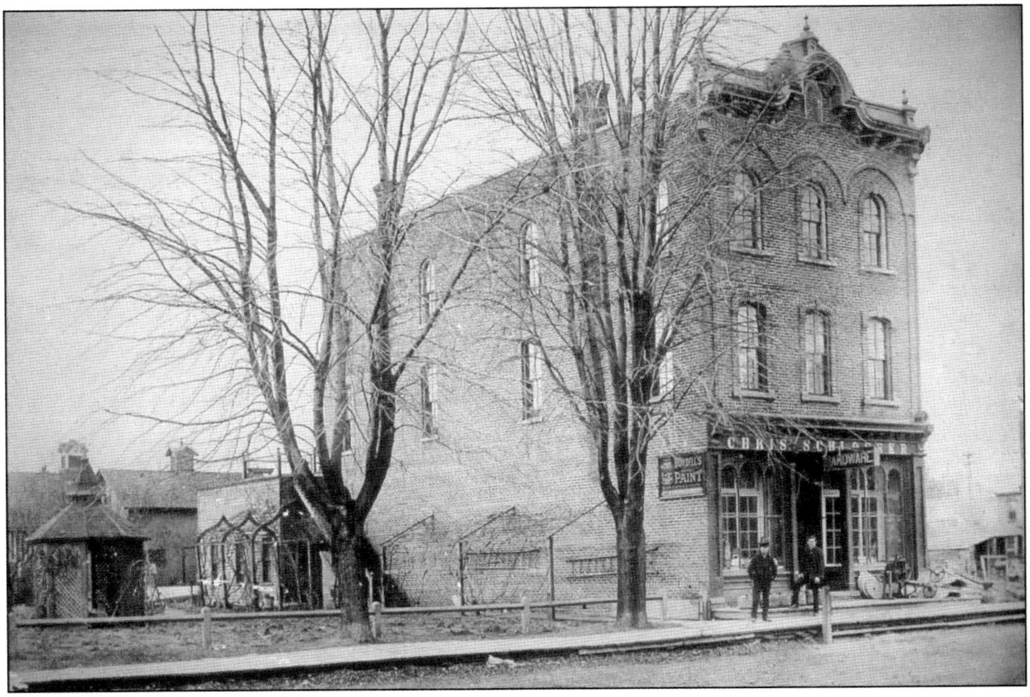

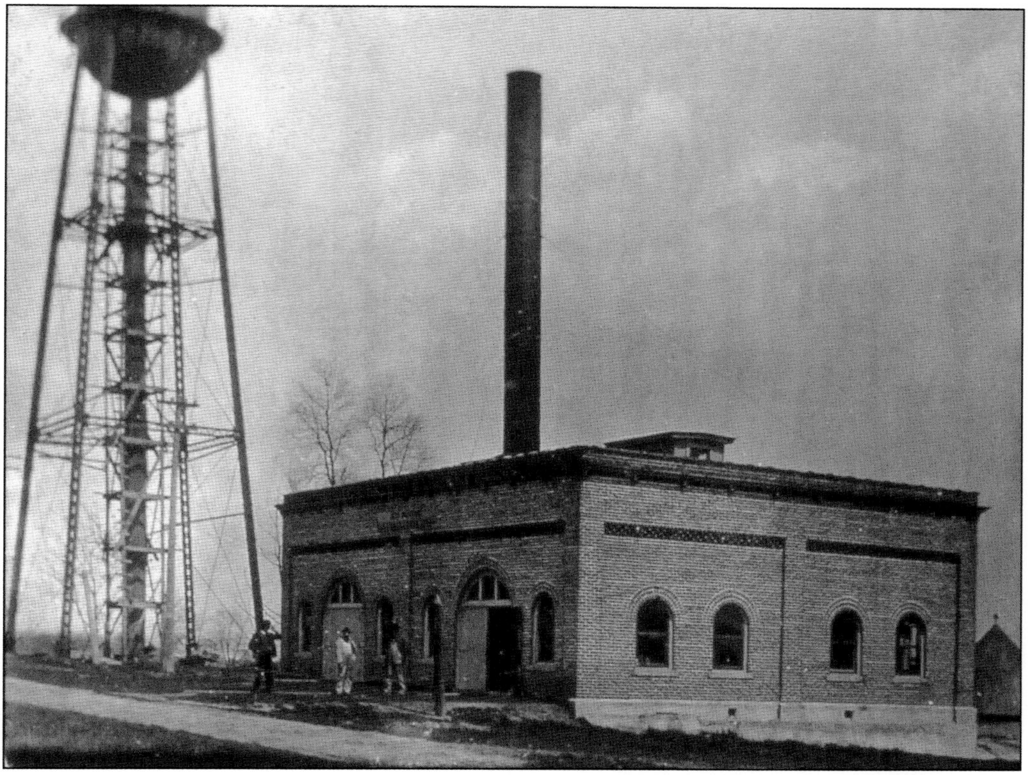

New Baltimore, due to its proximity on the water, attracted tourists from Detroit and surrounding areas. In the early days, prior to the railroad, they would come in by steamship. As of the late 1800s, the village had its own water plant and produced its own electricity in the building pictured above. Here are two versions of the water building, the one below showing it reconfigured and built up, and both were located in the same spot on Front Street near the city park.

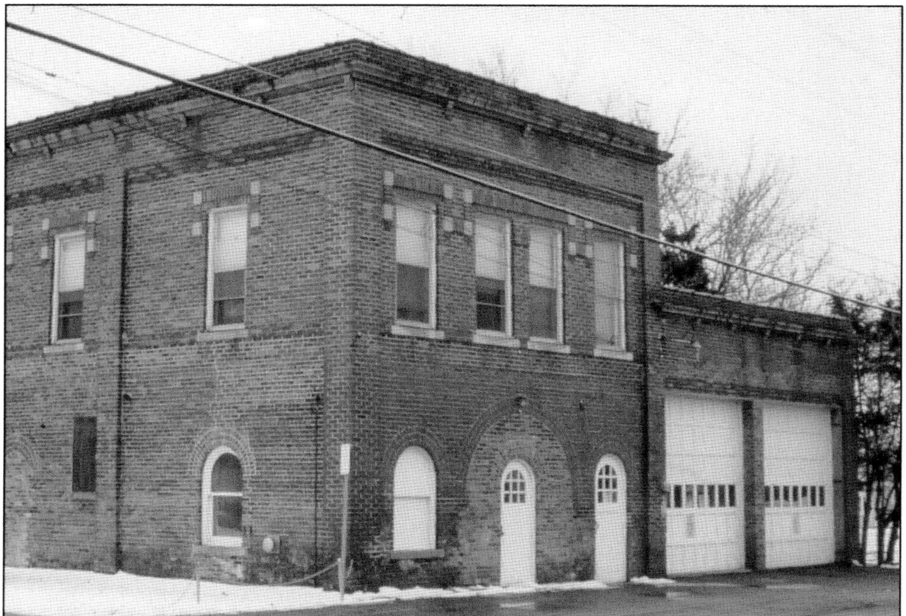

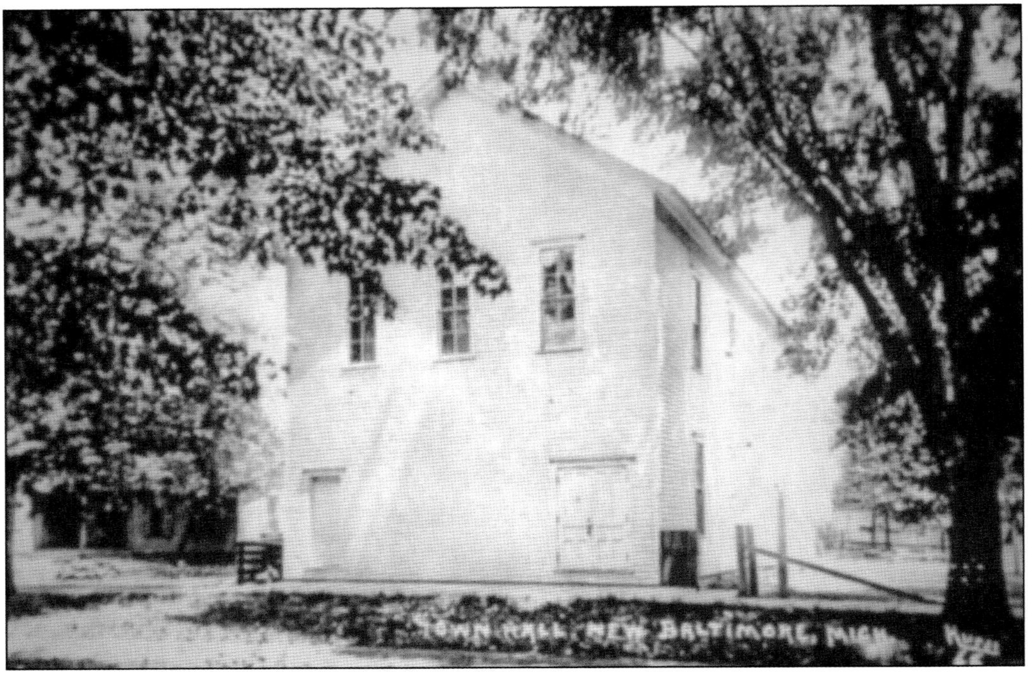

Other businesses flourished in New Baltimore. The village had breweries, movie houses, and bowling alleys. Pictured are an early municipal town hall (above) and the village Opera House (below), which is now the Bethel Temple Baptist Church.

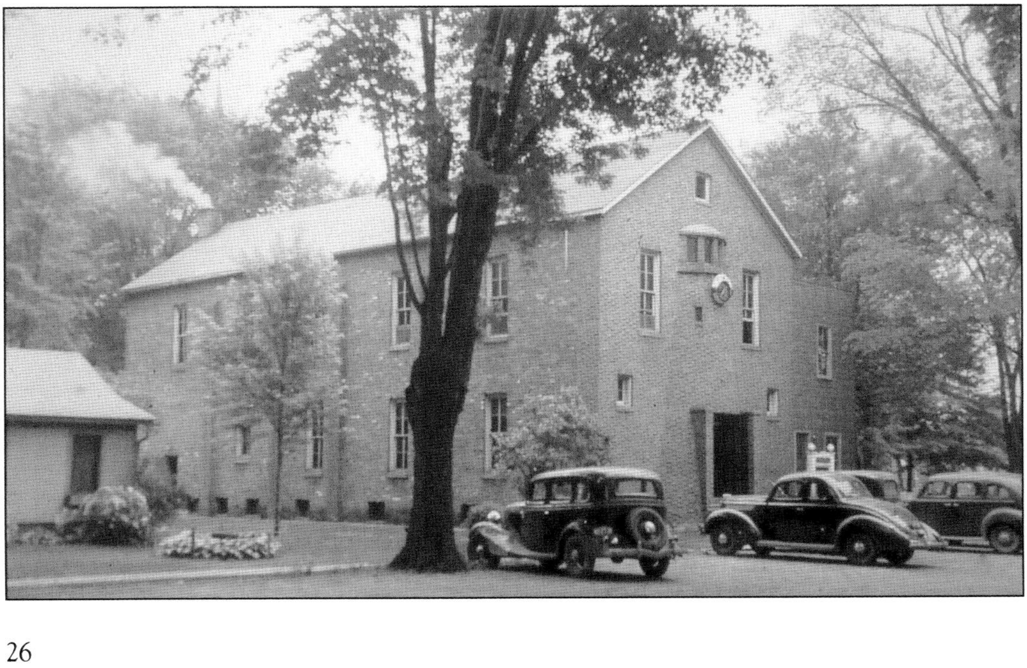

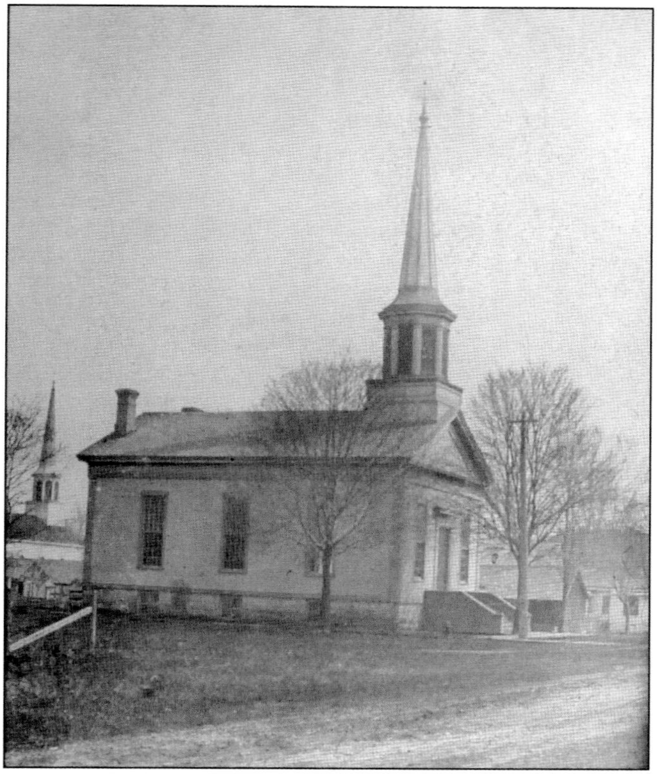

Two of the oldest structures in town are the First Congregational Church (right), at Base and Alfred Streets, and the St. John's Lutheran Church (below), on Maria Street near Green Street. Alfred Ashley, the town founder, was also one of the founders of the First Congregational Church.

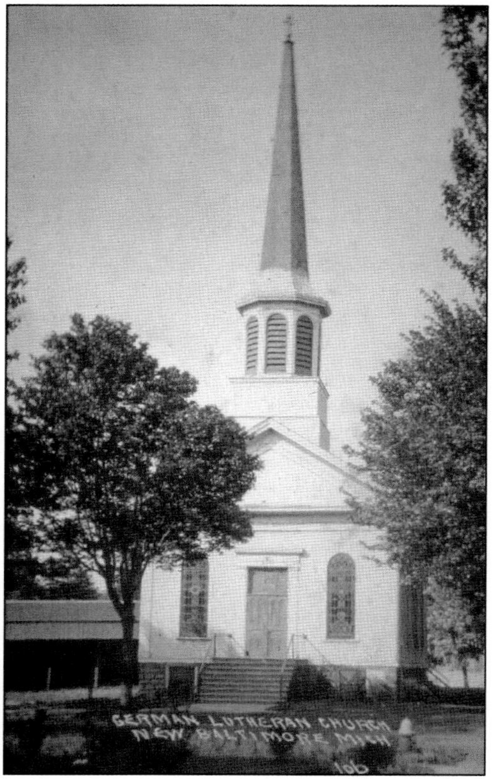

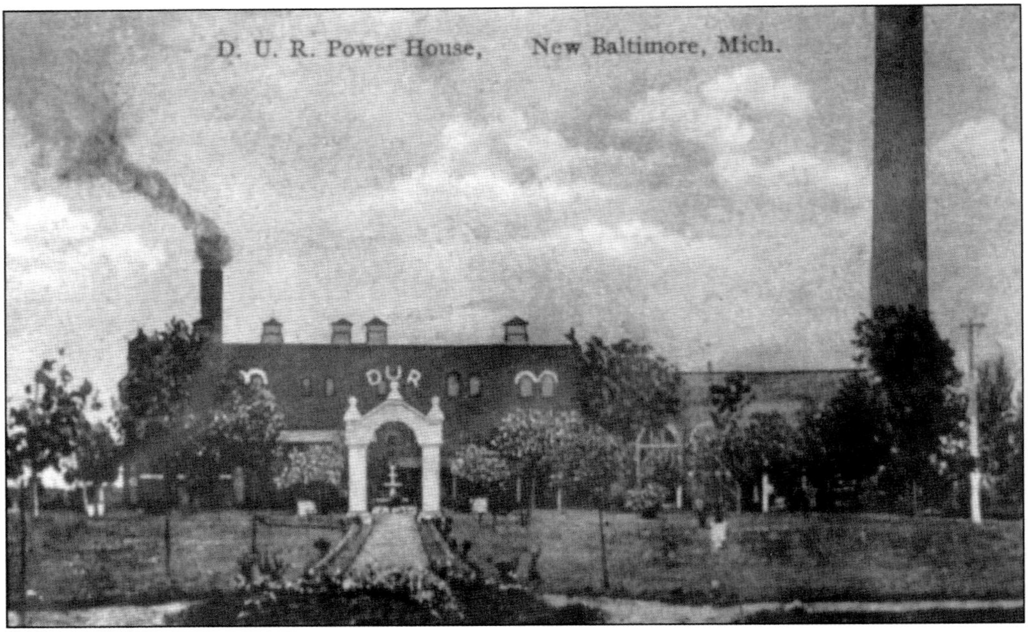

Beginning in 1870, the Detroit Urban Railroad (DUR) ran from Detroit to Port Huron and through Chesterfield and the New Baltimore area. Since it was in the middle of the route, the DUR Power Plant was built in New Baltimore. The train fare reportedly depended on the conductor and usually ranged from 3¢ to 7¢. Later, it was standardized to be 5¢ from Chesterfield to Mt. Clemens, with a trip all the way to Detroit costing 25¢. The tracks ran along Gratiot Avenue and down 23 Mile Road. These tracks were often used by vehicles when it was too muddy in the spring to use the roads. In fact, the mailman would wait until the train had gone by and then get on the tracks with his horse and wagon to deliver the mail.

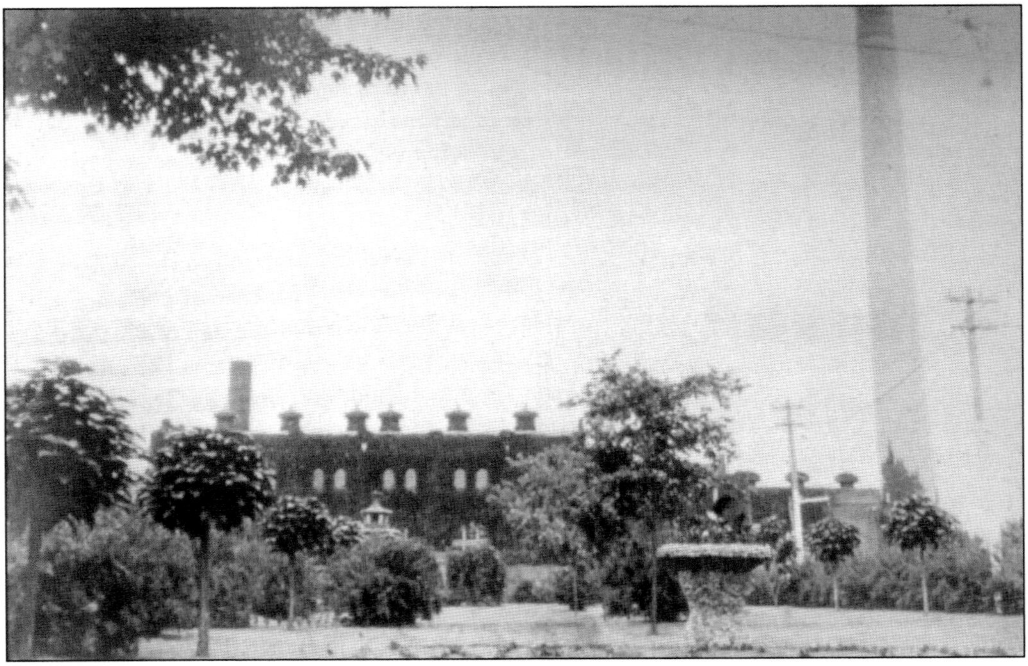

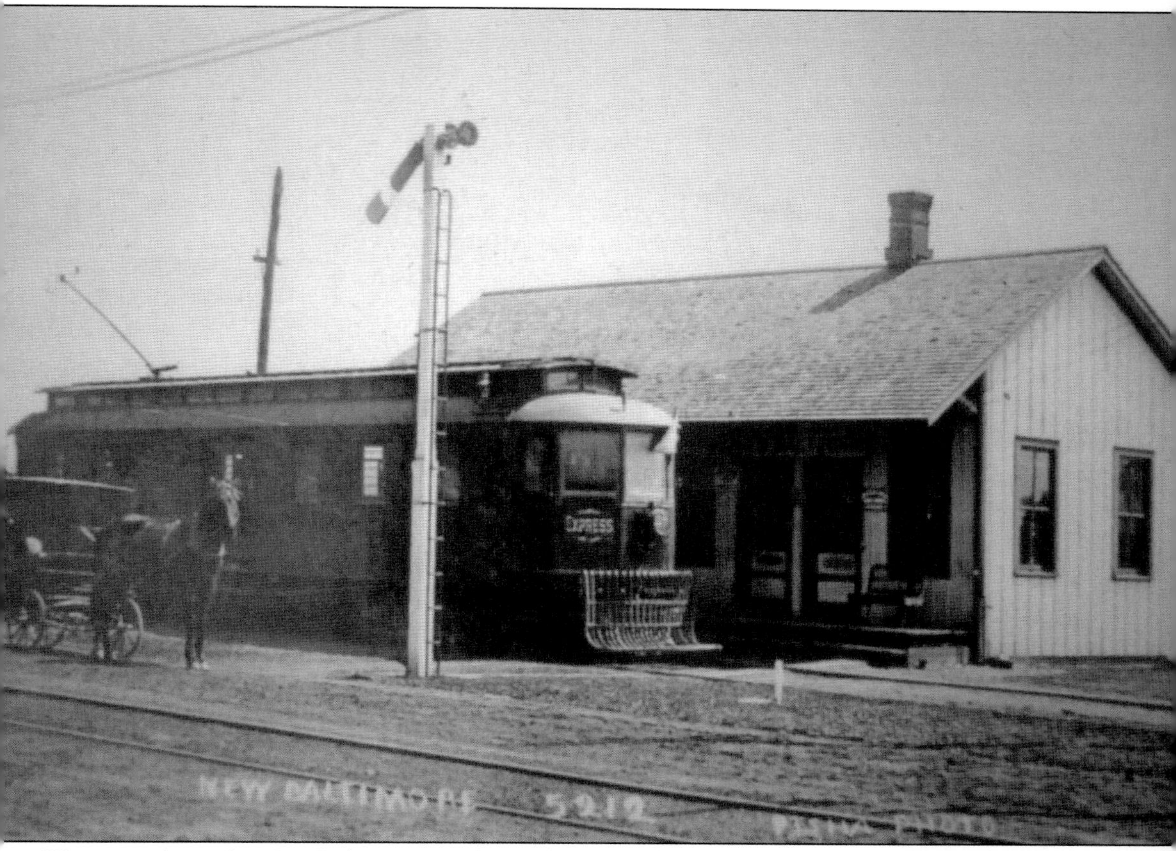

The train depot for New Baltimore was located in a building across the street from the present New Baltimore Municipal Offices on Green Street, also known as 23 Mile Road and M-29. The Interurban Railroad (IUR) lasted until the Great Depression of the 1930s. It had stops along Jefferson Avenue at Bay Court, Chesterfield near 22 Mile Road, Stewart Road (now Sass Road), and at Orr's Crossing, which was at 23 Mile Road and Gratiot Avenue. For the IUR, there were 14 local trains making seven round trips and 30 limited ones making 15 round trips from Detroit to Port Huron daily, thereby providing hourly service.

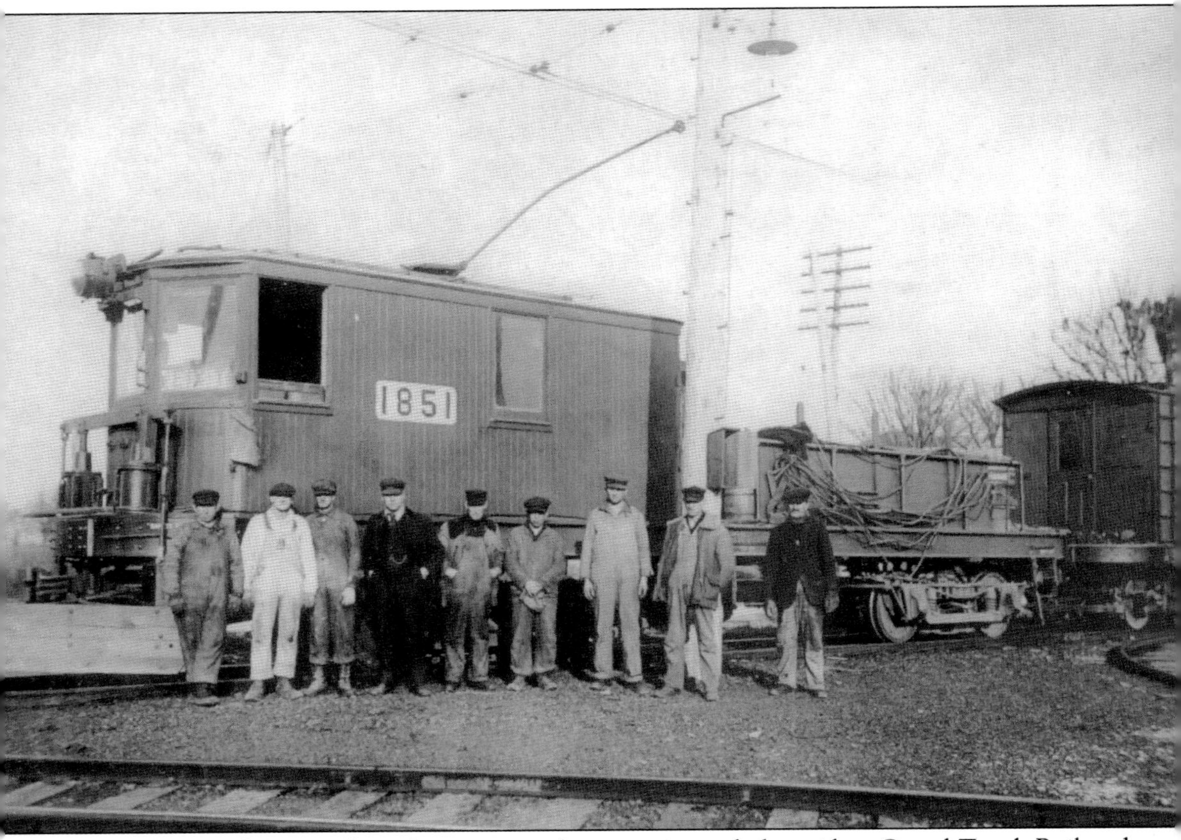

William and August Rivard are among the men pictured alongside a Grand Trunk Railroad train parked in Chesterfield. Besides the interurban passenger trains, Grand Trunk also ran trains through the area to haul freight, farm products, farm animals, wood and bricks, and more. (Courtesy of Roy Rivard.)

Three

Streets and Street Corners of Chesterfield

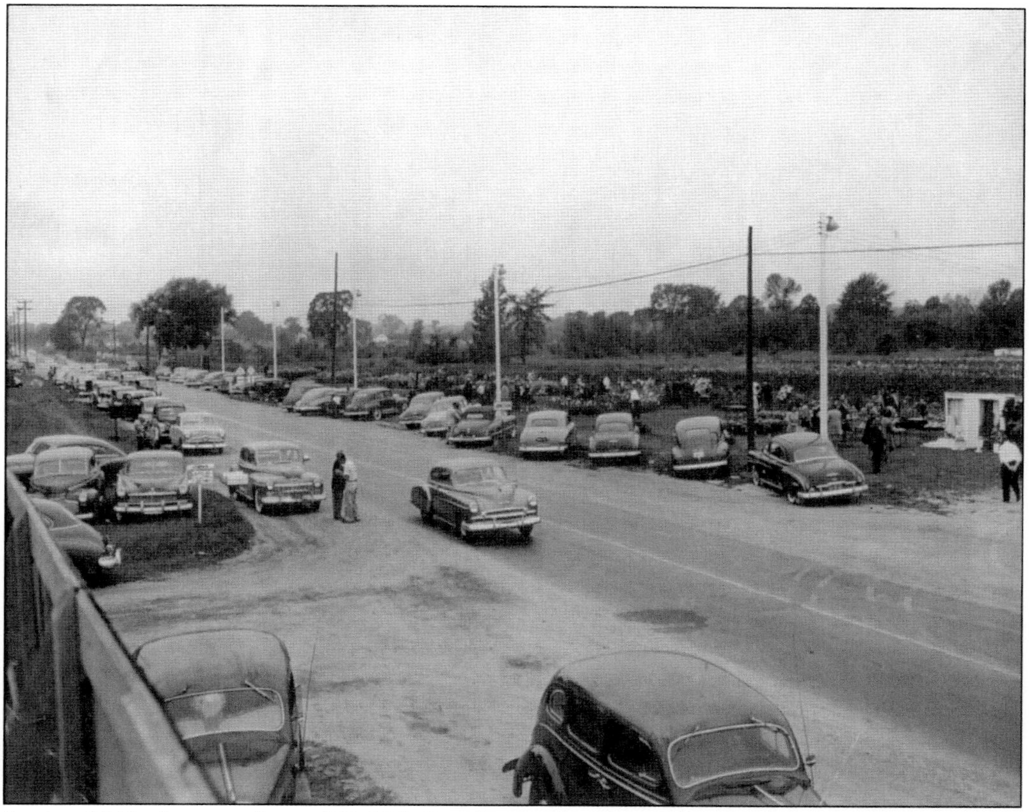

In this 1949 photograph is of 23 Mile Road near the New Baltimore border. Besides Gratiot Avenue, the dominant road through the township has always been 23 Mile Road. Mainly because of the Wayside Inn, once located on 23 Mile Road near Gratiot Avenue, and the inexpensive whiskey sold there, 23 Mile Road was nicknamed "Whiskey Road" east of Romeo Plank Road. (Courtesy of Jim Genso.)

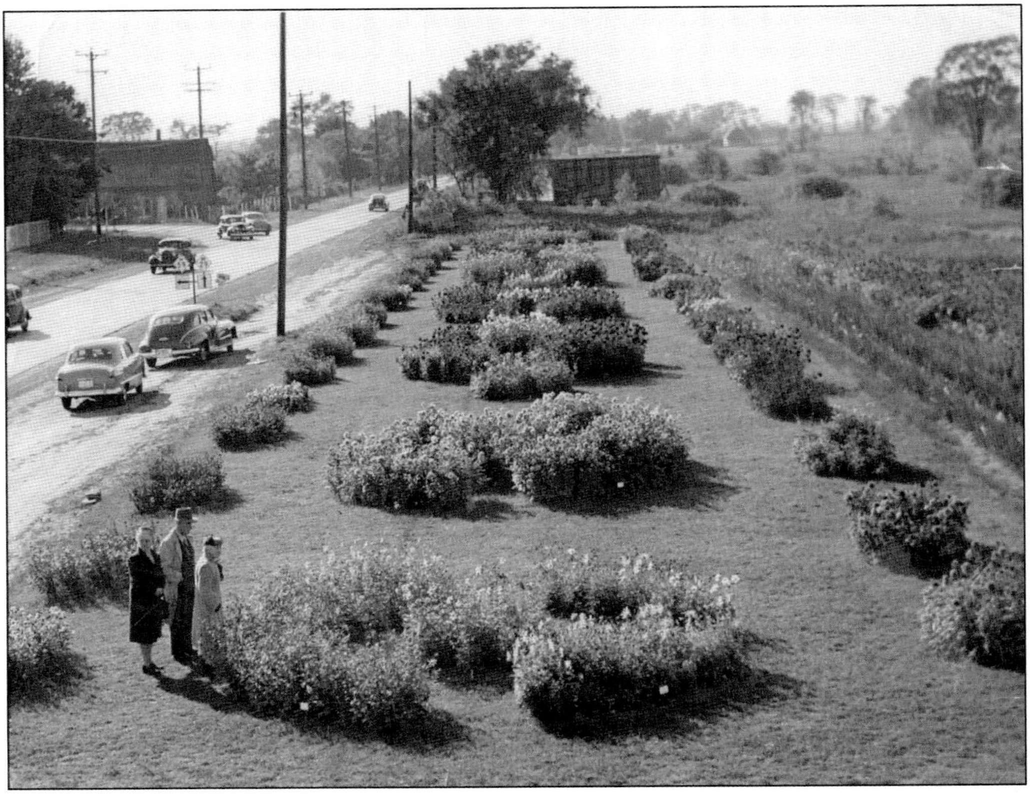

The part of 23 Mile Road near Gratiot Avenue was also known as the Irish section, while the eastern part of 23 Mile Road was referred to as "Cold Water Road," supposedly the non-Irish drink of choice. Other names included Telegraph Road (because telegraph lines ran along 23 Mile Road) and the New Baltimore Highway. (Both, courtesy of Jim Genso.)

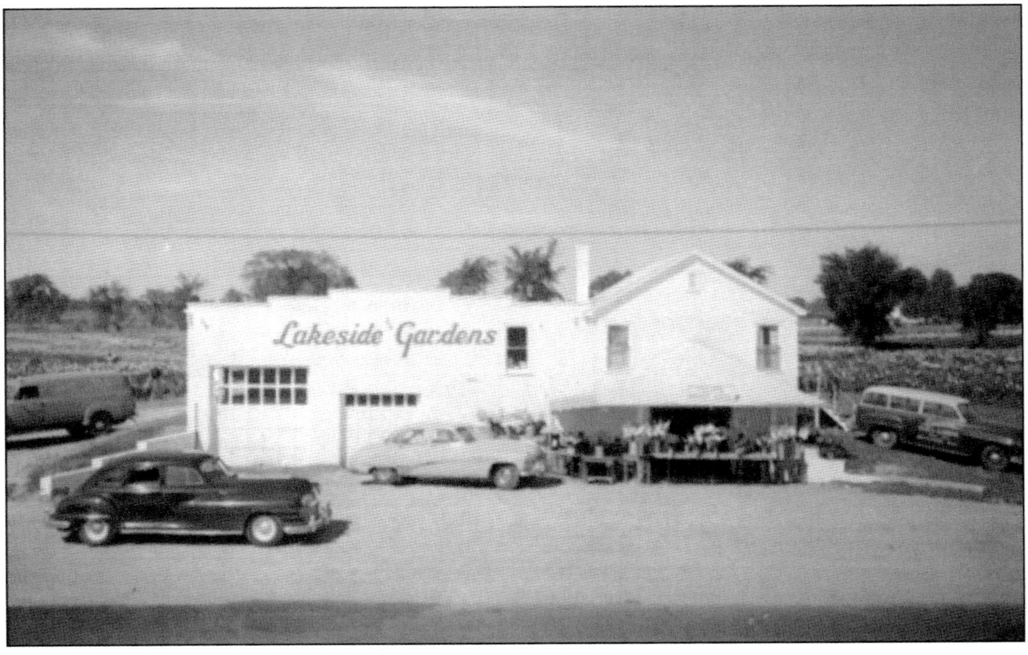

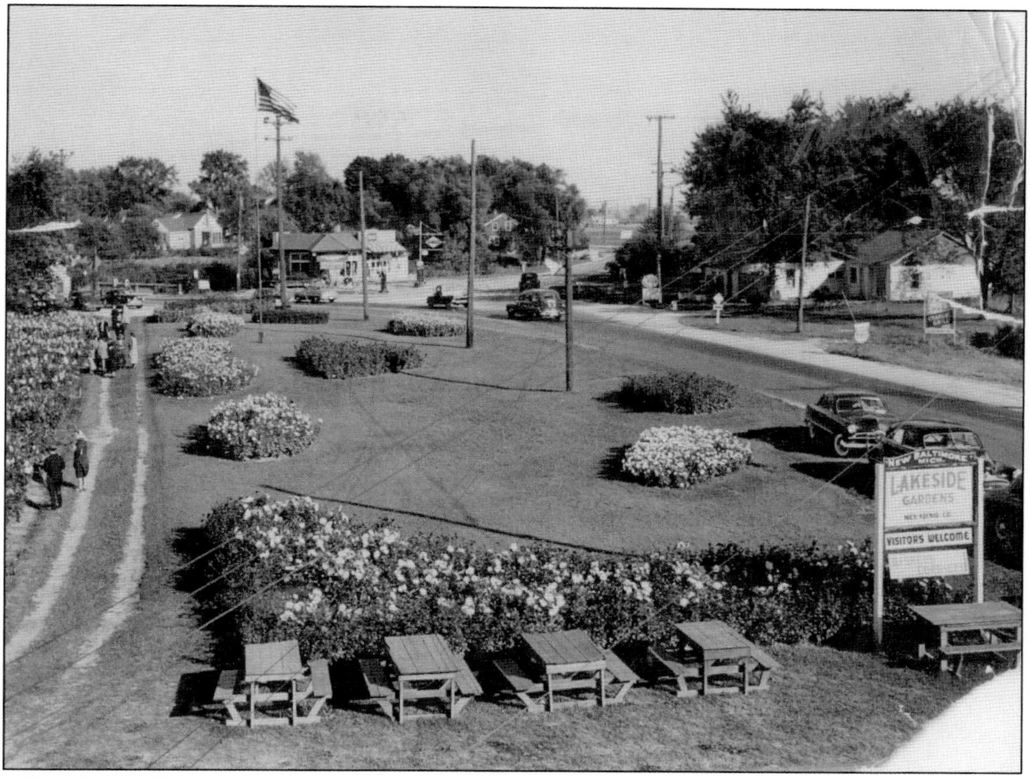

Lakeside Gardens was owned by the Koenig family and located at 23 Mile Road near Main Street. They deservedly caused the area to be known as the "Dahlia Capital of the World." (Both, courtesy of Jim Genso).

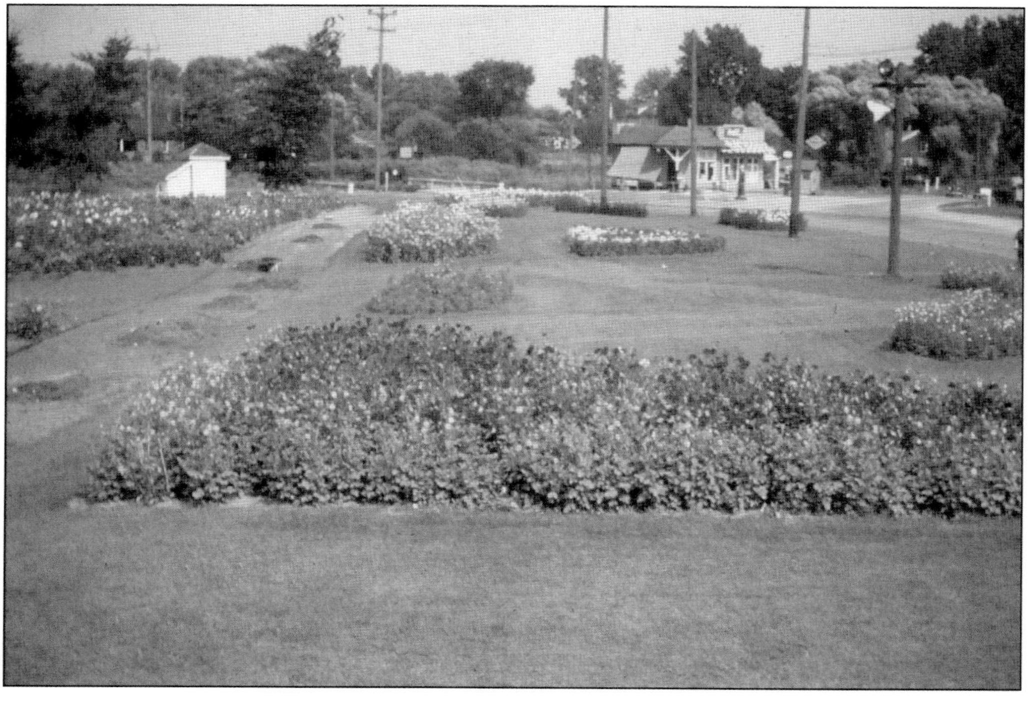

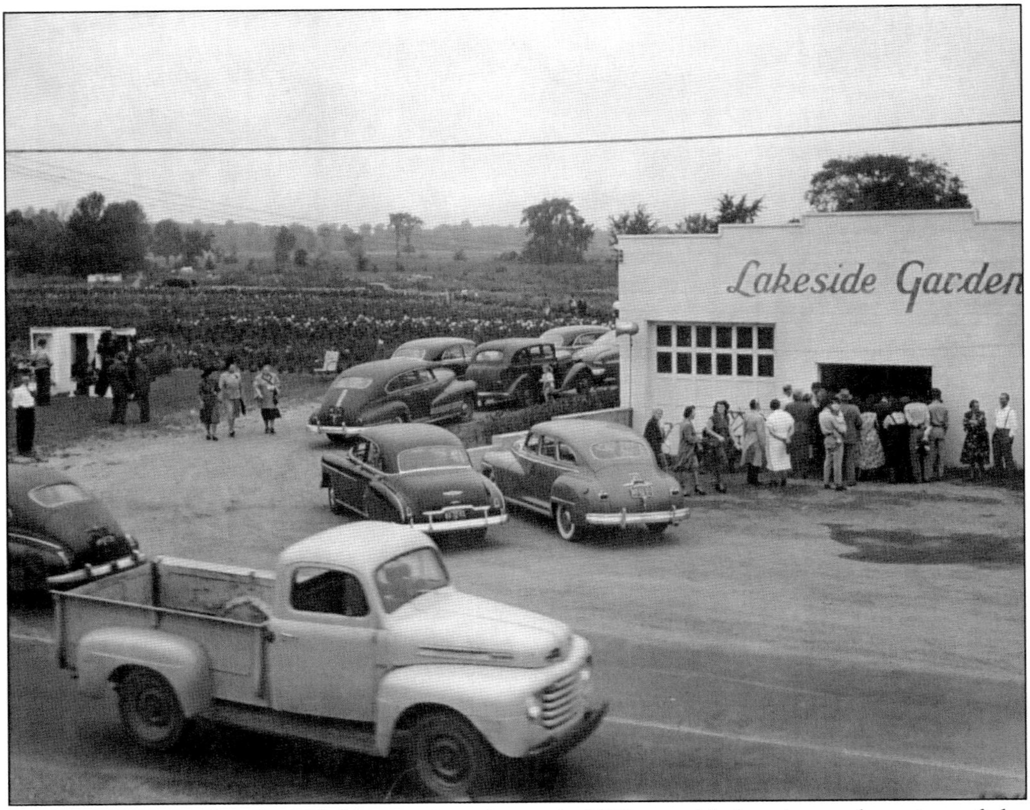

Above is a view of early 23 Mile Road in the early 1950s, and below is another view of the Koenig dahlia fields. Lakeside Gardens created its own types of dahlias, named after the Koenig grandchildren. There is now a memorial (with dahlias, of course) dedicated to the Koenigs at the entrance to Walter and Mary Burke Park in New Baltimore. (Both, courtesy of Jim Genso.)

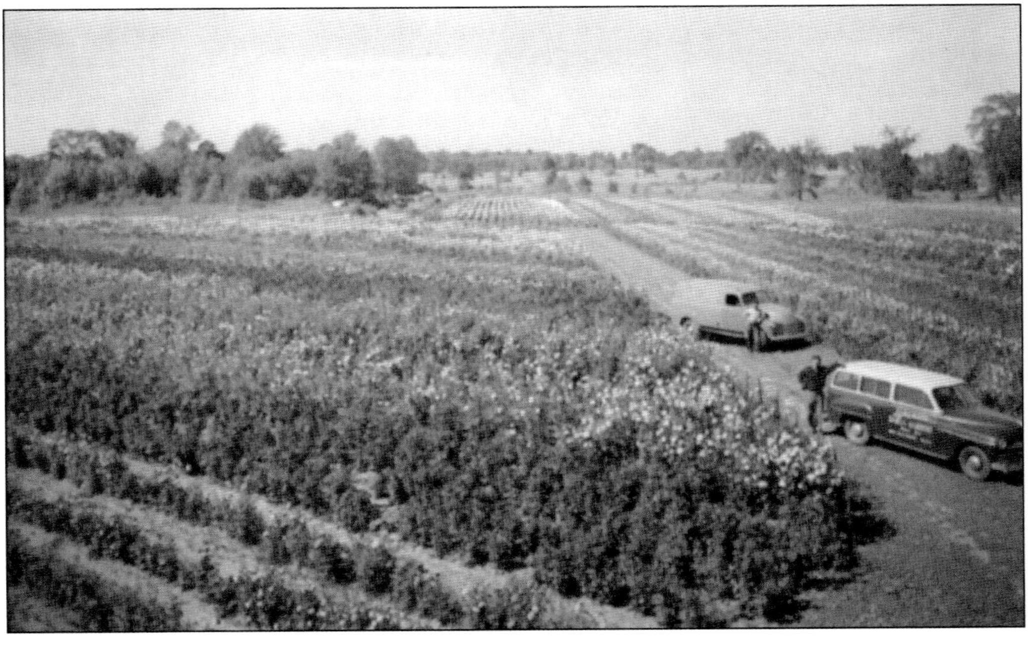

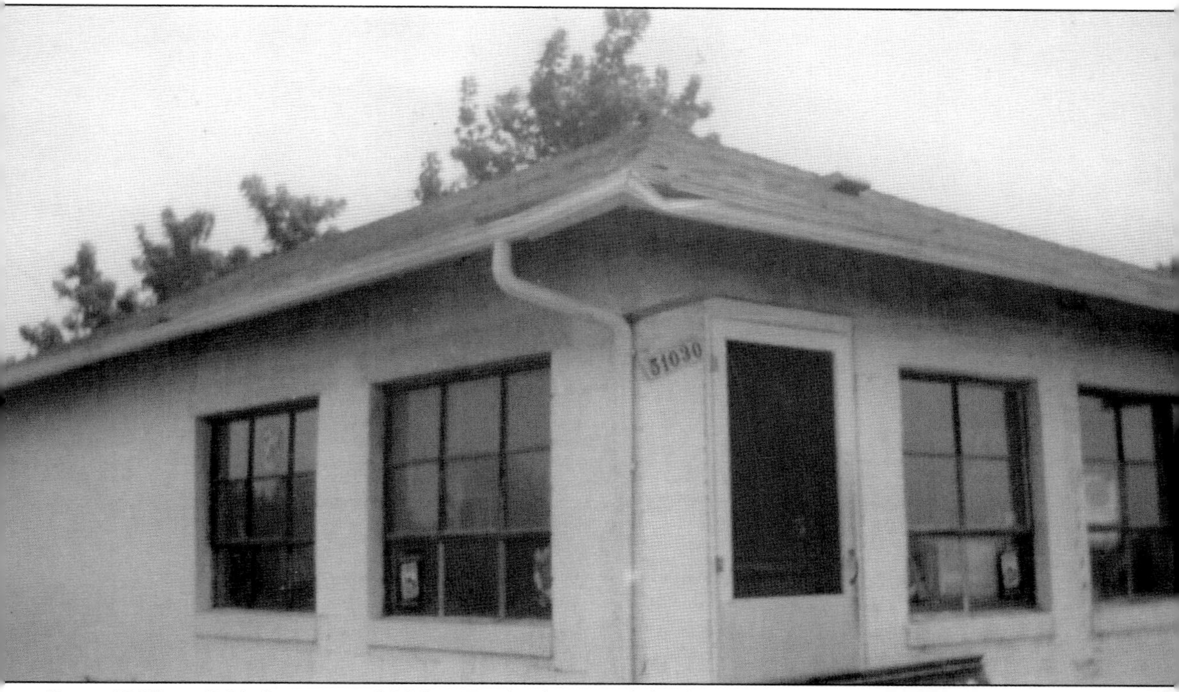

From 1925 to 1974, Jerome and Helen Zischerk owned the business on the southeast corner of 23 Mile Road and Gratiot Avenue. Originally a brick building with a gas station called Jerome's Corner, the building was renovated and converted into a restaurant called Jerry Jo's. (Courtesy of Marion Allemon.)

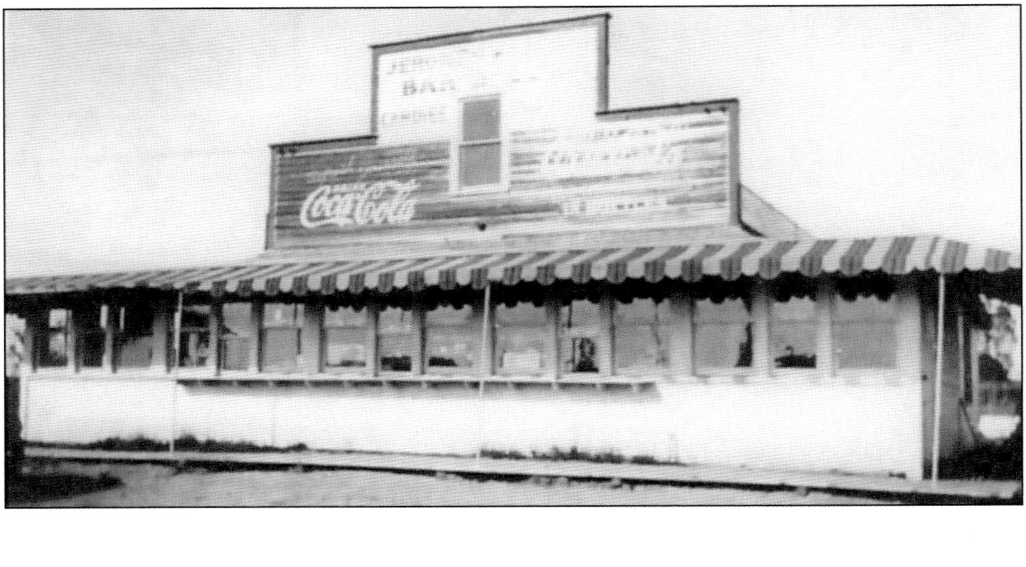

Above is what the building at 23 Mile Road and Gratiot Avenue looked like after being converted. The image below shows the structure behind the other building, which was a drive-in restaurant; one could walk up to the window and order. In the 1940s, the porch and top of the building were removed as the structure underwent a renovation. (Both, courtesy of Marion Allemon.)

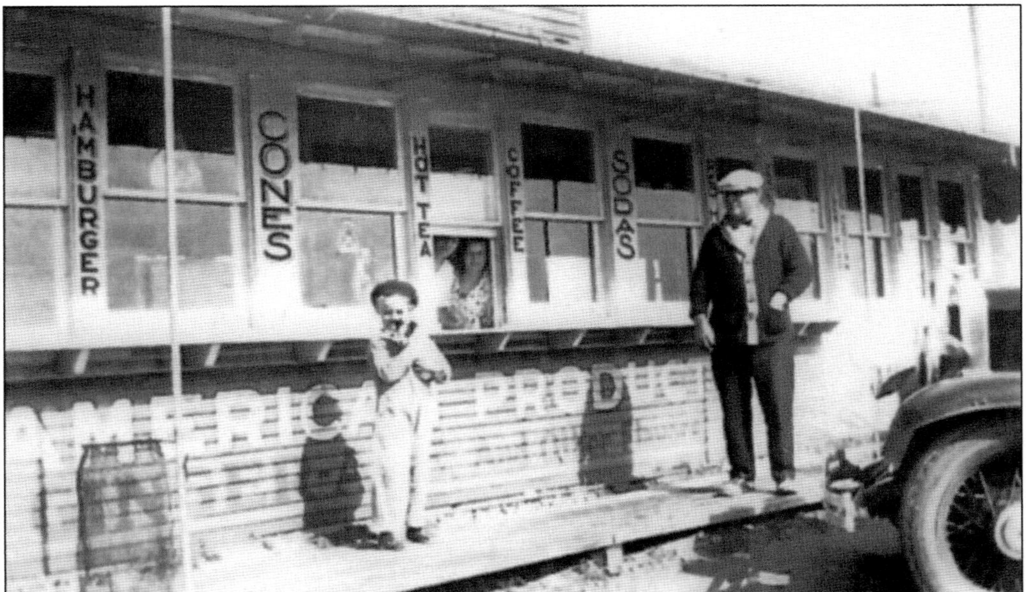

Here are two views of the restaurant. In the photograph at right, taken during the 1930s, are Evelyn, Jerome A., and Jerome W. Zischerk. Since Gratiot Avenue was the main street in Macomb County, it was the main thoroughfare for trucks to make deliveries from Port Huron to Detroit. Therefore, the businesses Jerome's Corner and Jerry Jo's Restaurant were on one of the busiest corners of the township. Even in the 21st century, the corner of 23 Mile Road and Gratiot Avenue is still one of the busiest in Michigan. The building was modified in 1937 to appear as it does on the cover. (Both, courtesy of Marion Allemon.)

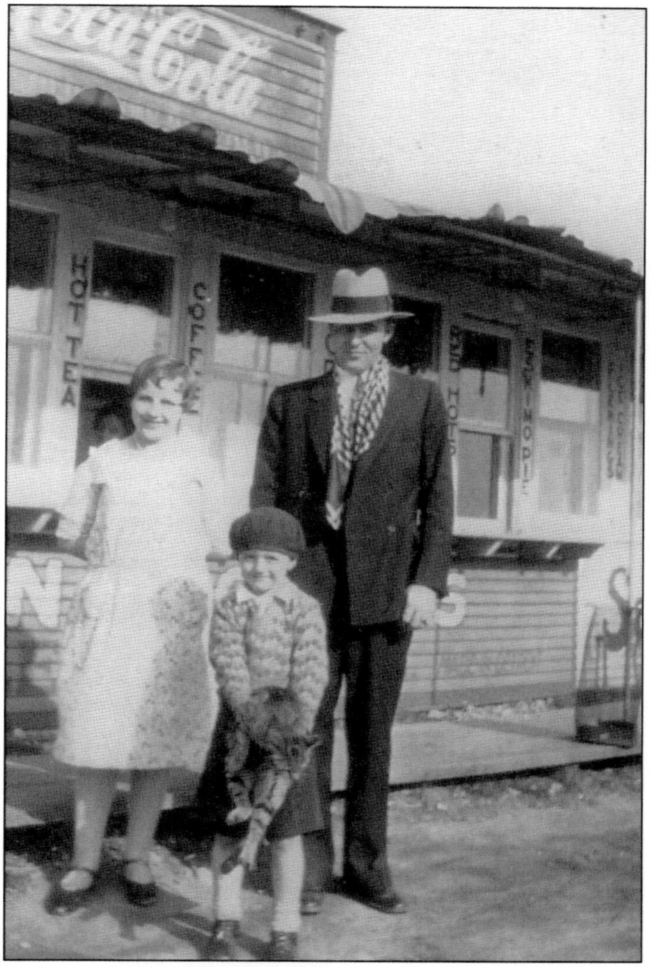

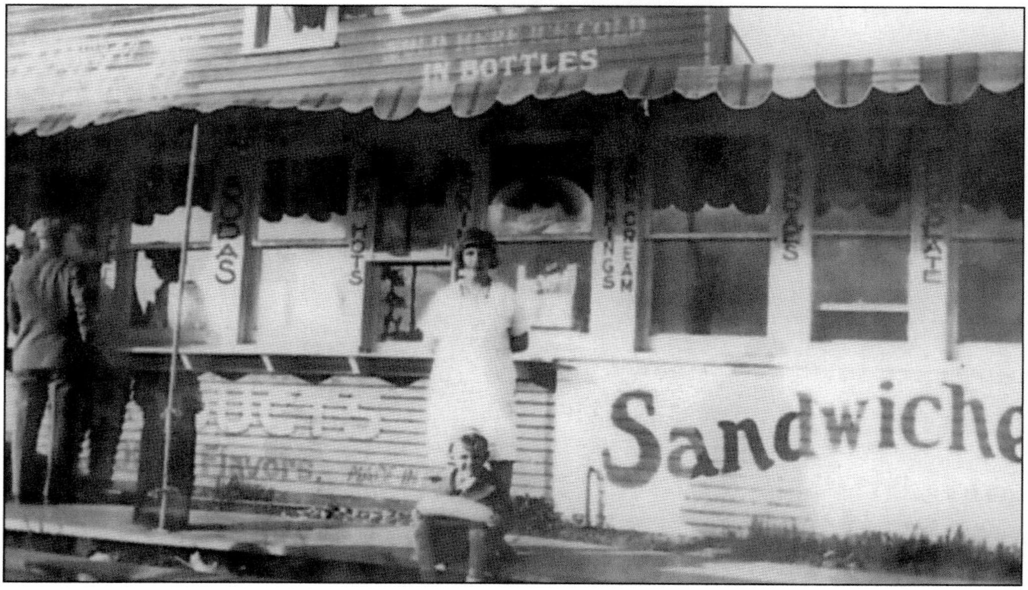

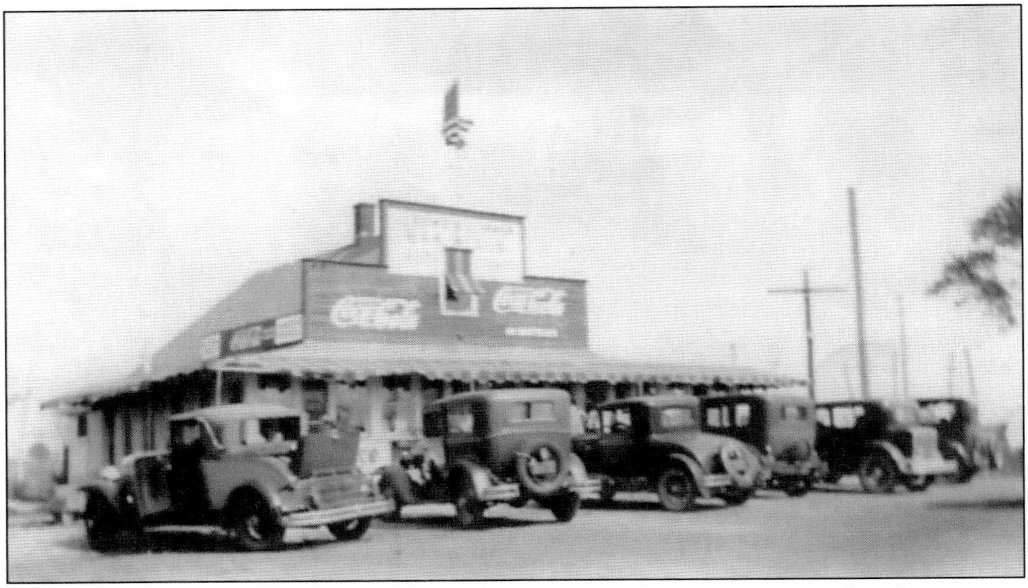

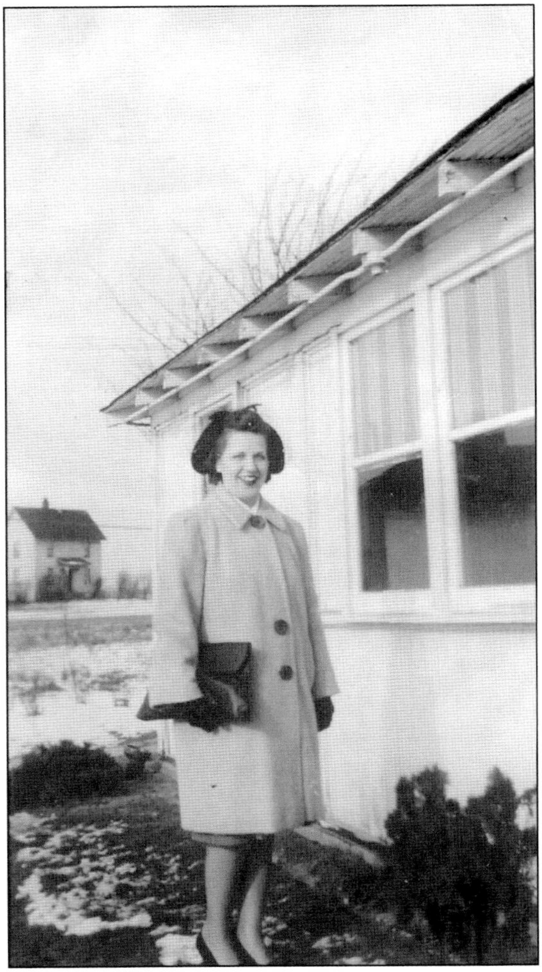

Jerome's Corner continued to thrive through the 1930s, 1940s, and 1950s. Open 24 hours a day, it served hamburgers, ice cream, soda, tea, coffee, sandwiches, and other food items. Also sold were cigars, Copenhagen snuff, and stay-awake pills that appealed to truck drivers. In the photograph at left, Evelyn Zischerk is standing by the side of the building with the Sans Farmhouse at the other corner of Gratiot Avenue. A gas station is now on the corner where the farmhouse stood. (Both, courtesy of Marion Allemon.)

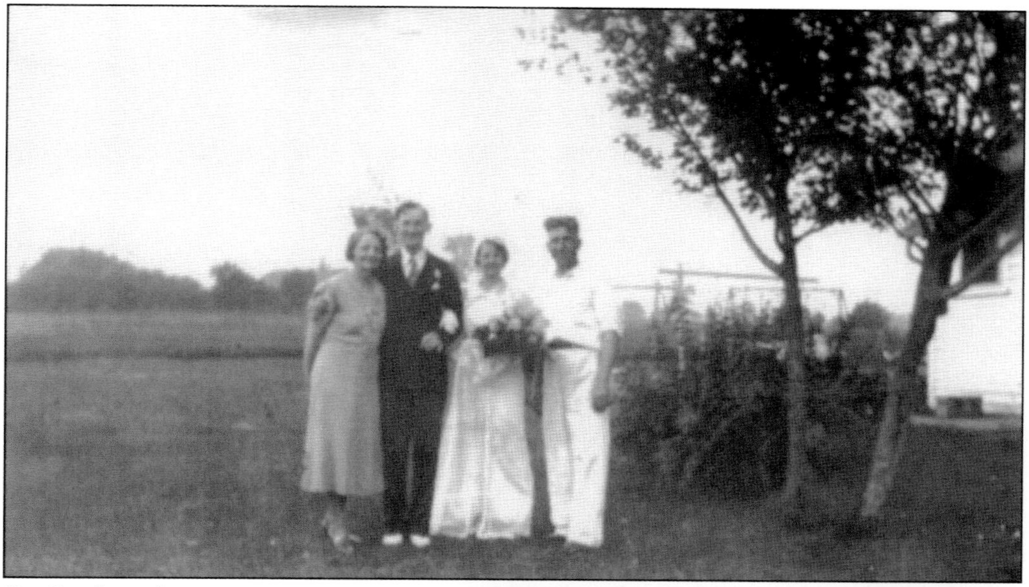

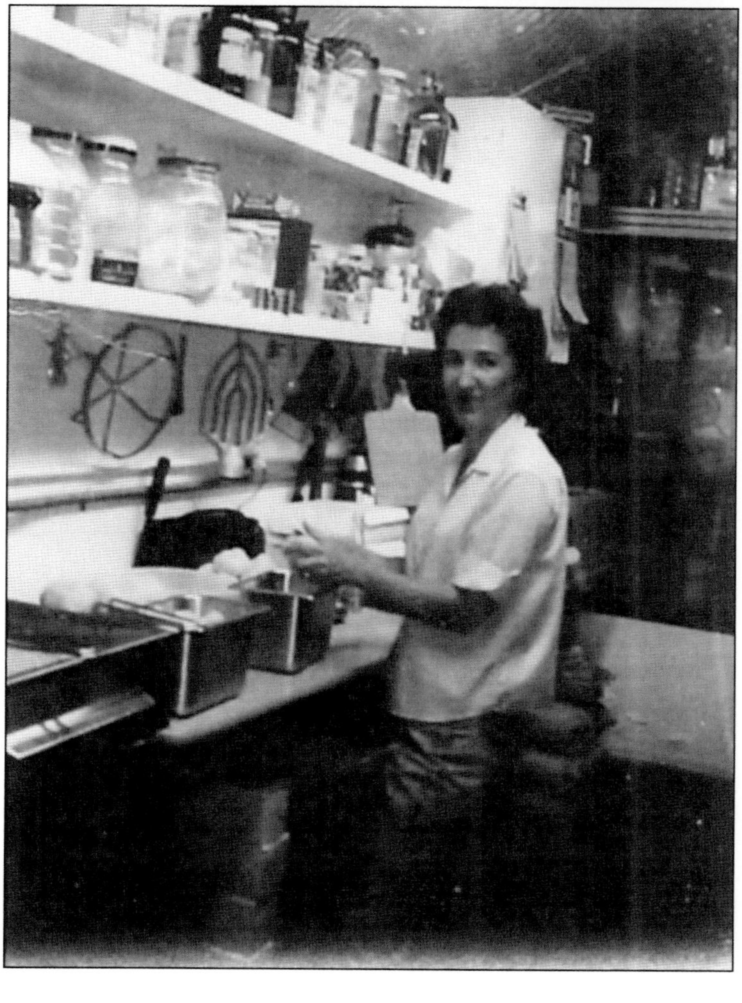

On Sundays, the restaurant used carhops, and in 1956 Marion Allemon was the first one to perform this function. Pictured above from left to right are Helen and Anthony Finnigan and Helen and Jerome Zischerk standing in front of the Jerome's Corner driveway. Anthony and Helen were Helen Zischerk's parents. Seen at right is Joanne Zischerk in the kitchen at Jerry Jo's. (Both, courtesy of Marion Allemon.)

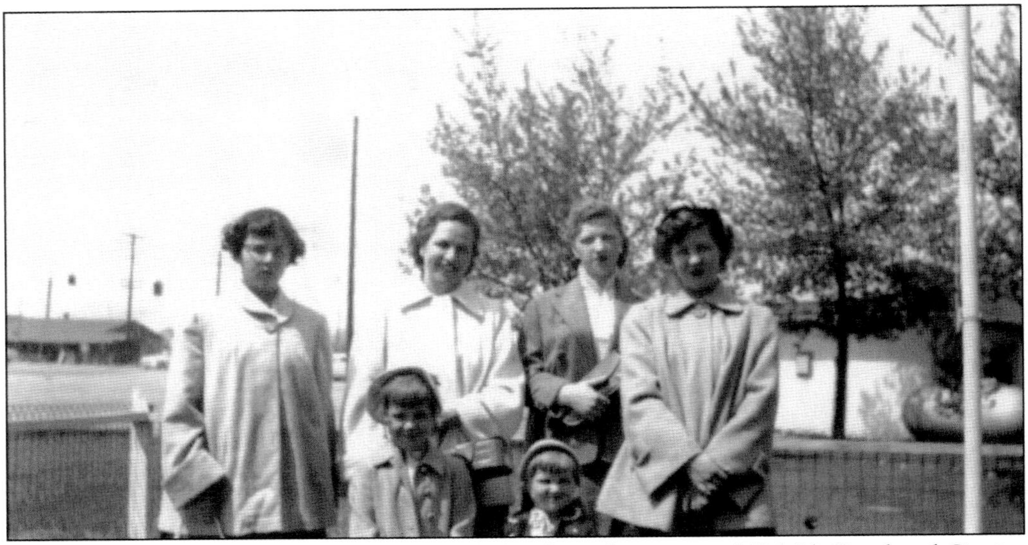

Pictured here on May 3, 1955, is the Zischerk family at the corner of 23 Mile Road and Gratiot Avenue. They are, from left to right, Viola, Evelyn Joan, Marion, Dorothy, and Audrey Weingartz. Seen in the background on the corner is Phil's Fruit and Vegetable Market. On the right is Jerry Jo's. Today, there is a stoplight at this intersection. (Courtesy of Marion Allemon.)

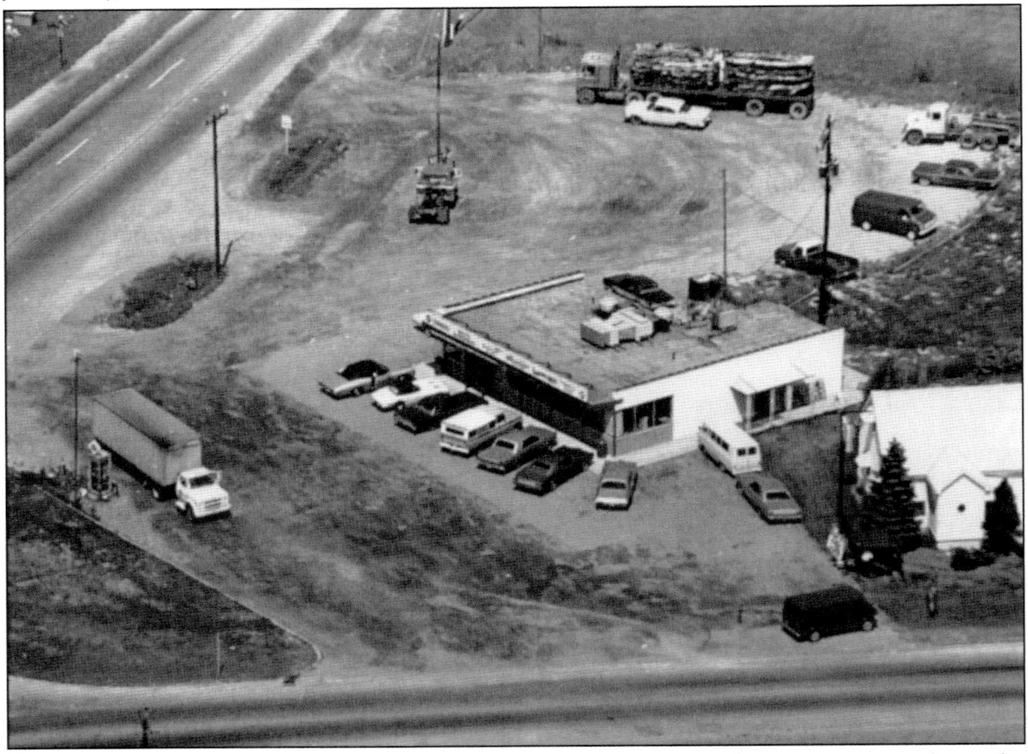

This early-1960s aerial view of Jerome's Corner at 23 Mile Road and Gratiot Avenue shows the original gas station/restaurant and the house that faced 23 Mile Road. Around 1970, the buildings were demolished and a Hardee's Restaurant was later built on the site. A shopping center was constructed to the east of the corner. In early 2000, the Hardee's was torn down and a Walgreens drugstore was built on the corner. (Courtesy of Marion Allemon.)

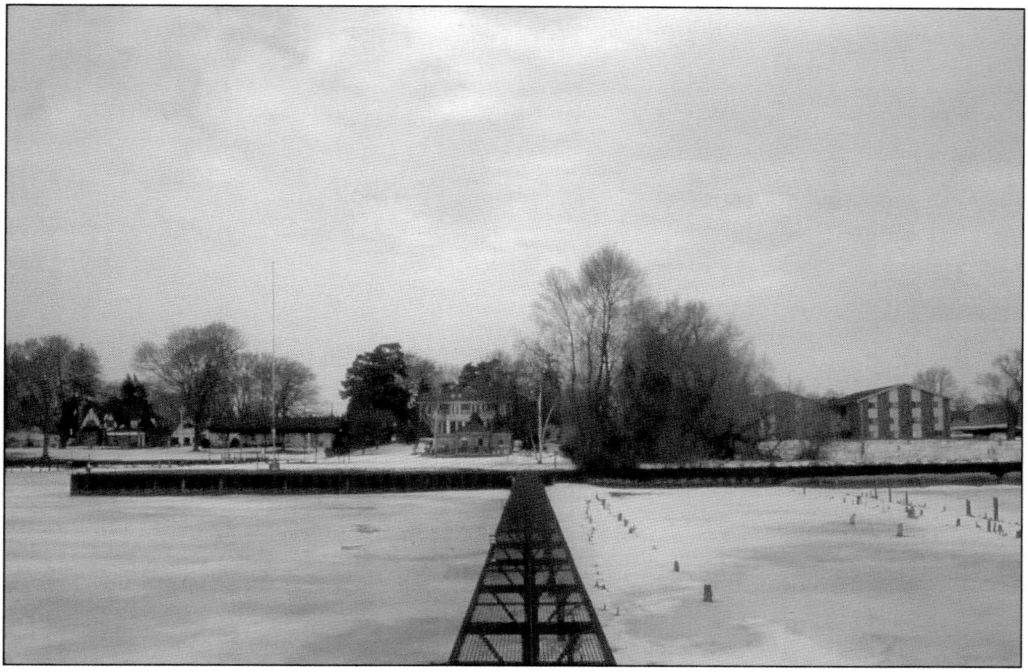

An interurban stop was at Bay Court, a street off from Jefferson Avenue on Lake St. Clair. Right on the border between Chesterfield Township and New Baltimore, Bay Court was the last stop before the train would enter New Baltimore.

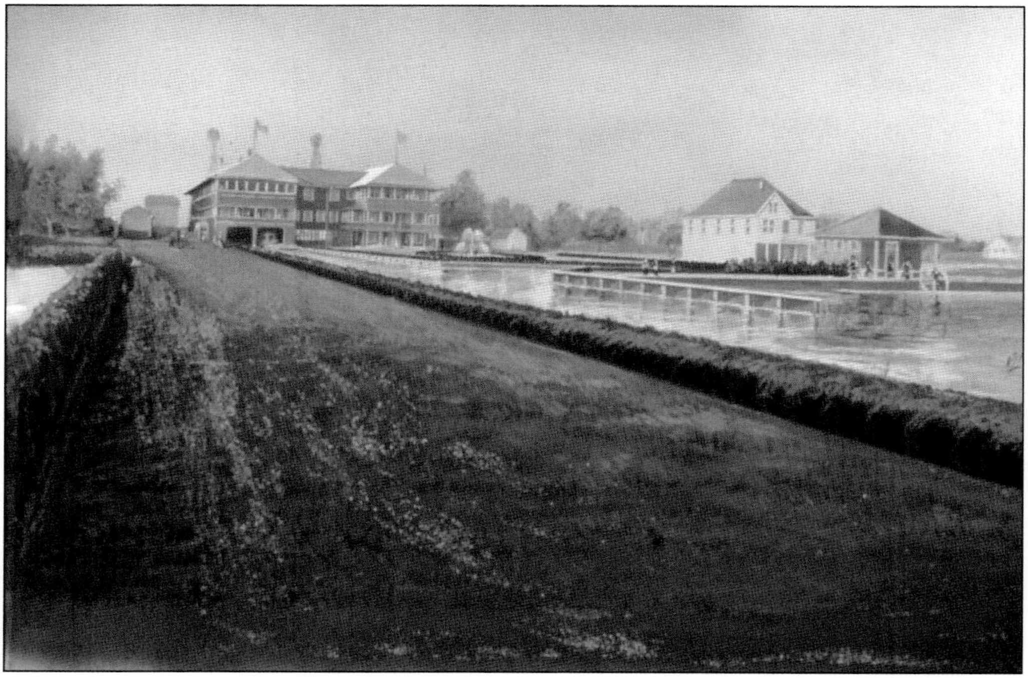

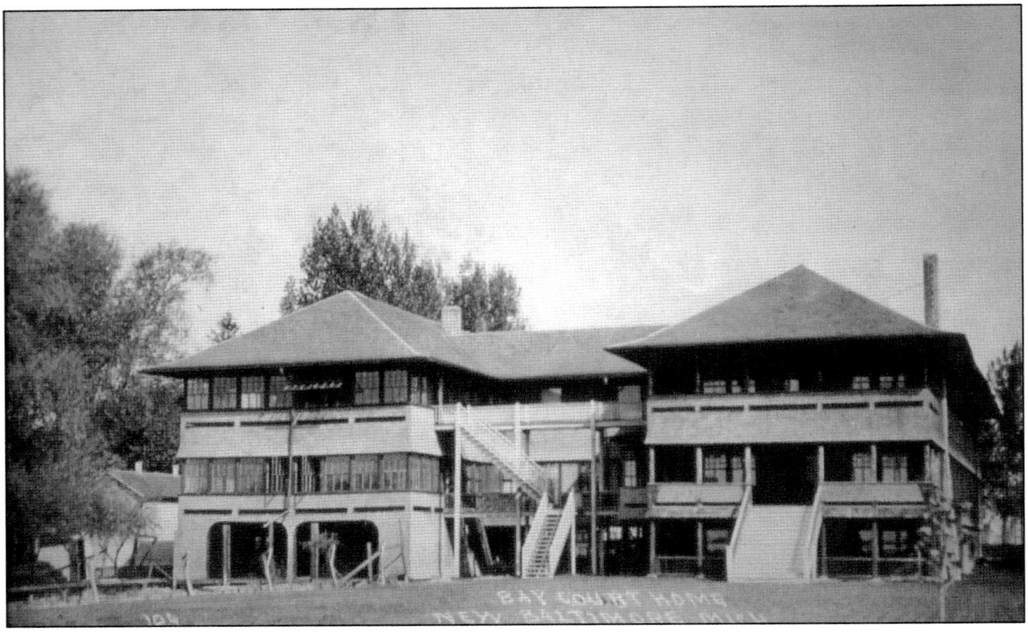

Nearby county seat Mt. Clemens, with its mineral bath industry, and New Baltimore, with hotels and its proximity to Lake St. Clair, appealed to Detroit tourists. Chesterfield also made its bid for the tourist dollar by renting out log cabins for hunters and fishermen to use on Bay Court. Both from around 1910, above is an image of the Bay Court Home, and below is an advertisement for Shore Haven cabins.

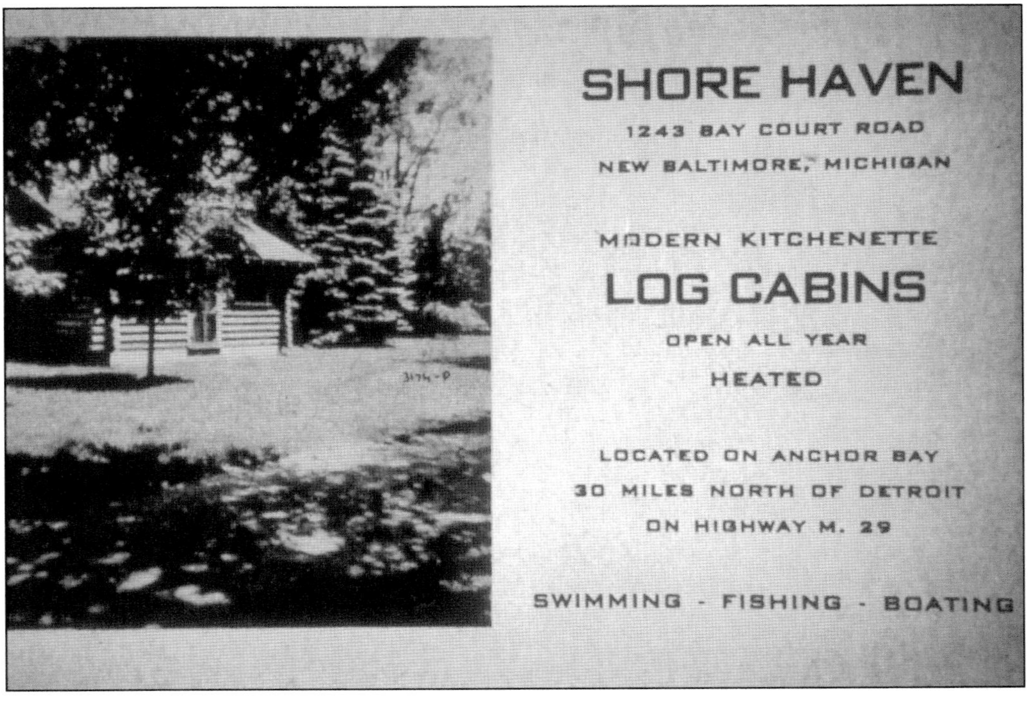

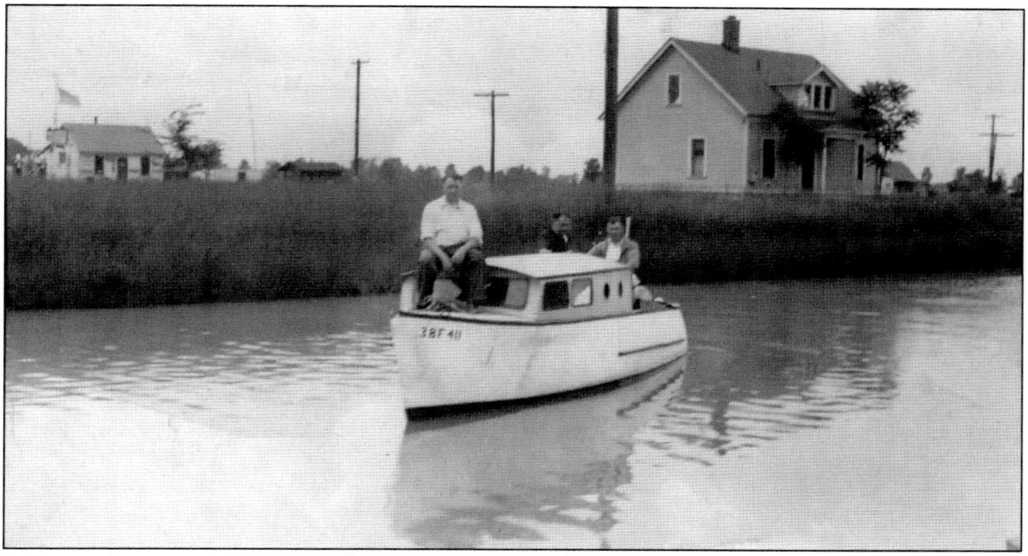

Jefferson Avenue in Chesterfield was not a very stable road; every year from the 1920s through the 1940s, it would flood in the spring. Residents of the area would always get ready for the annual flood season, especially depending on how close their houses were to the lake. (Courtesy of Kraft family.)

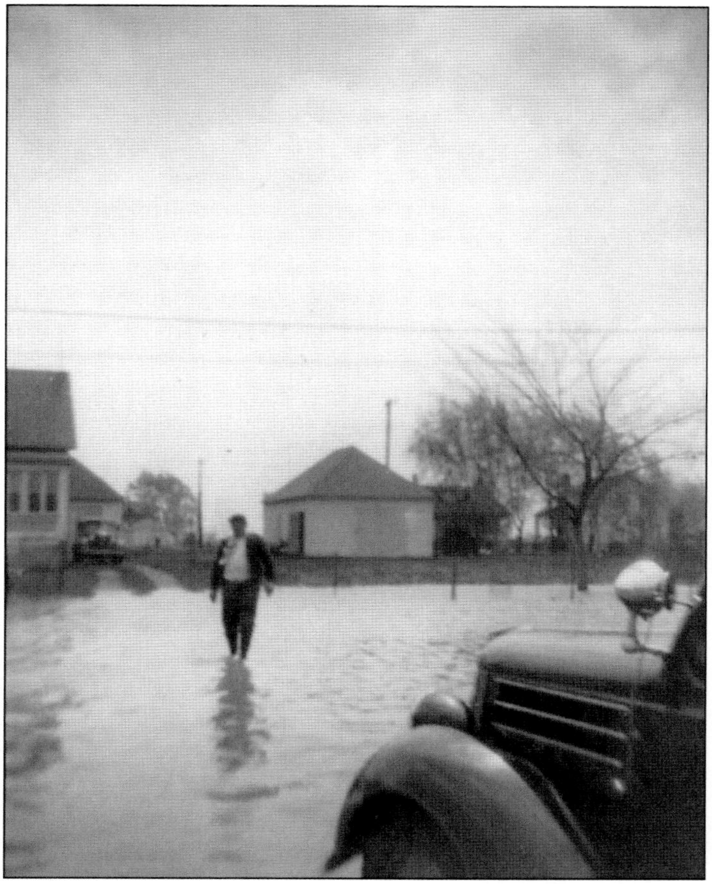

Even in more recent years, seawalls have had to be strengthened and sand bags used to shore up the rising waters. Many of the most affected homes had boats, which unfortunately came in handy in the spring. (Courtesy of Kraft family.)

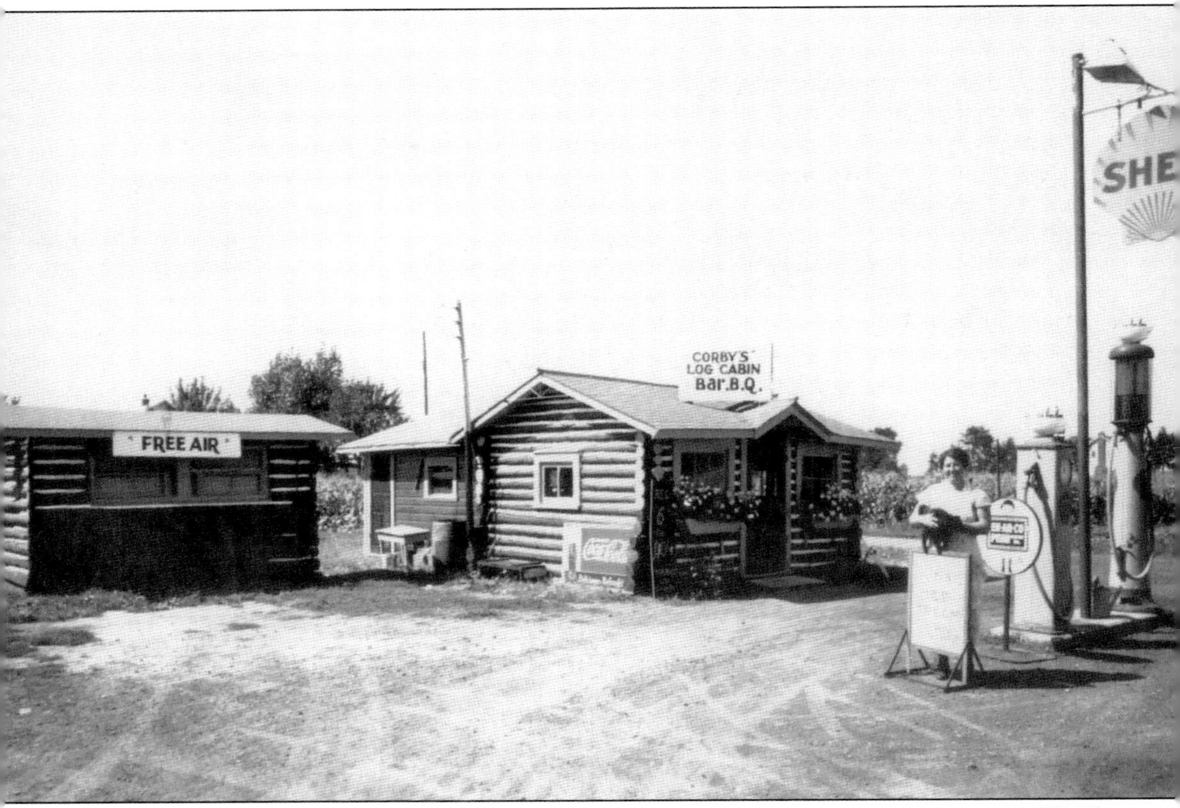

Adeline (Dolly) Neighbauer Corby is in this photograph with her black cat on August 29, 1937. This log cabin gas station was located north of 21 Mile Road (then known as Shoemaker Road), on the west side of Gratiot Avenue, just across from the barns of the Brandenburg Farm on the northeast corner of 21 Mile Road and Gratiot Avenue. (Courtesy of Helen [Priehs] Foss-Bohm.)

Four

Businesses of Chesterfield

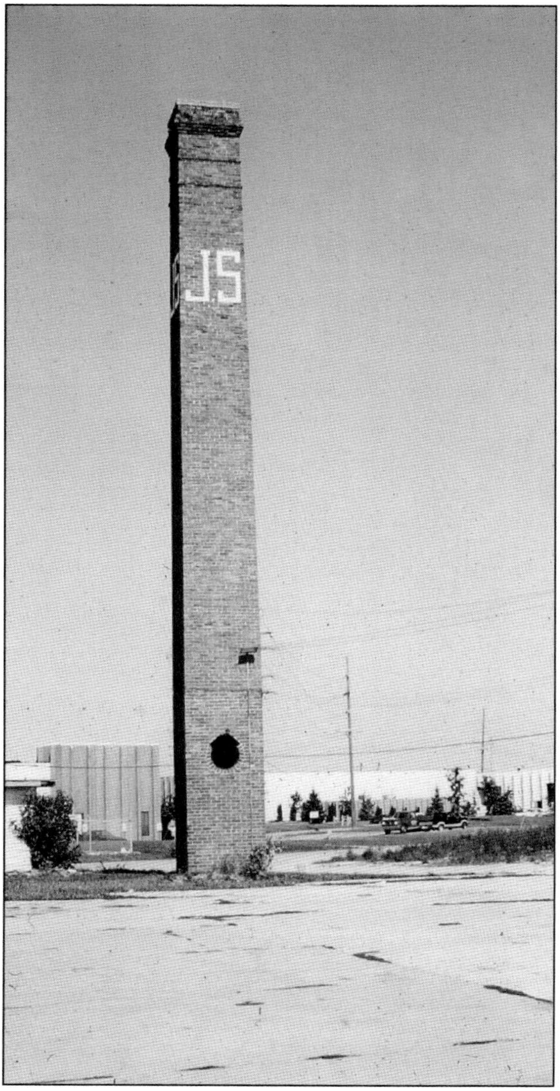

Many Chesterfield farmers raised cattle, mostly Jersey. Around 1916, the dairy industry was so big in Chesterfield that the Chesterfield Creamery at Cotton Road and Gratiot Avenue was said to be world renowned. It was started by George H. Nichols when he bought the 16-acre Fairchild farm. One of the most successful in Michigan, it sold 110,000 pounds of butter and other dairy products in 1904. John Schlaff eventually bought the operation. The initials "J.S." on the top of the chimney stood for John Schlaff. When the creamery burned, its tall chimney continued to tower over Chesterfield until it was torn down in June 2003. As of 2010, the house was still there and being used by Rossel's Farm and Garden.

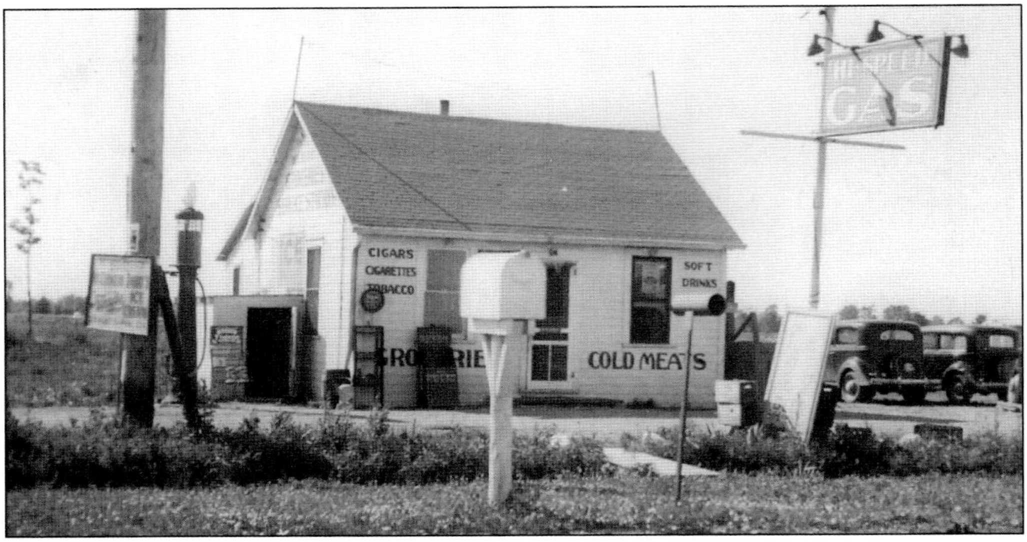

The late-1930s photograph above shows the original building for Kraft's Market. In the image below is a later view of Kraft's Market from the 1950s. The building underwent some renovations, including the addition of a beer store. (Both, courtesy of Kraft family.)

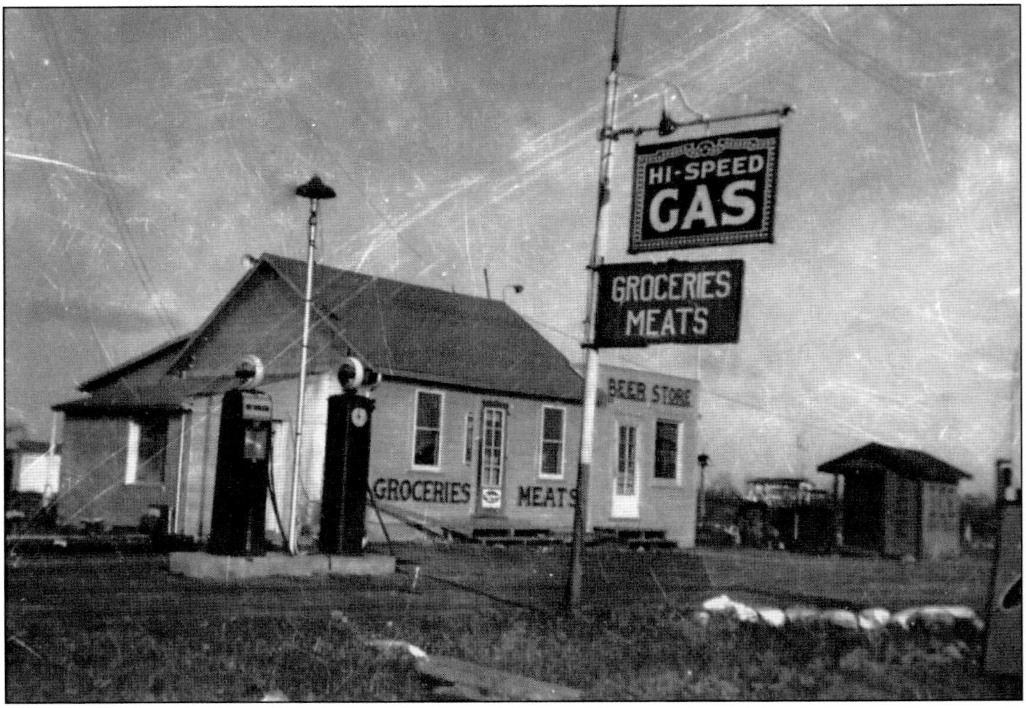

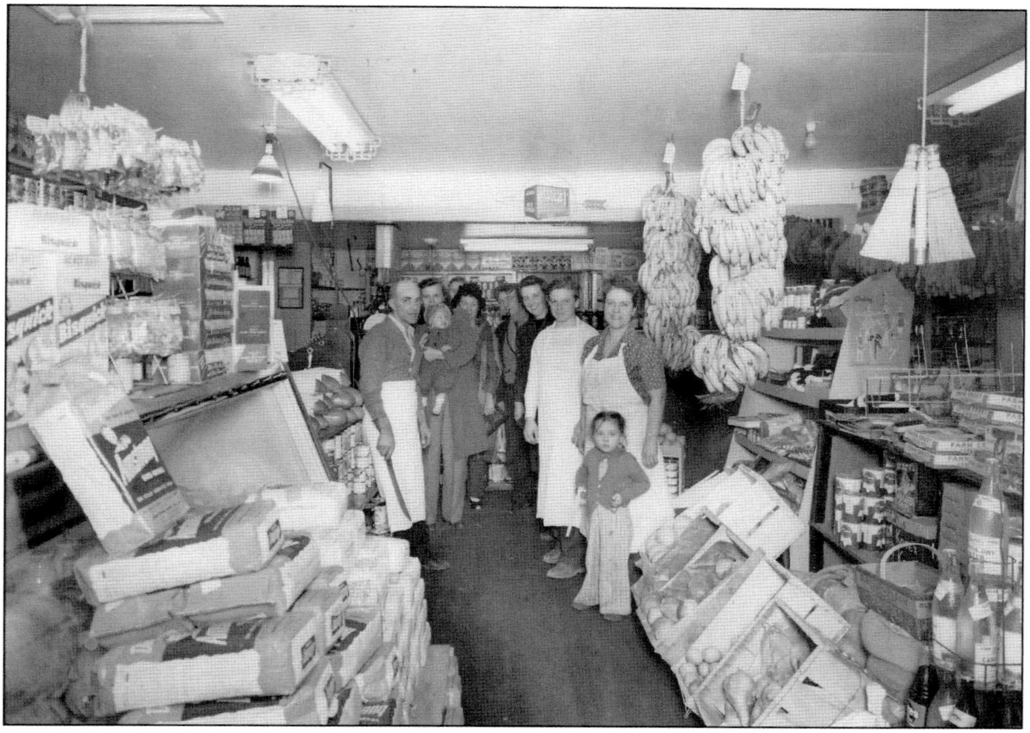

Pictured are Kraft's Market employees with Helen Kraft in front. Run by "Grandma Kraft", the store featured fresh vegetables, nationally known brands of canned goods, high-quality meat, and beer and wine. Notice the bananas suspended from the ceiling and the crates of fruits and vegetables stacked on the floor. The store also sold gasoline. By the late 1960s, the business also carried a liquor license, as a wide range of the alcohol available can be seen behind Grandma Kraft in the image below. (Both, courtesy of Kraft family.)

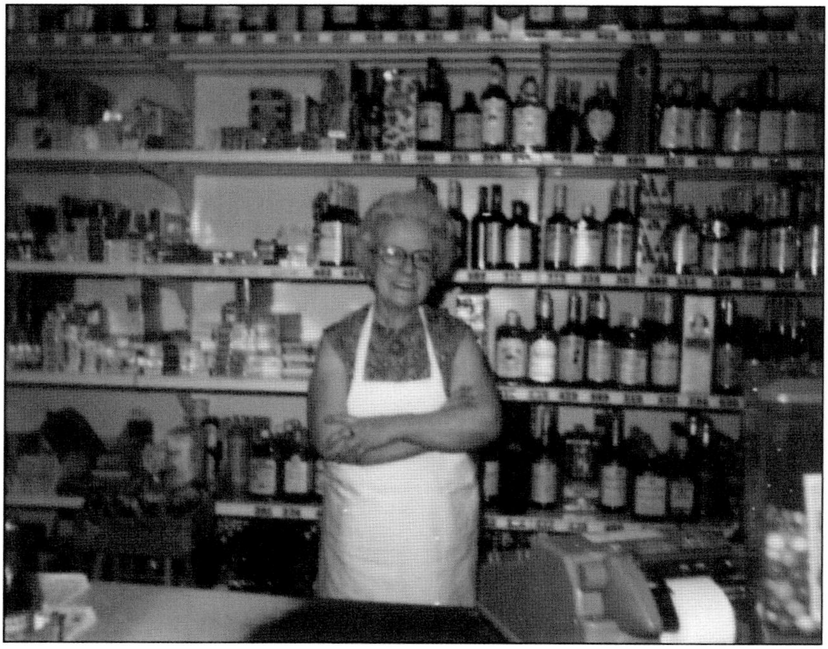

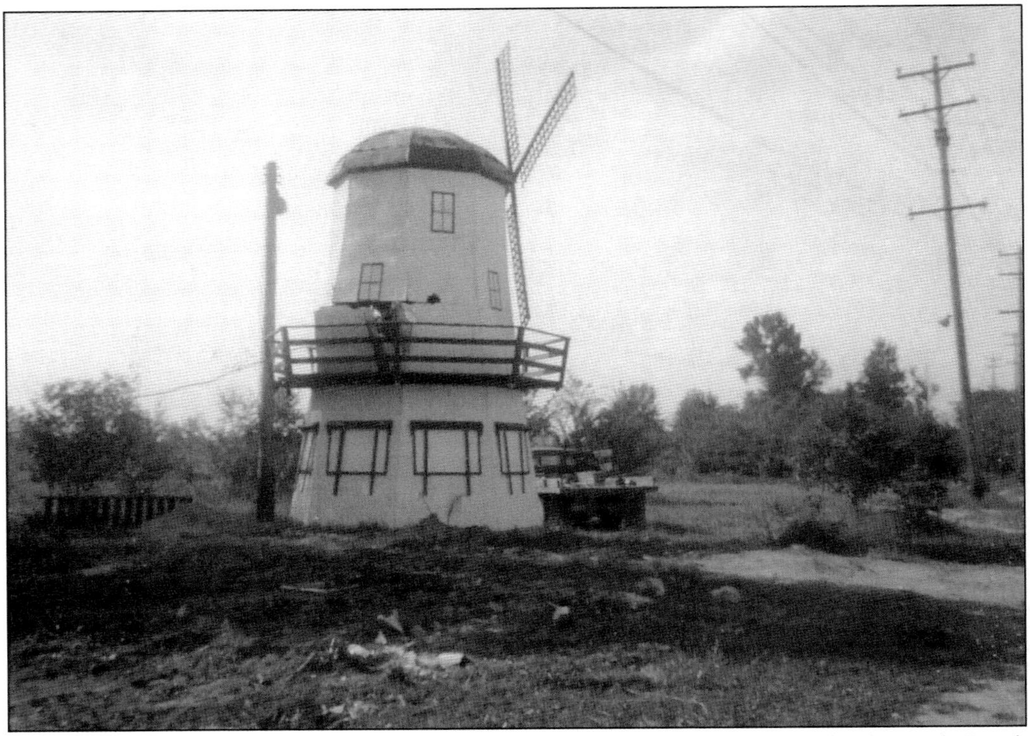

The Kabel tulip farm was located on the east side of Gratiot Avenue just south of 22 Mile Road. Marked by this windmill, the tulip farm was a local landmark until a tragic airplane accident. According to Wilma Kabel Henry, in 1960 an aircraft tanker failed to get proper liftoff from Selfridge Air Force Base and crashed just south of the windmill. The plane leaked fuel all the way from Selfridge to 22 Mile Road and Gratiot Avenue, causing the land to have to be plowed for miles. (Both, courtesy of Trinity Archives.)

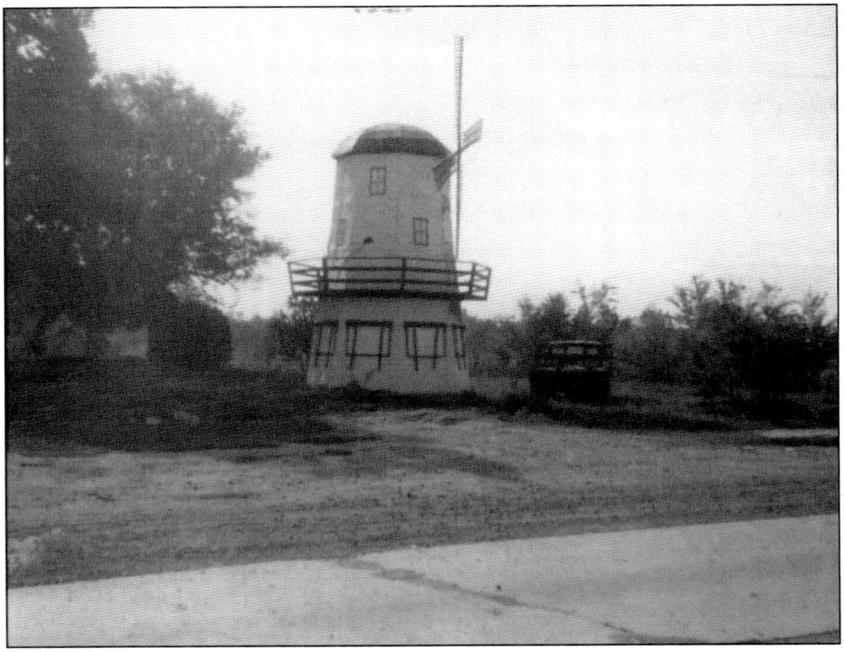

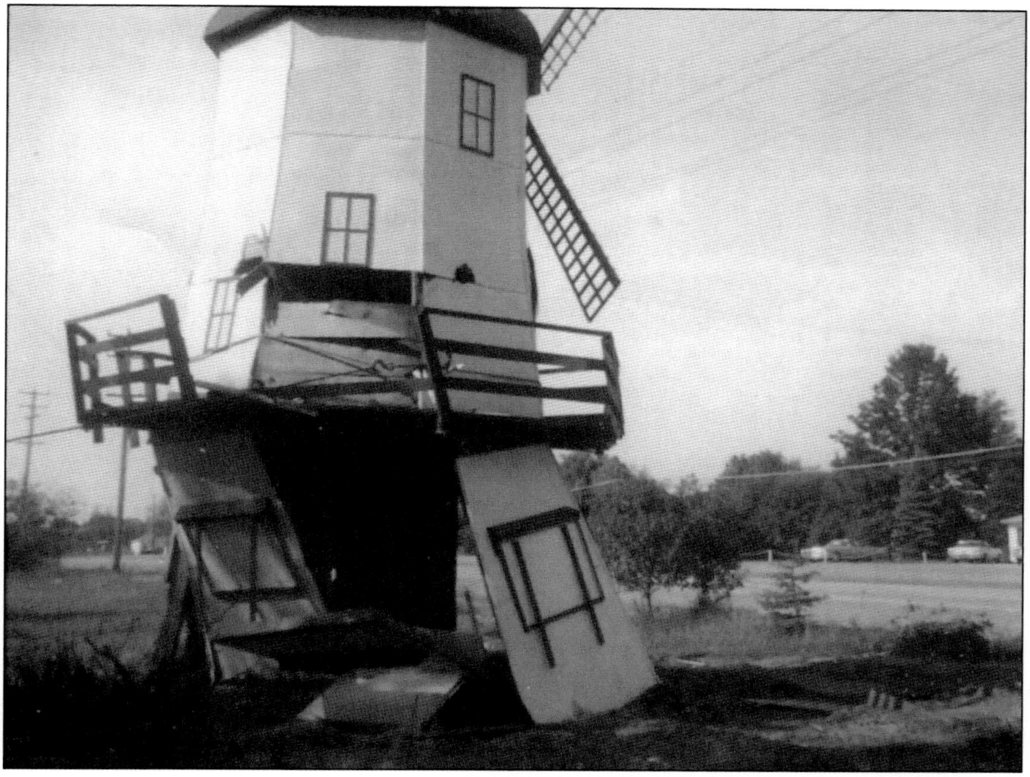

The plane crashed at the Kabel farm, sending pieces of it all over the property. Parts of the wing crashed into the barn, causing Gerald Kabel, who was inside, to see only flames and think, "The world is coming to an end." After lots of anxious minutes, everyone in the Kabel family was accounted for. Unfortunately, all five of the servicemen in the plane perished in the crash. Kabel would find body parts for years while plowing the farm and would notify the air base to send someone to pick up the remnants. (Both, courtesy of Trinity Archives.)

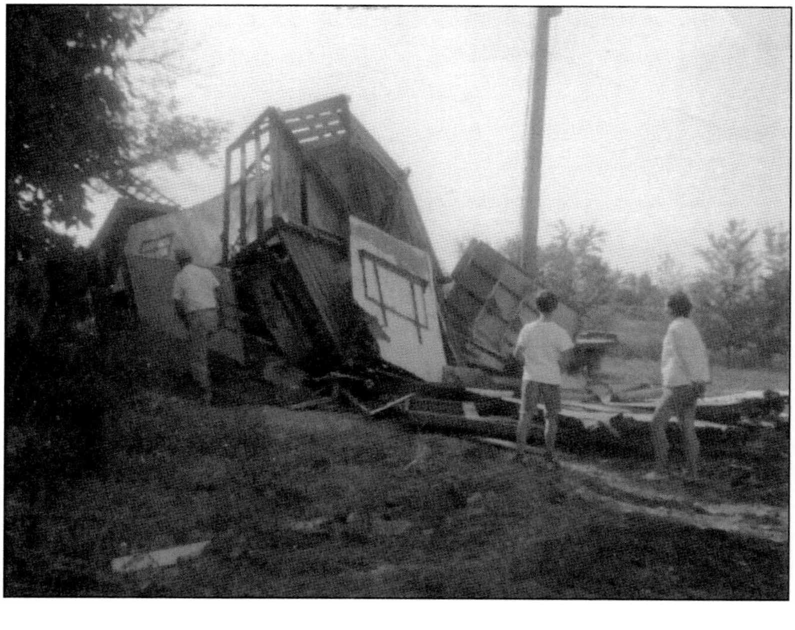

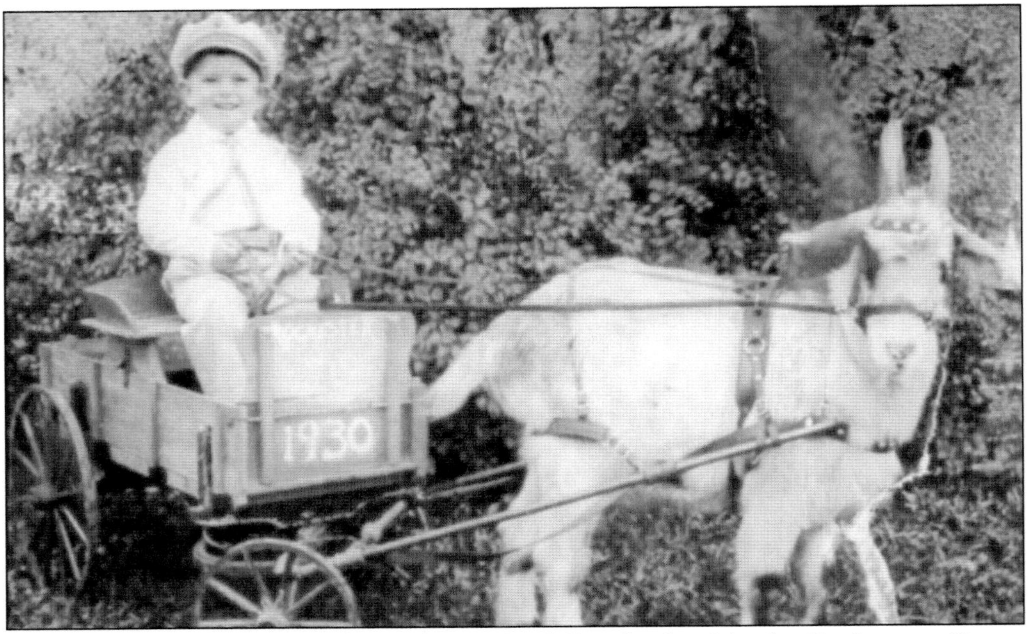

At one time, the huge Book Brothers Lakeview Stock Farm bordered Anchor Bay between Cotton and Sugarbush Roads. Up to the 1960s, Chesterfield was primarily a farm area with many French families, including the Furtons, Gardners, Marsacks, Meldrums, Peltiers, Rivards, and Pelkies. In the early 1900s, their version of Shrove Tuesday, the day before Lent begins, was called "Shone Tuesday," also commonly known as Pancake Tuesday. Parades, parties, dancing, and games lasted until midnight before Ash Wednesday, the first day of Lent, which began six weeks of prayer and abstinence; no couples got married until after it was over. After Lent, for Easter everyone would wear their best clothes and go to church. Pictured here is Joseph Allemon being pulled by a goat in his Easter finery. (Courtesy of Dolly Allemon).

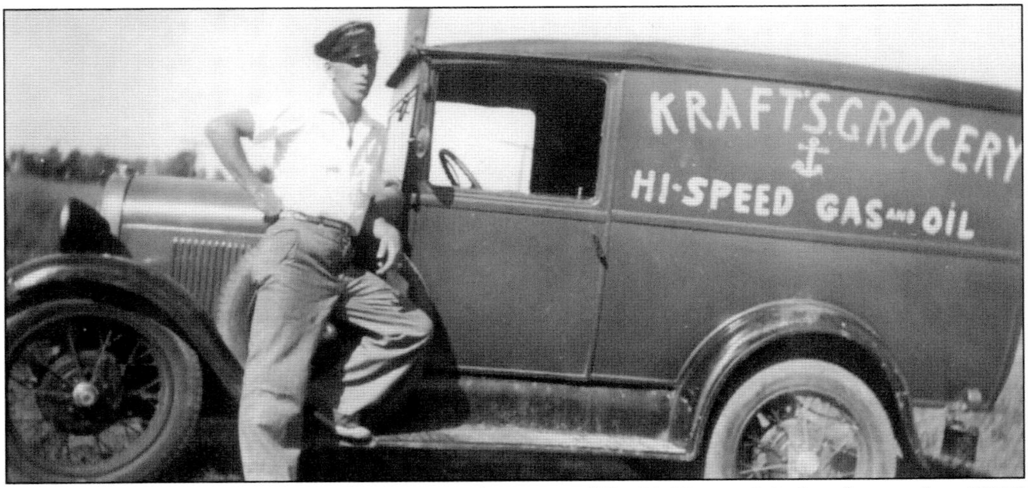

Typical of businesses back in the 1930s was the story of Kraft's Korner Market. Located at 45935 Jefferson Avenue near the cross street of Anchor Drive, it was in business for over 25 years as a local grocery store. Helen Kraft and her family lived above the store, which was expanded a few times. They would take phone orders and deliver groceries in a truck. Back in the day when there would be only one car per family, which was generally used by husband to commute to work, delivery was a big part of many grocery businesses. (Courtesy of Kraft family.)

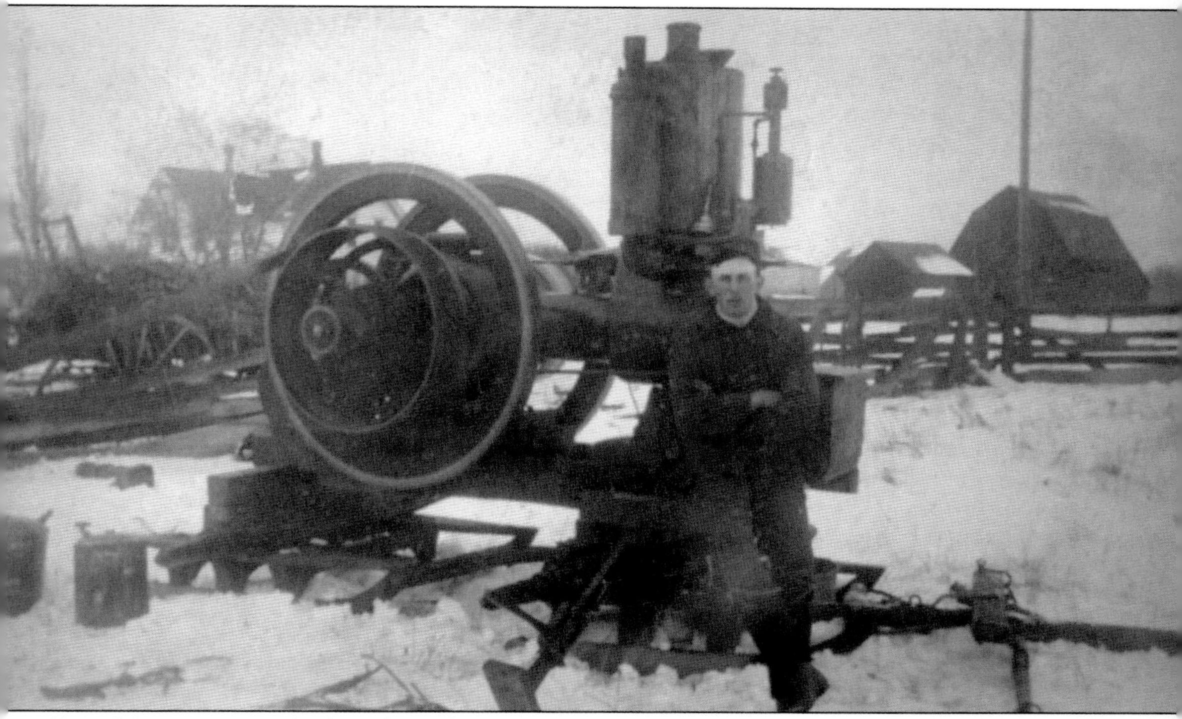

Farm life was not easy back in the early 1900s. A typical farm raised oats, wheat, and barley with fields being plowed by horse or mule. Crops were at the mercy of the weather, and some summers were so hot and dry that nothing would grow. Rare winters lasted so long that there would still be snow in May. A small vegetable garden was usually maintained for family use, and livestock and poultry were also raised. Work was done in the spring through the autumn from dawn to dark. An annual income would often be in the area of $1,200 per year, although cash was not needed for many things. Heat in the winter came from wood stoves, and all a family could eat was produced right on the farm. Hunting and fishing helped diversify meals.

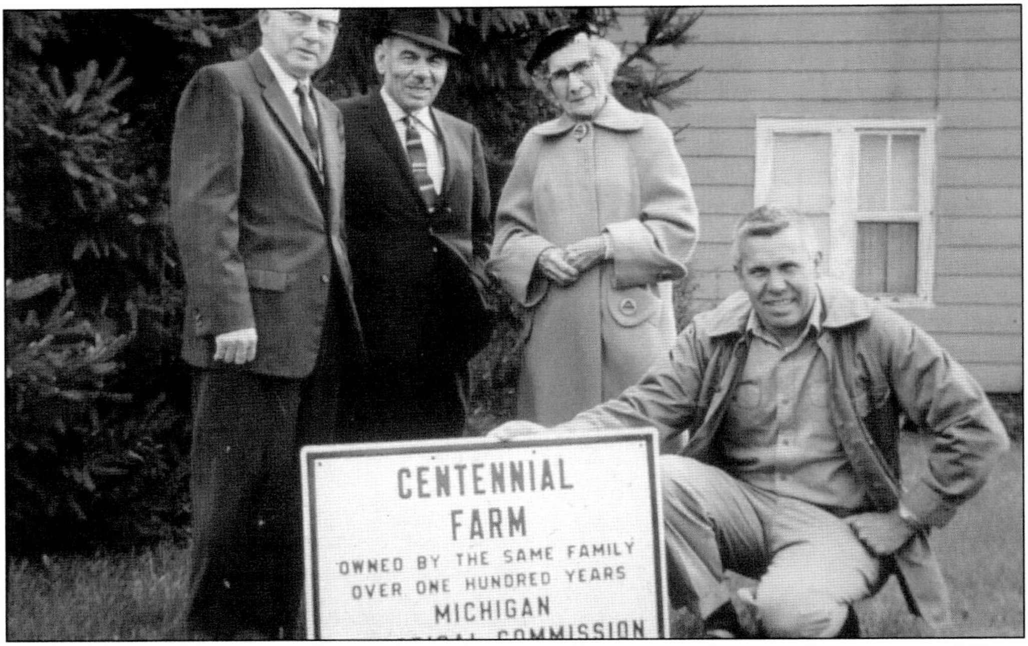

Built in 1826, the Fullers' farm was on Callens Road, and it was designated a Centennial Farm for having been in the same family for over 100 years. Each one is certified by the Centennial Farm Program and must be a working farm of over 10 acres.

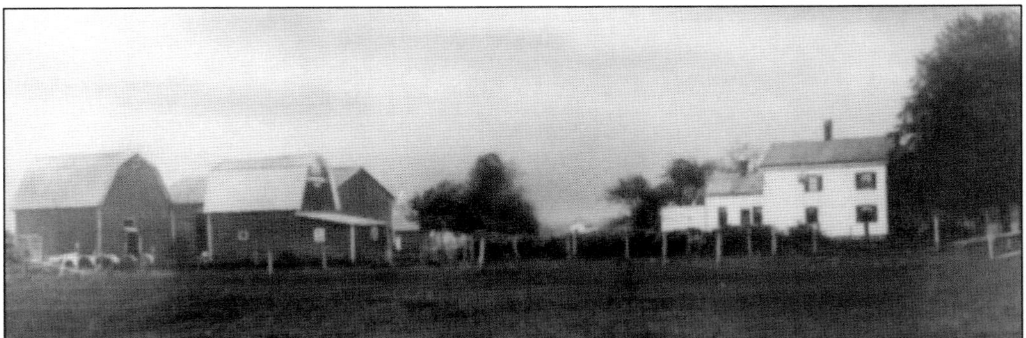

Cotton Road in Chesterfield Township was named for Otis White Cotton, the patriarch of the Cotton family, who purchased the family farm at Fort Gratiot Turnpike and Cotton Road. Originally from the state of Vermont, he acquired 128 acres in Section 20 of Chesterfield Township. Otis built a log cabin close to the Fort Gratiot Pike, which he had graded and completed under a government contract. Otis married his neighbor Martha Fairchild, and they raised nine children in the original cabin. In 1852, they replaced the cabin with a white clapboard house. (Courtesy of Russell Smith.)

Five

The Tornado of 1964

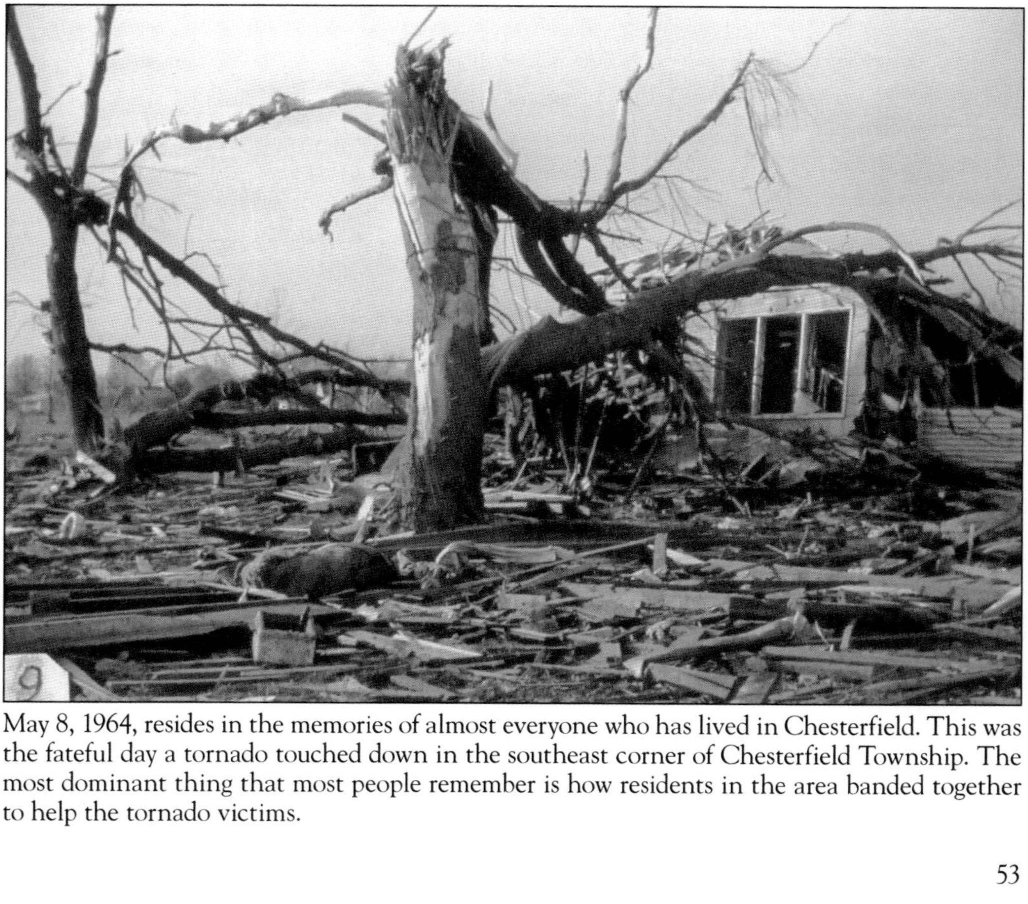

May 8, 1964, resides in the memories of almost everyone who has lived in Chesterfield. This was the fateful day a tornado touched down in the southeast corner of Chesterfield Township. The most dominant thing that most people remember is how residents in the area banded together to help the tornado victims.

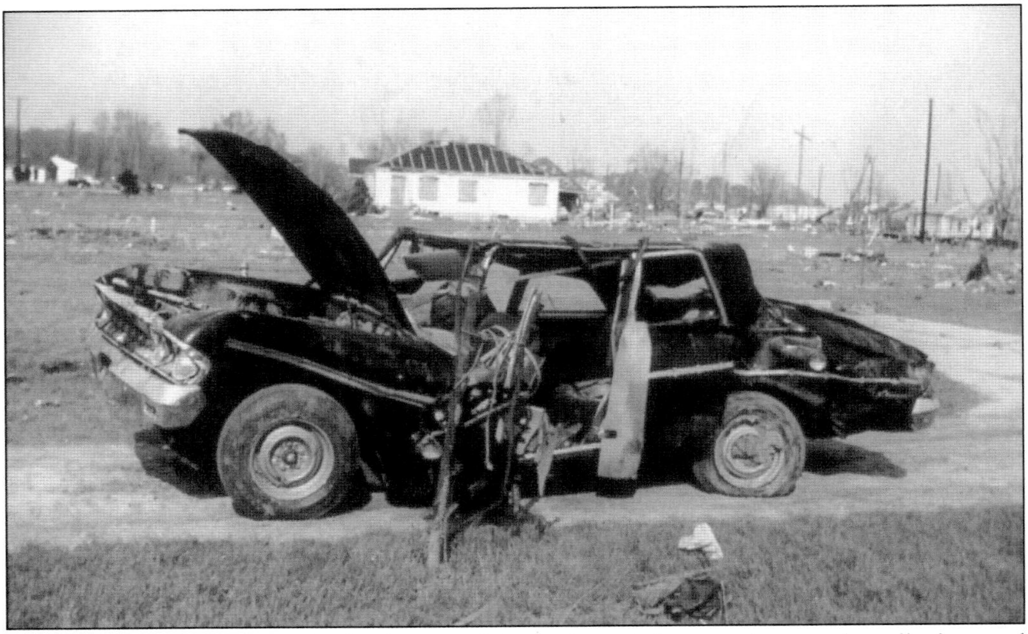

Immediately after the tornado, for the rest of the night and the next day, people walked around looking for displaced family members and friends. Unfortunately, many people ended up at the county morgue at Martha T. Berry Hospital on Groesbeck Avenue. However, the number of victims would have been much higher than it was if not for the quick work of emergency and medical personnel. All of the hospitals in the area, including St. Joseph, Anderson Memorial, Mt. Clemens General, Martha T. Berry, and the Selfridge Air Force Base Hospital went into immediate action to help the victims. So many people ended up in these hospitals that newspapers printed the names of tornado patients in order to inform people looking for friends and relatives.

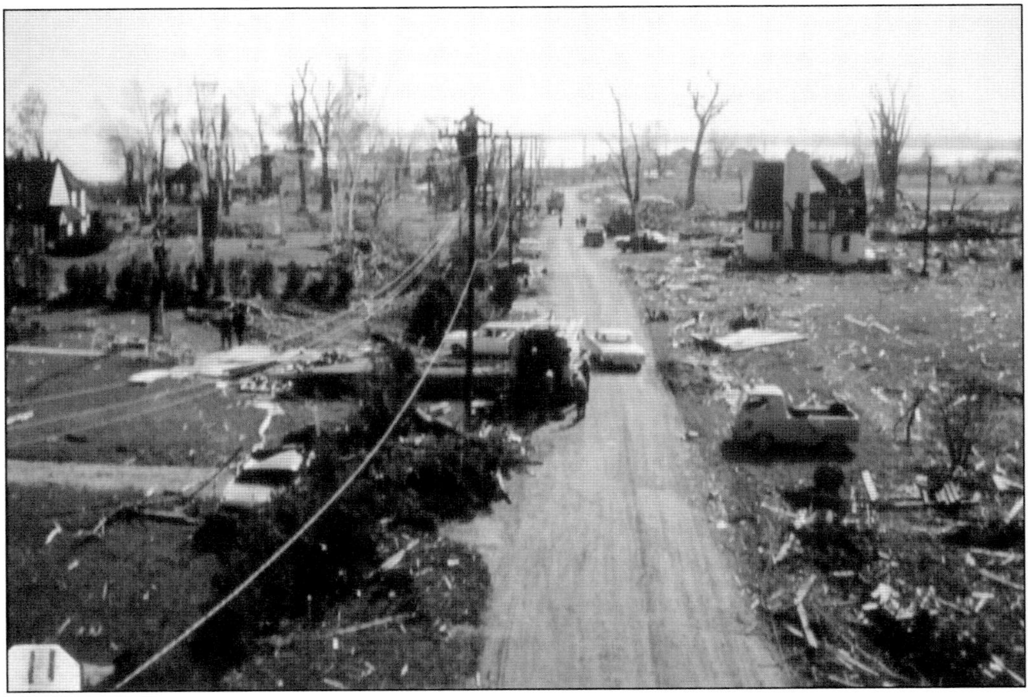

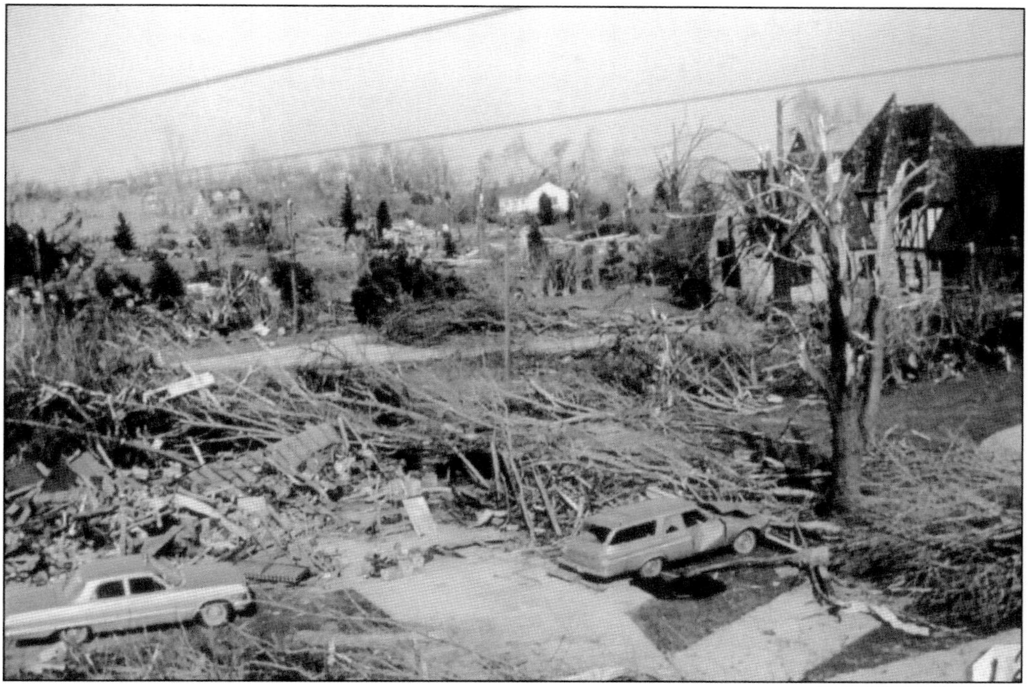

It was at first reported that the disaster area was the land between 21 and 23 Mile Roads, flanked by Gratiot Avenue and the lake. In fact, the tornado, although not encompassing as large an area as first thought, only lasted 30 seconds but covered a two-mile-by-three-quarters-of-a-mile area. It included the section bounded by Cotton and Sugarbush Roads and Jefferson Avenue down to Lake St. Clair. Almost everything was destroyed in its wake, as whole side streets off Jefferson Avenue were reduced to rubble.

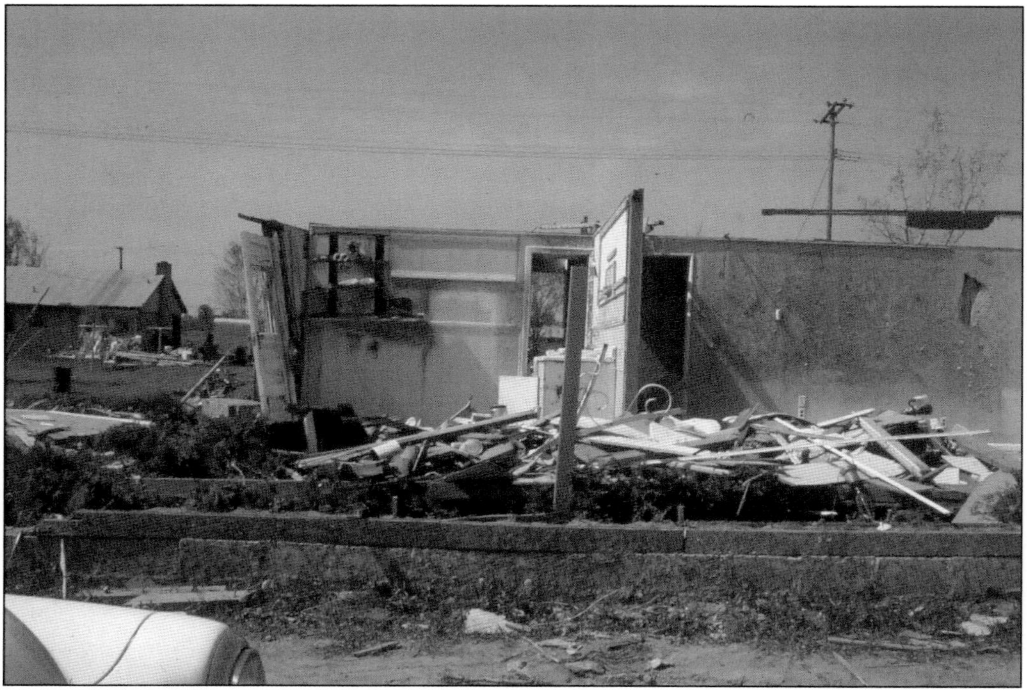

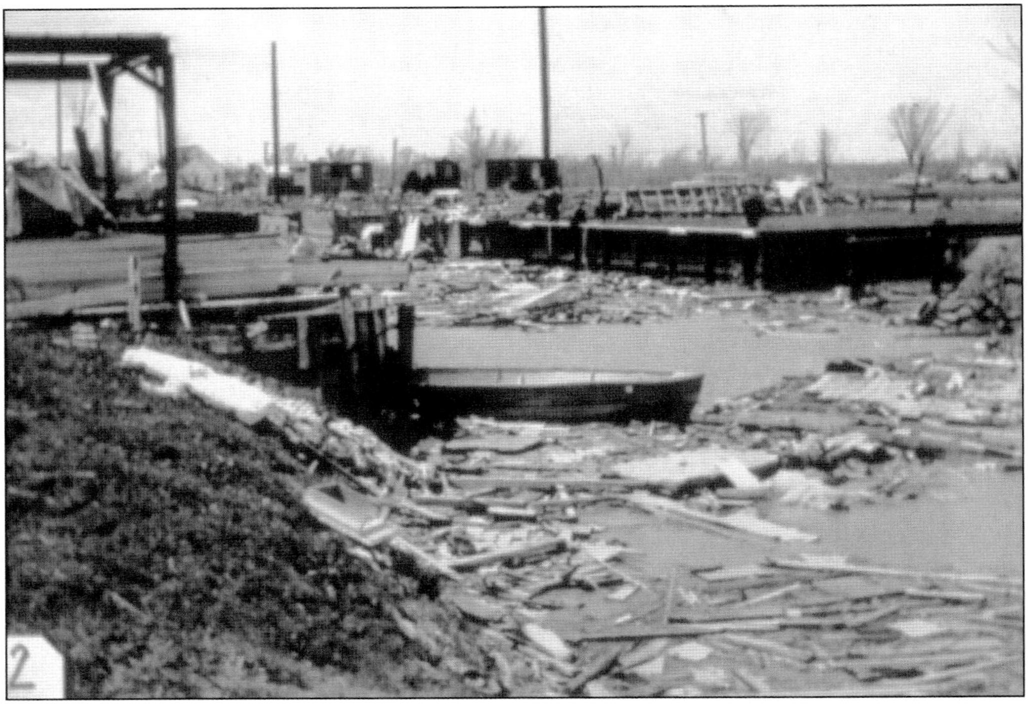

There were a few examples of the freak wind's whim with some lucky little pockets in areas left unscathed. For instance, the tornado skipped the Naldrett Elementary School on Sugarbush Road and most of the Sebille Manor military housing complex across the street, but it struck properties around them. In other spots, entire streets would be decimated except one house that remained untouched, while entire streets would remain unscathed except for one lone house that was destroyed. It was later possible to follow the circuitous route of the tornado via aerial photographs.

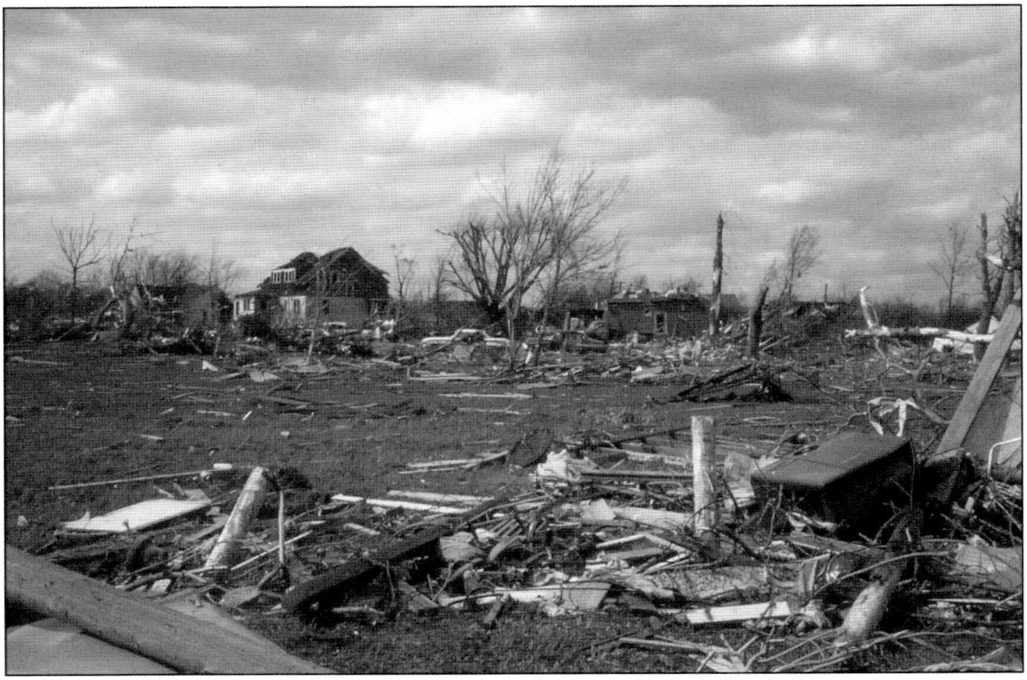

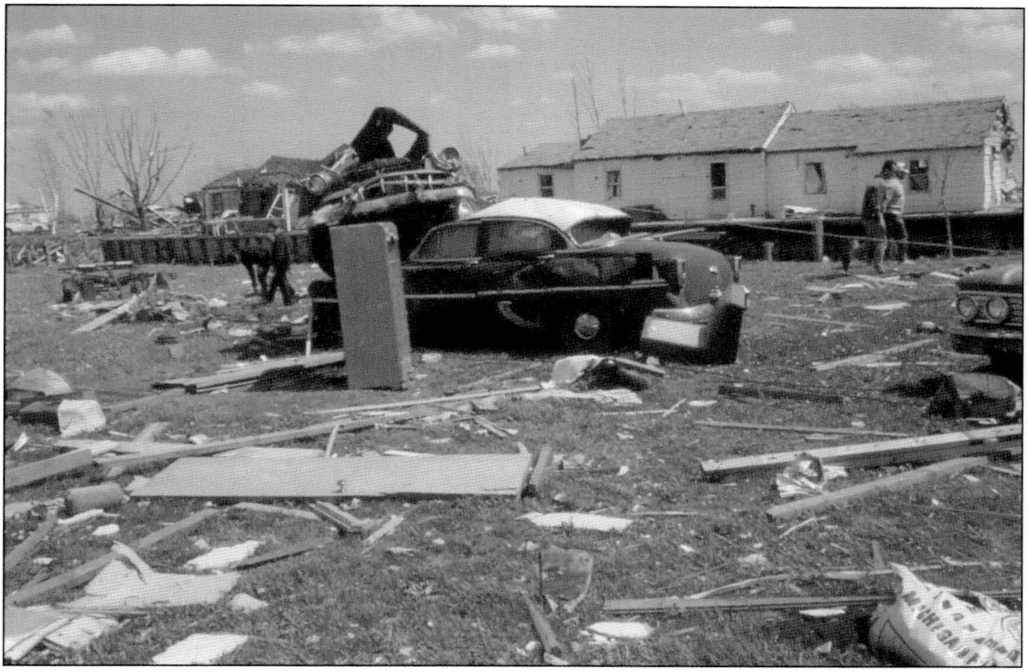

The governor and the Red Cross declared the section of Chesterfield hit by the tornado a disaster area, and State Police set up a temporary headquarters at the Green School. Also at the Green School, a lost and found station was established to collect the various found objects suspected of belonging to tornado victims. Thousands of items were dropped off—enough to fill two vans. Most items were claimed, and those that were not were brought to the Macomb County Sheriff's Department in Mt. Clemens. Although most of the items found were clothes, many other objects included golf clubs, small appliances, money, and even a clock that had stopped at the exact time of the tornado—4:59 p.m.

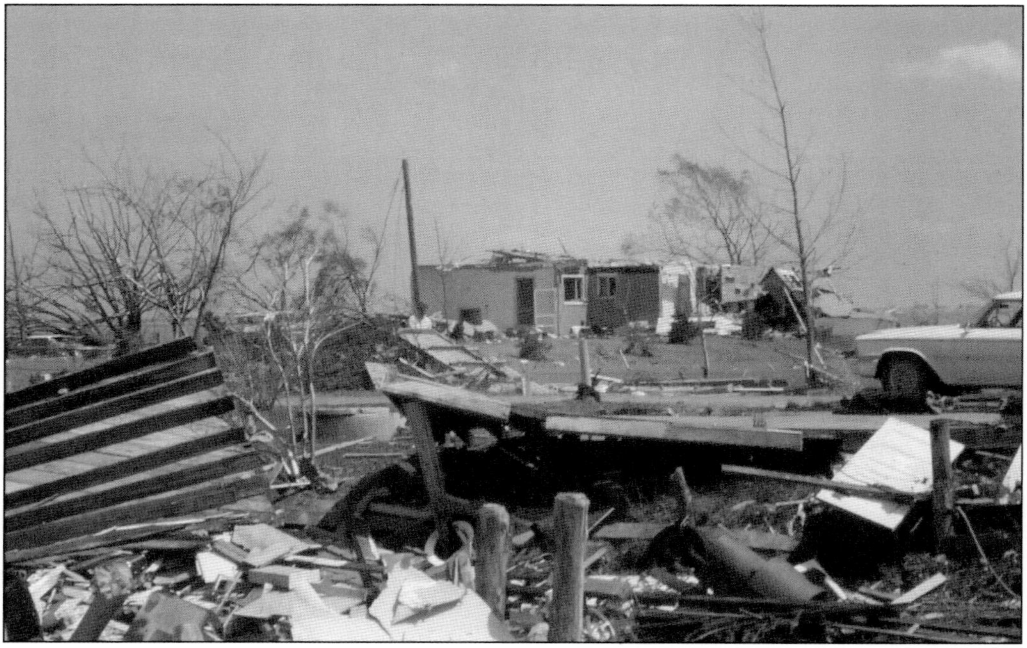

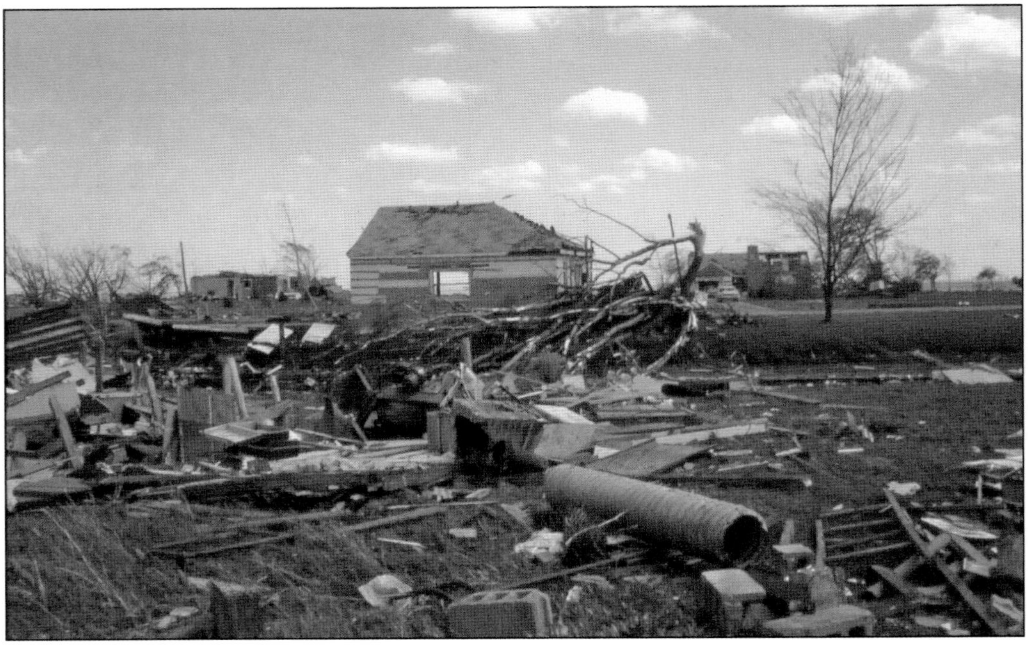

At first, 368 National Guardsmen, called out by Gov. George Romney, were in the area. Romney left the Republican state convention in Grand Rapids to come to the area; he visited three times in all. The supervisor of Chesterfield Township at the time was Carl Brandenburg, and he helped coordinate much of the relief effort. The majority of the police work was handled by the Macomb County Sheriff's Department, headed by Lester Almstadt, and the Michigan State Police. Sheriff Almstadt cancelled all officers' leaves and put his full complement of over 90 men on 12-hour shifts working in the disaster area. They set up an emergency control point at the intersection of Jefferson Avenue and Pheasant Ridge Drive.

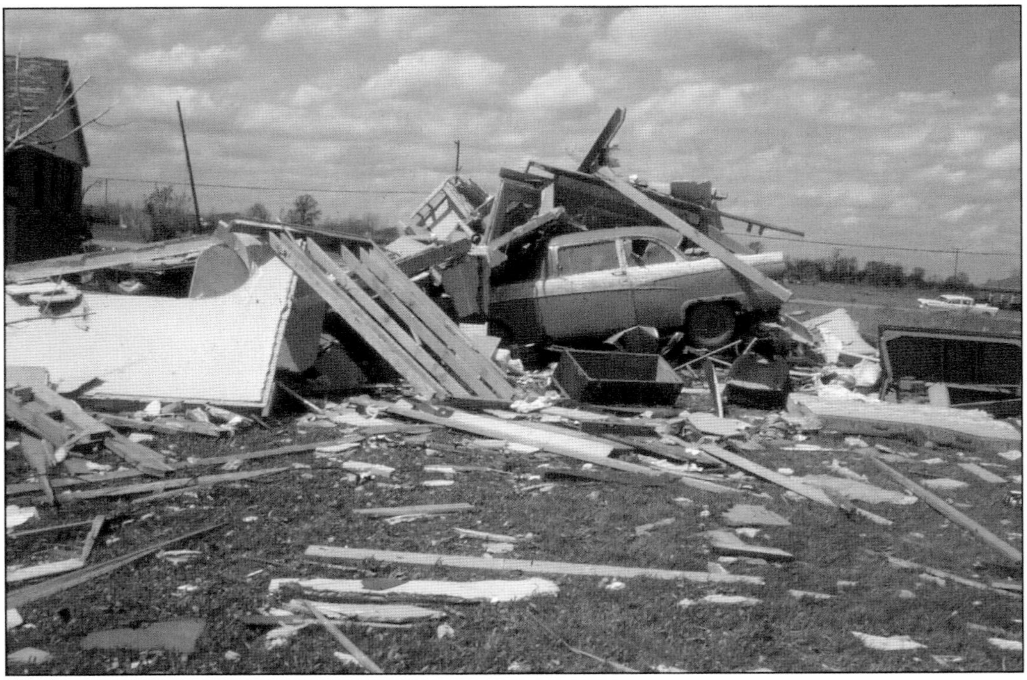

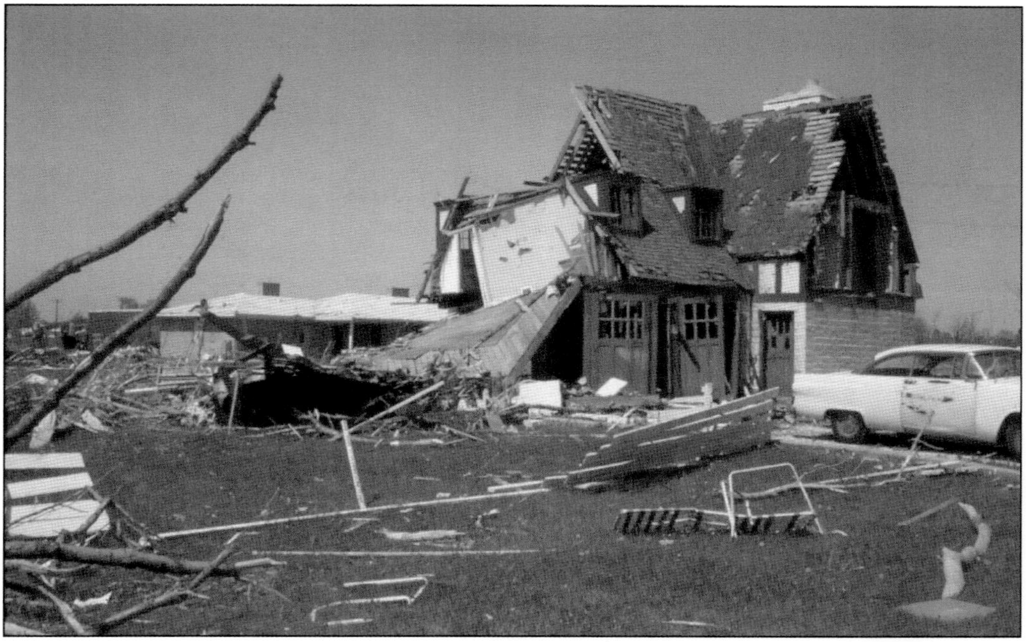

Sixty state troopers, with commander Capt. Fred E. Davids, immediately came to the area to seal it from sightseers. The area was at first closed to anyone except victims and their families, persons affiliated with rescue operations, and news personnel with limited rights. County police began conducting a house-to-house search for survivors within minutes after the tornado struck. Also assisting was the Mt. Clemens Police Department. Many other departments in the area furnished men and equipment, including Warren, Romeo, Roseville, and the Oakland County and St. Clair County Sheriff's Departments.

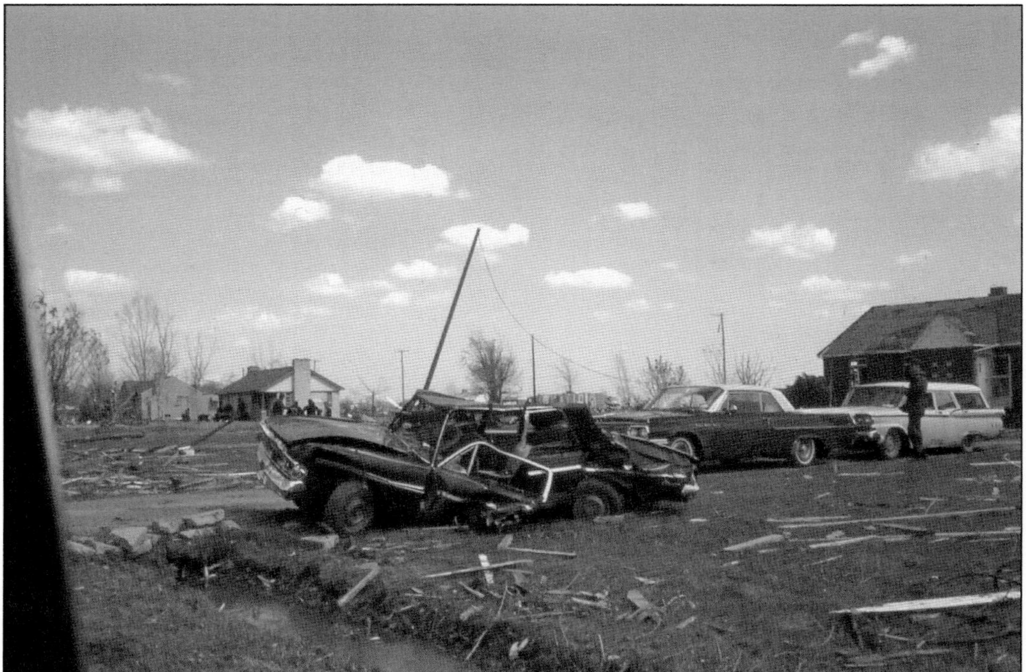

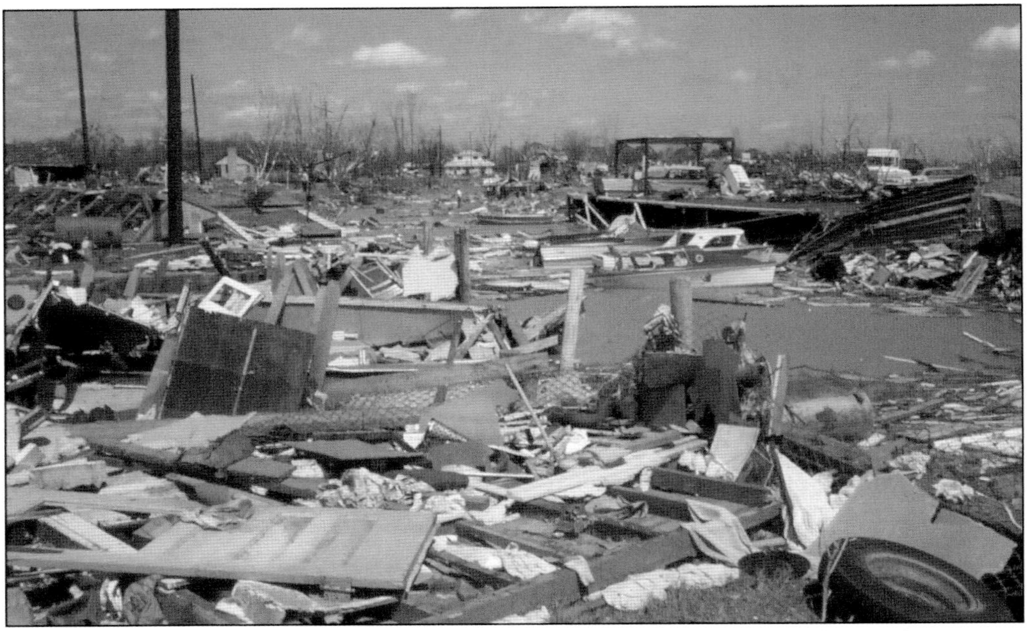

Casualties of the tornado included 13 people killed and 75 seriously injured, while 46 homes were destroyed and 108 more severely damaged. Volunteers from all over rushed to the area to help, so much at first that all could not be used effectively. The disaster plan implemented by the county was very efficient. With all agencies filling their roles so well, much of the volunteer equipment and manpower made available by neighboring areas was not needed. Some of the other agencies involved in relief efforts included the utility companies, the Red Cross, the Salvation Army, the county road commission, the welfare department, the Michigan Humane Society, many insurance organizations, and the coroner's office.

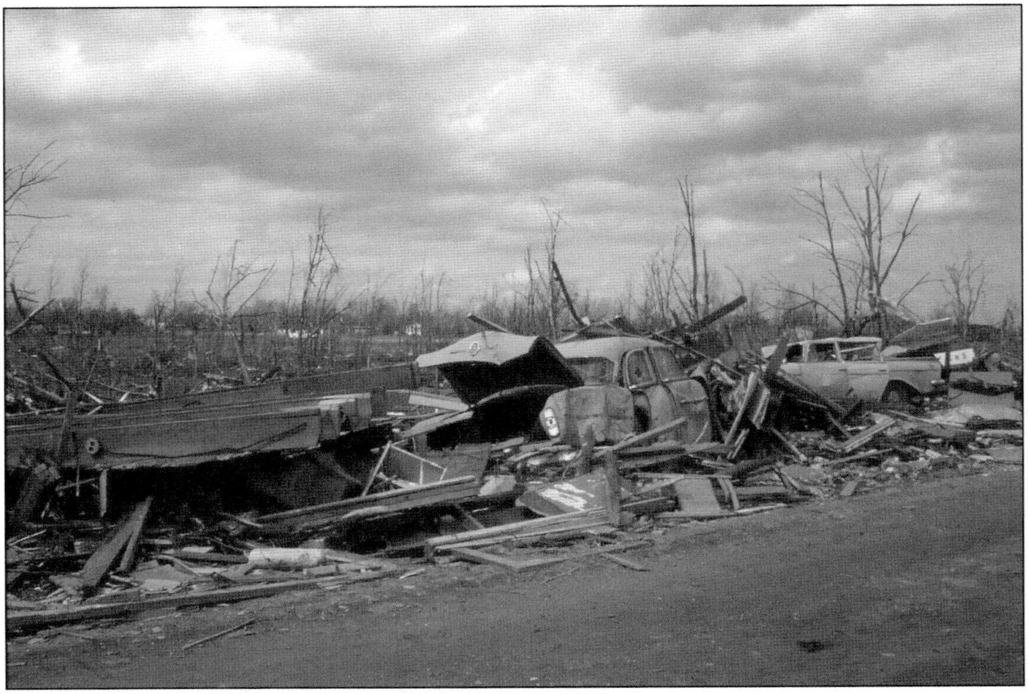

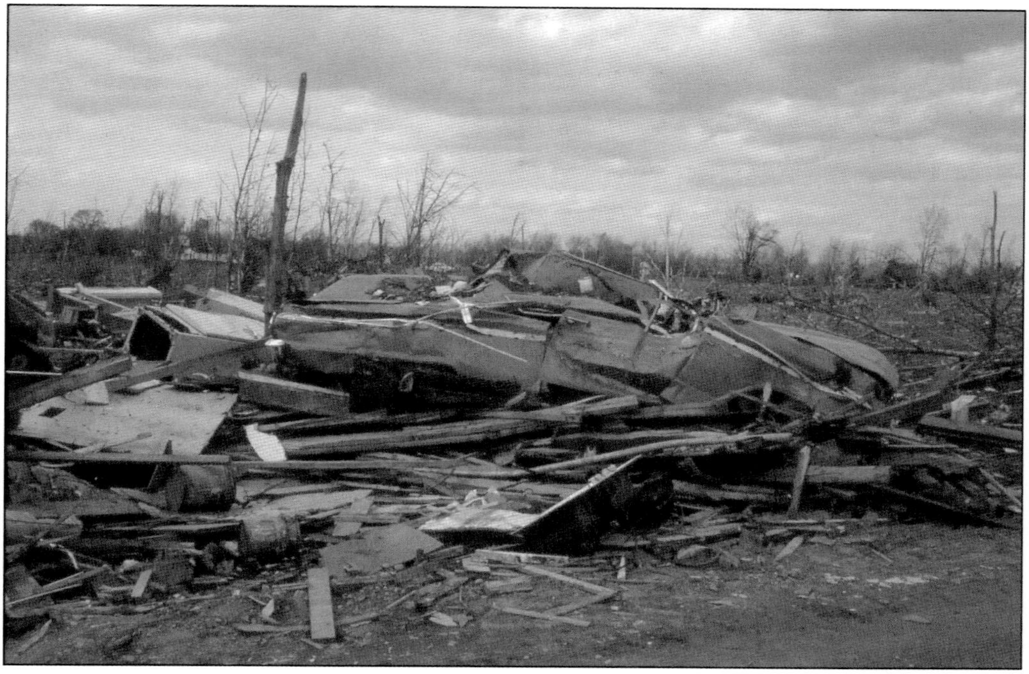

There were 218 people treated in hospitals with another 418 treated at the scene. The hospitals, like the community as a whole, rallied to help the many victims. Dr. Wallace Carrothers at St. Joseph Hospital, who had assisted after a major tornado in Sarnia, Ontario, in 1953, was one of the few doctors who had disaster experience. He arrived at the emergency room that Friday at noon and did not leave until 8 a.m. on Saturday morning. He remarked upon how the patients acted very admirably and that they were very cooperative and thoughtful.

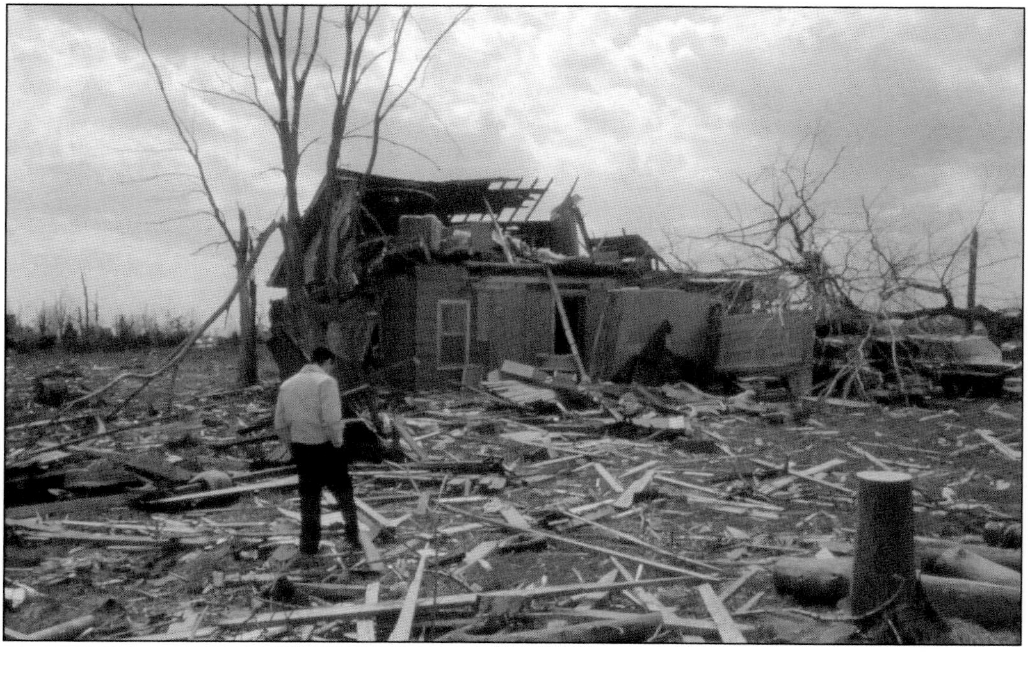

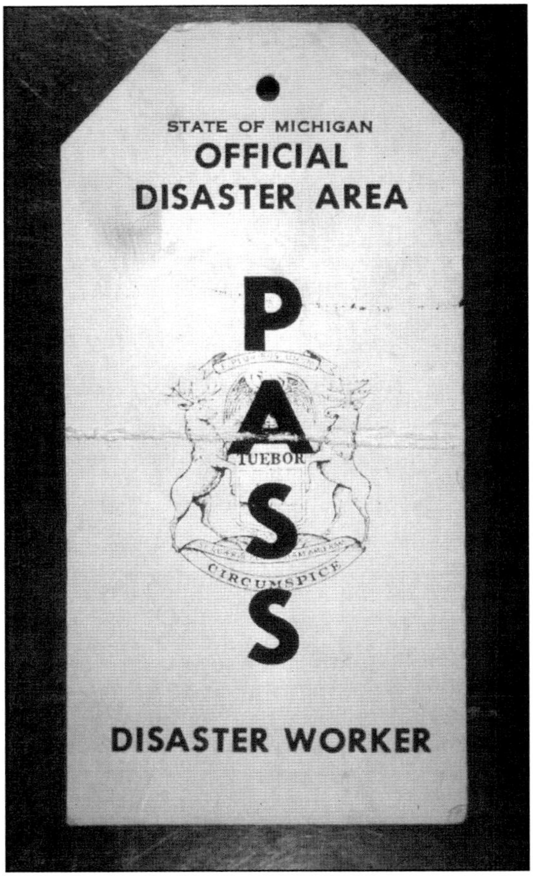

A special pass was needed to get into the tornado zone, and over 1,000 were eventually issued. Much of the damage was centered on Jefferson and Sugarbush Roads. One of the duties of the National Guardsmen and police was to keep unauthorized people out of the area. Many houses were just piles of rubble that would have to removed, and this made it very dangerous for the general public to be allowed access. Also, there was the fear of looting. When the boundaries of the area were finally opened to the public over a week later, the traffic down Jefferson Avenue was bumper-to-bumper for days because of all the people who wanted to view the damage.

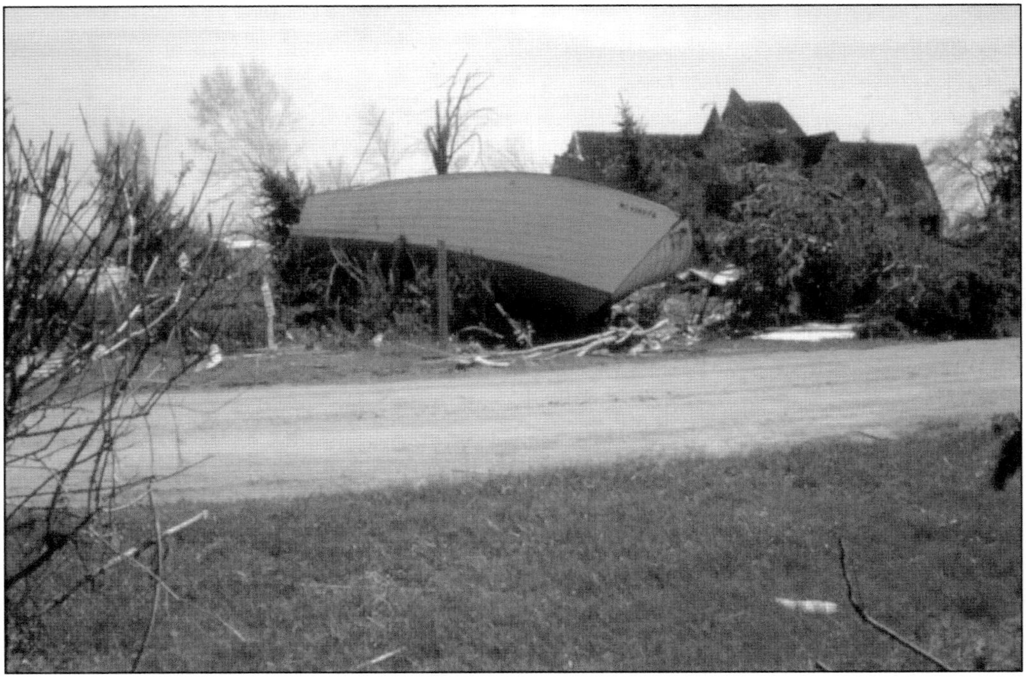

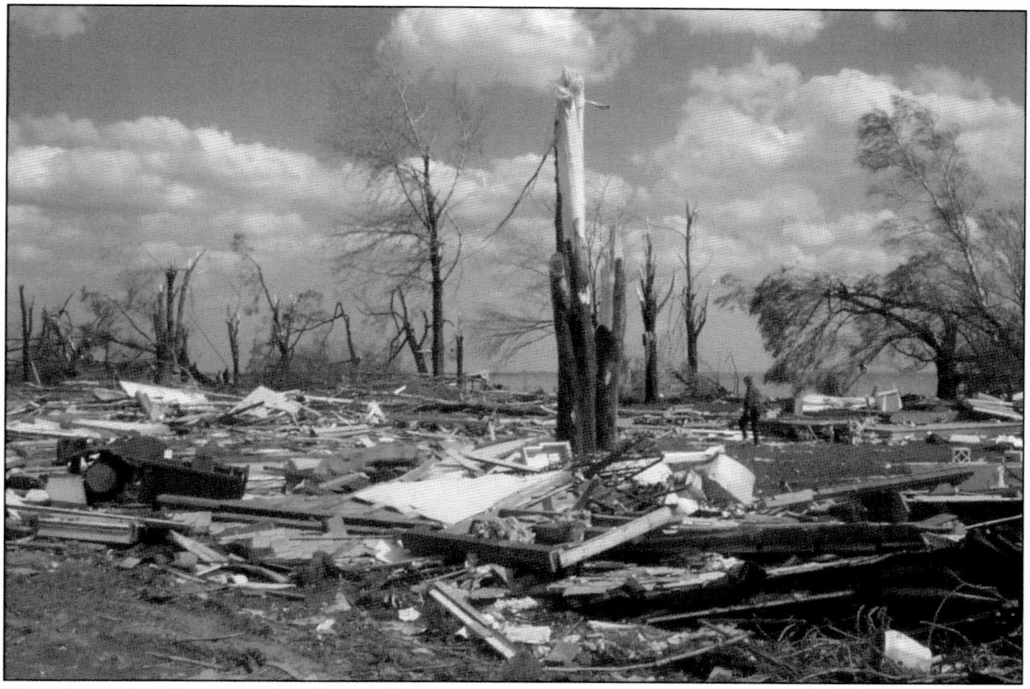

Four days after the tornado, the *Daily Monitor-Leader*, the newspaper of Macomb County at the time, reported that eight youths, five from Warren and three from Centerline, had been arrested for "creating a disturbance" and trespassing. They were arraigned and a trial date was set. This fact was reported in the headline story no doubt to serve as a deterrent to others thinking of trying to slip through the tight security. Warren and Centerline were far from the tornado area, illustrating the fact that it was a temptation for gawkers.

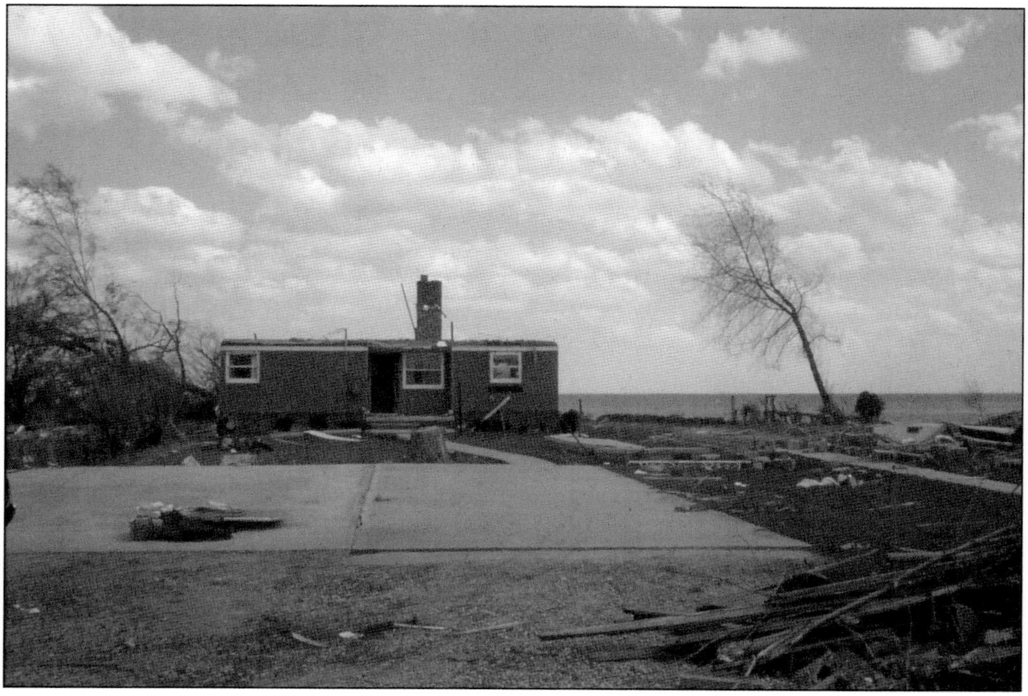

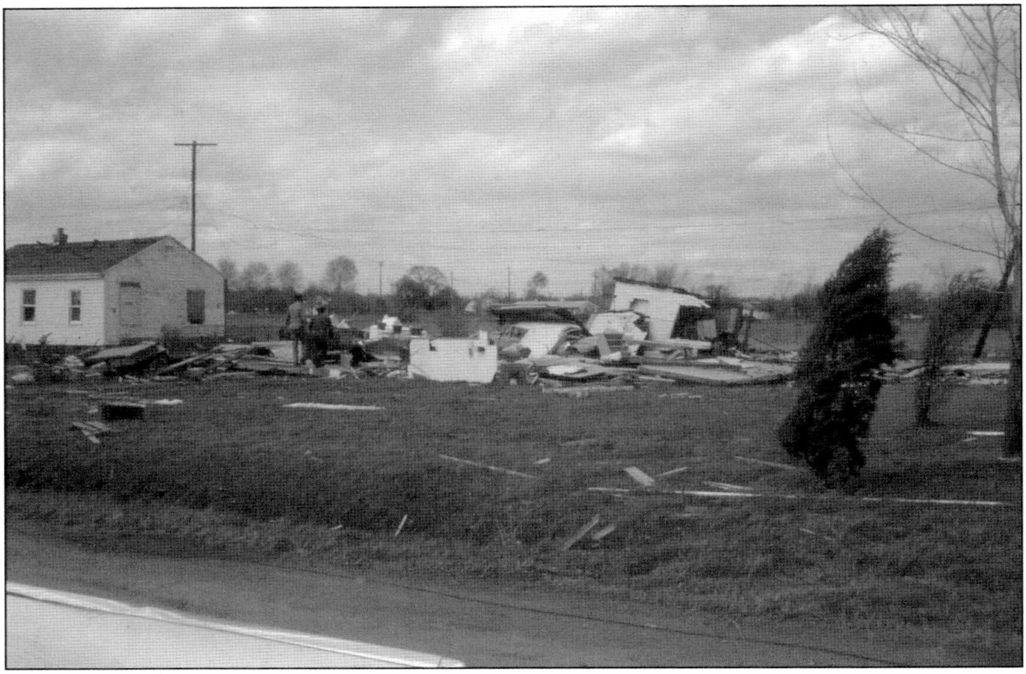

The press reported incidents to dissuade other people intent on viewing the wreckage. One was about an inebriated motorist who slurred that he was in the area to visit his parents on Sugarbush Avenue, but when the trunk of the car was opened, three people were found inside, obviously trying to sneak into the area. Over 60 tickets were issued to people stopping or parking in the restricted area. The state police, the Red Cross, and over 150 National Guardsman stayed in the area for over a week after the tornado struck.

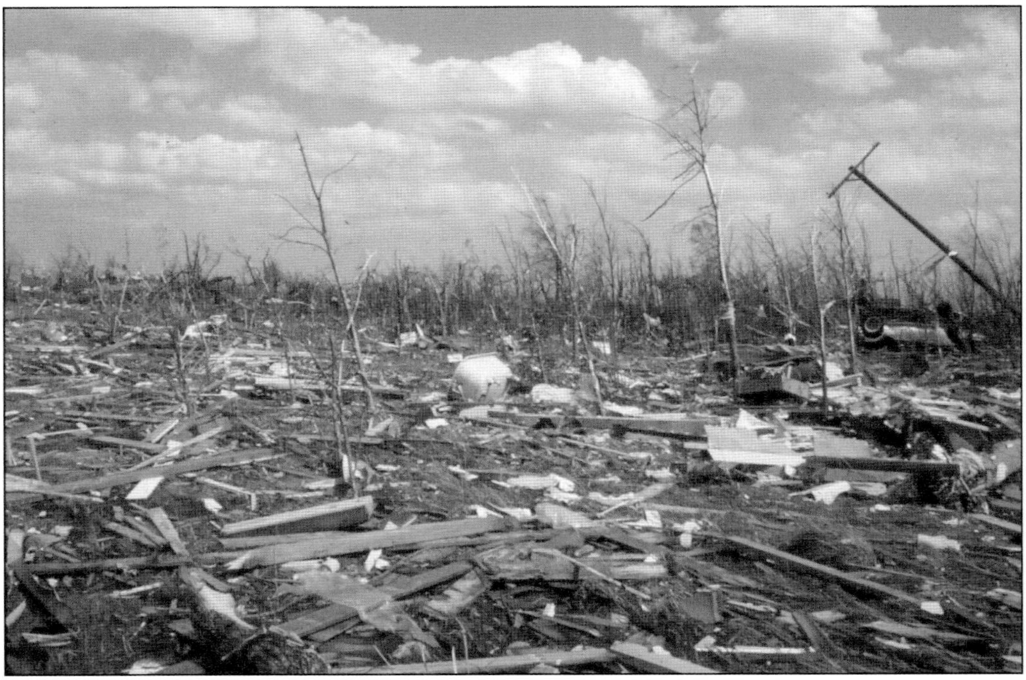

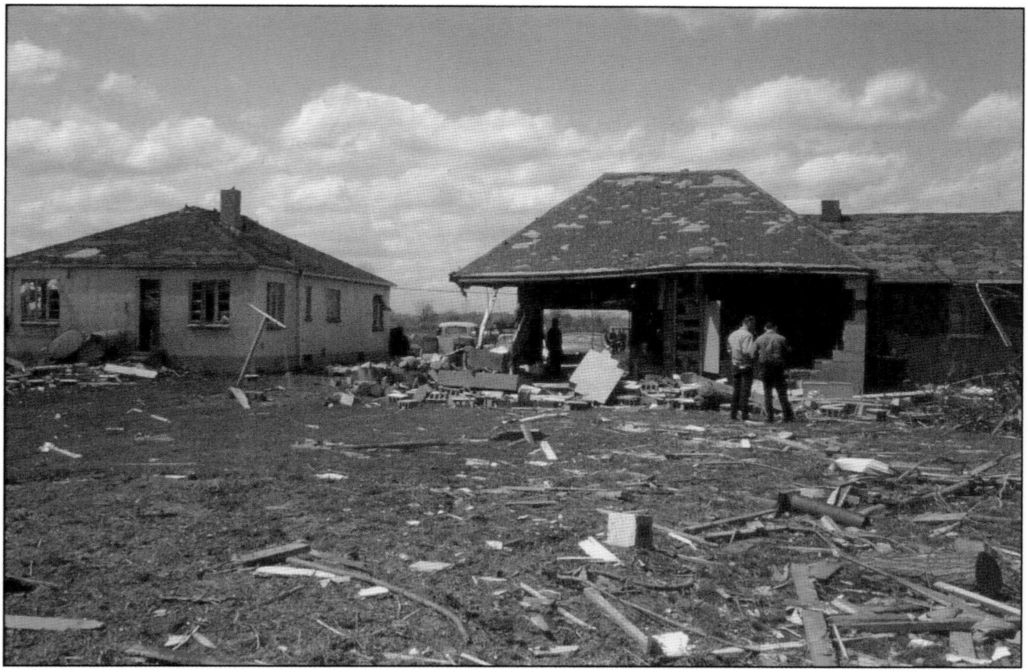

The scene at the morgue in the two small rooms in the basement of the Martha T. Berry Hospital was very somber. Victims of the tornado lay on stretchers placed neatly in a row. Many of those looking for friends and relatives lined up. One of those people was machine shop operator Joseph Soloc, who sadly found his wife, Donna Mae (24 years old) and daughter Wendy Lou (six months old). He was away from his house when the tornado hit, and by the time he returned the winds had totally destroyed his home. He searched for his family and found his sons Joseph six years old) and Alan (five years old). After arranging for them to get some medical help, he had resumed the search for his wife and daughter and ended up at the morgue.

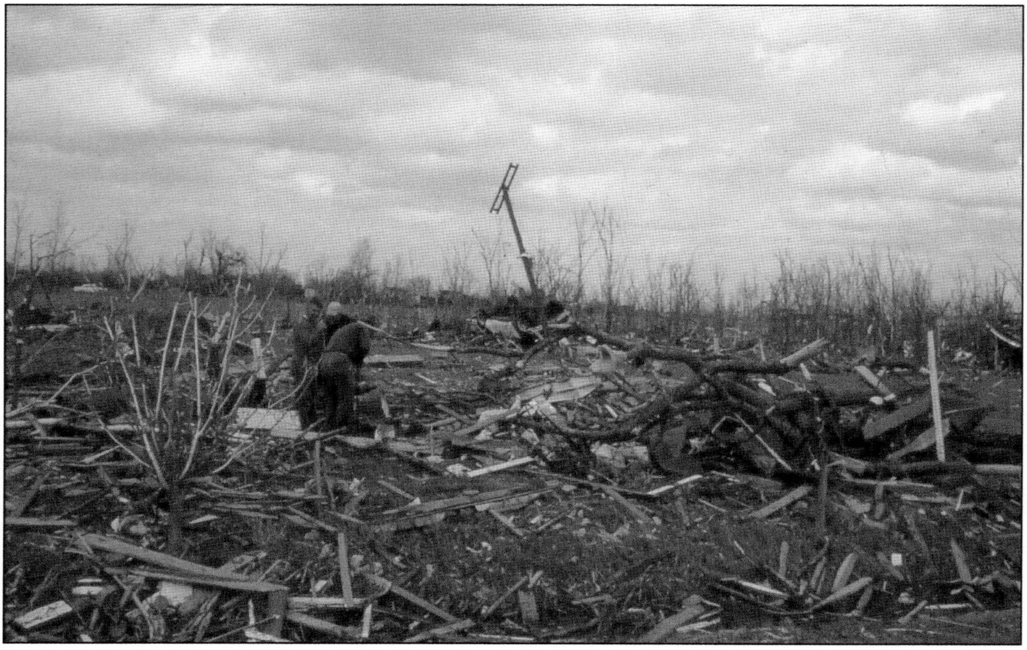

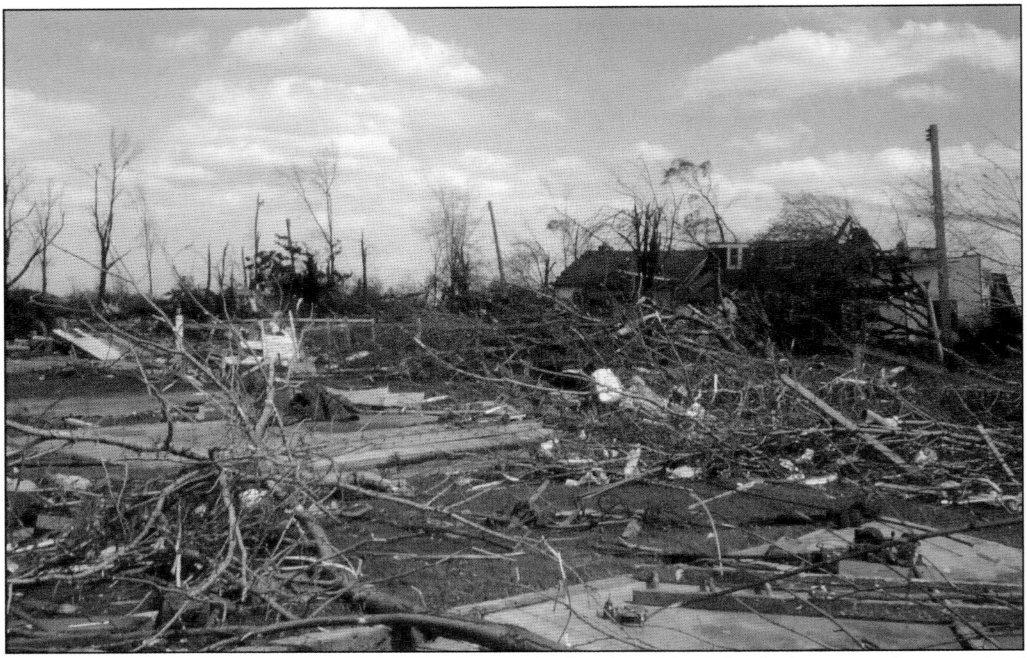

Other victims of the tragedy included the Burroughs family on Sugarbush Avenue, who crouched under a kitchen table in the basement of their two-story house. When the tornado left the area, all that remained was the table in the basement with the family underneath, fortunately unharmed. Sadly, 28-year-old Barbara Forton of Forbes Street, expecting her fifth child, was found dead beneath the rubble of what was her home, but her four children were found alive in the debris. The Chesterfield Township Hall, pictured on page 14, was a collection point of aid for tornado victims. It was soon requested by township supervisor Carl Brandenburg that no more clothing be donated, not only due to the volume donated by charitable neighbors, but also because many people had no place to store additional outfits at that time. Because of the amount of clothing stored at the Chesterfield Fire House, fire engines had to be parked outside. Detroit Edison put eight men in the field in order to contact every person whose property was affected. They also announced that manufacturers of electrical appliances had agreed to provider loaners, through Detroit Edison, to families who lost their appliances.

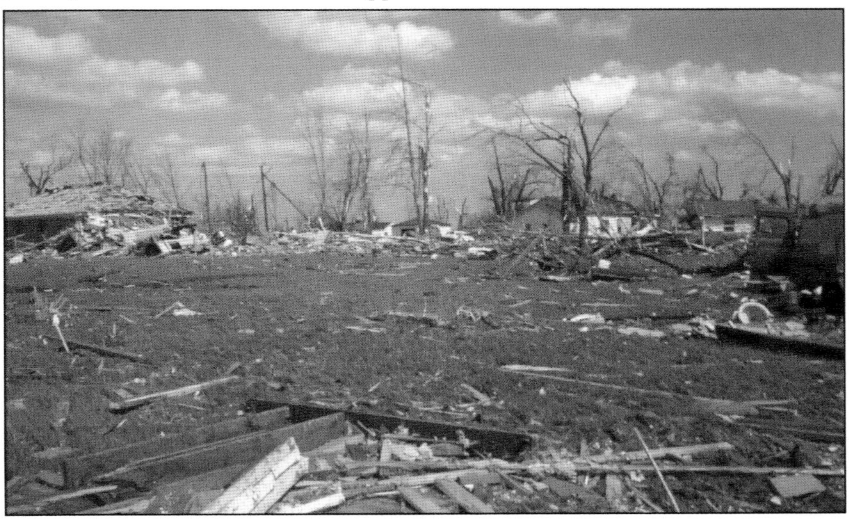

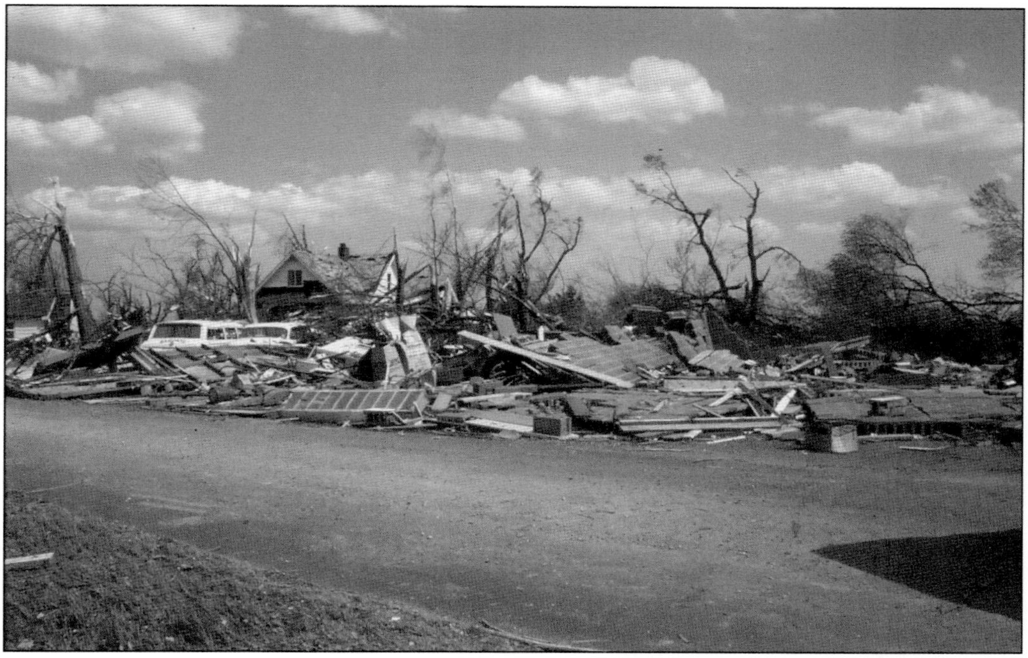

Dr. E. J. Dudzinski, who was the chief of staff at St. Joseph Hospital in Mt. Clemens, said that at least 30 doctors arrived at the hospital shortly after the first victims came in. Some victims came by ambulance, but most arrived by private passenger cars. Dr. Dudzinski said that most medical personnel worked until the rush was over, which wasn't until late in the evening. The doctors and about 125 additional hospital personnel were called to the hospital or went in voluntarily. The hospital staff successfully followed a disaster plan previously established for emergency situations.

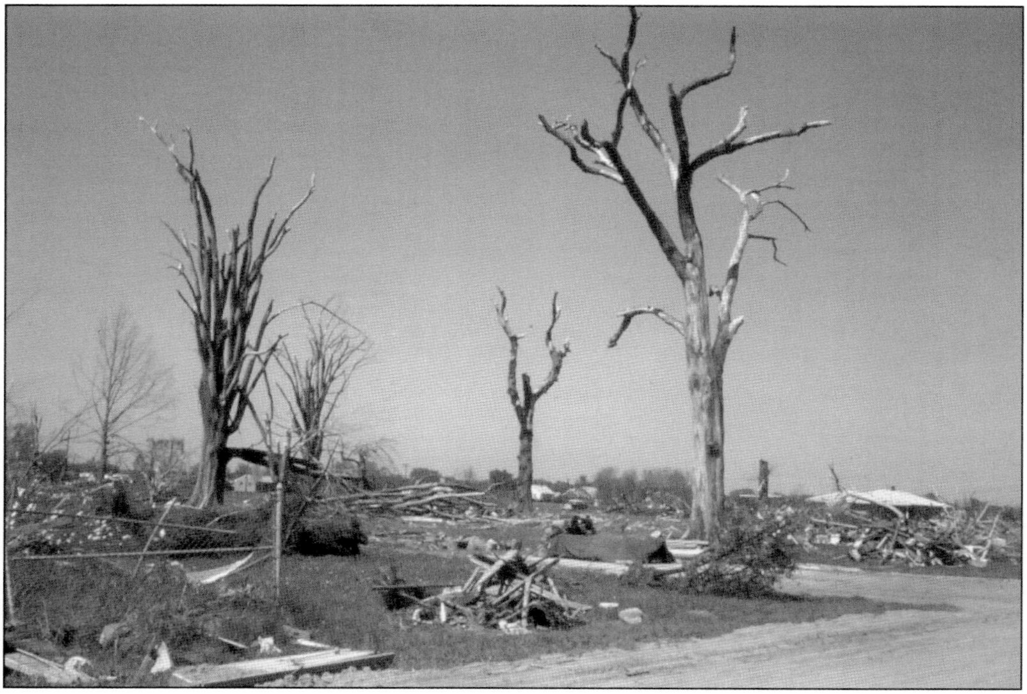

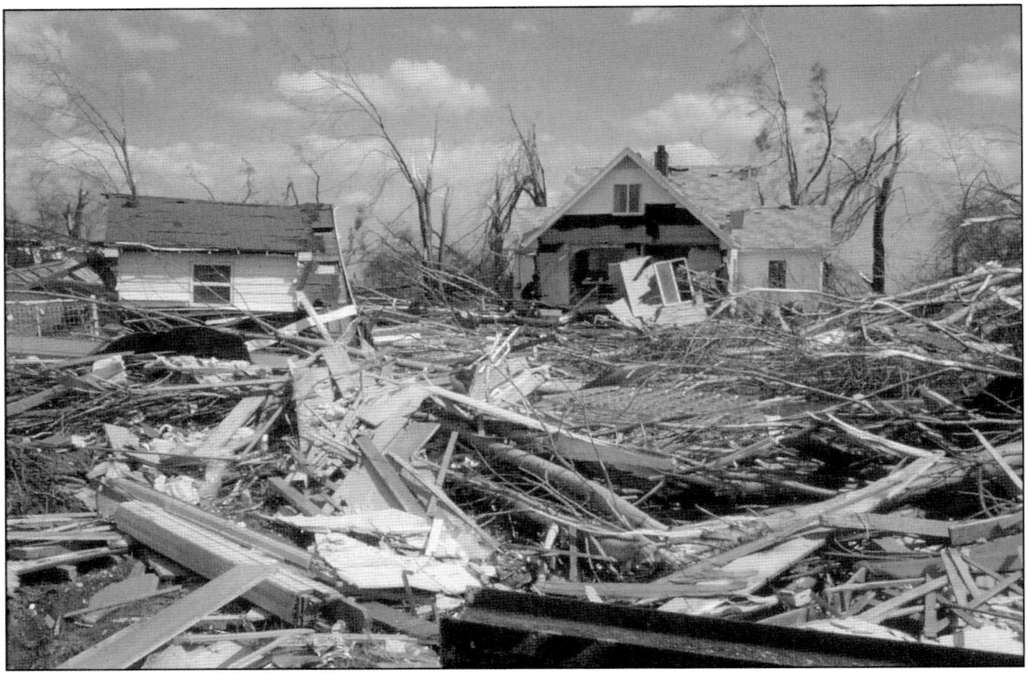

Many of the side streets along Jefferson Avenue also suffered damage. Besides the 13 people killed, 75 were seriously injured. Forty-six homes were destroyed, and 108 more were severely damaged. The initial damage estimate, in 1964 currency, was $6 to $8 million. Margaret Abbott of Jefferson said that the tornado sounded like 1,000 horses and that the sky was very dark. Others described it as sounding like many freight trains going by at the same time.

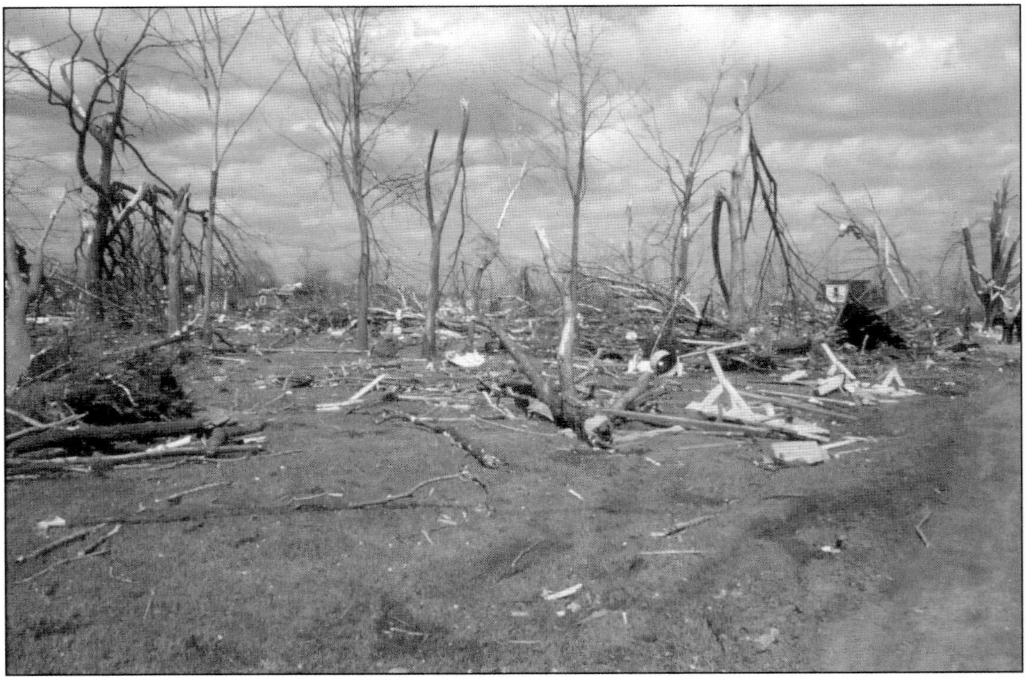

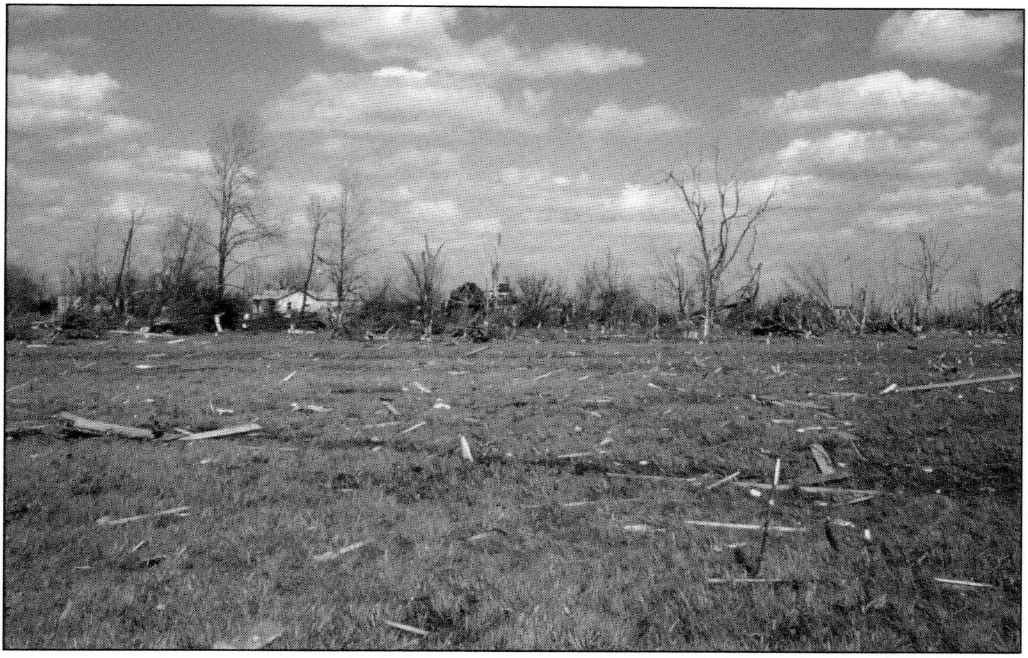

The victims of the tornado included Barbara Forton (28 years old), Joseph Giroux (72 years old), Anthony Lesher (40 years old), James Anthony Rivard (79 years old), Wanda Jo Sancrant (36 years old), Louise Sancrant (eight years old), David Sancrant (four months old), Tina Marie Sancrant (20 months old), Donna Mae Soloc (24 years old), Wendy Lou Soloc (six months old), Gladys Sparwasser (63 years old), Susan Westfall (seven years old), and Louis Winters (92 years old). After the initial ceremony by the township hall, the memorial was moved a few years later and rededicated in the Chesterfield Historical Village.

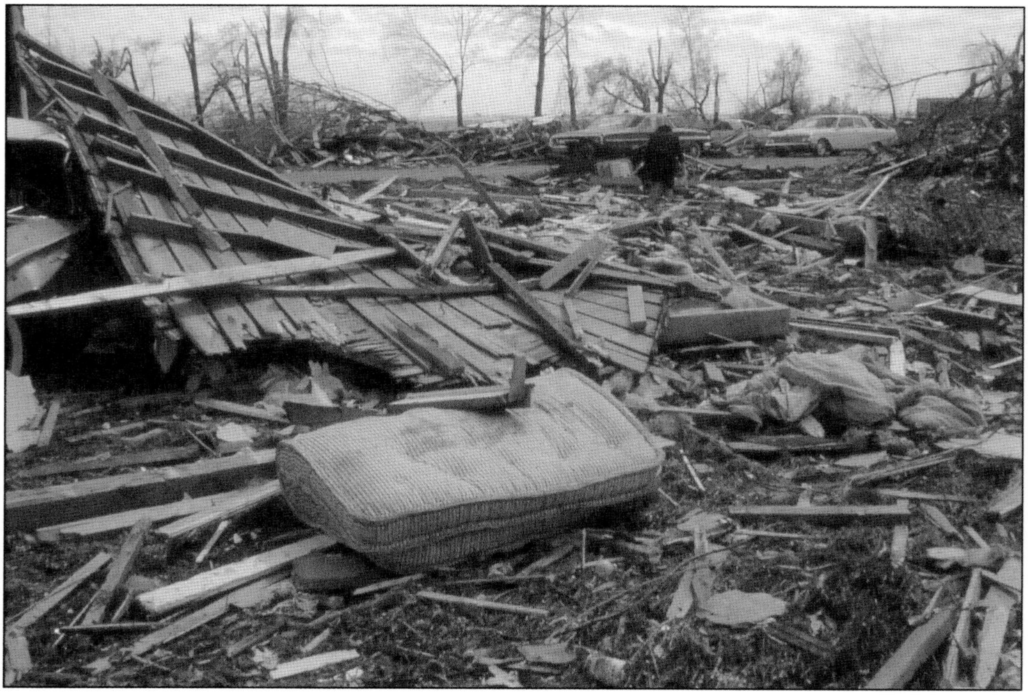

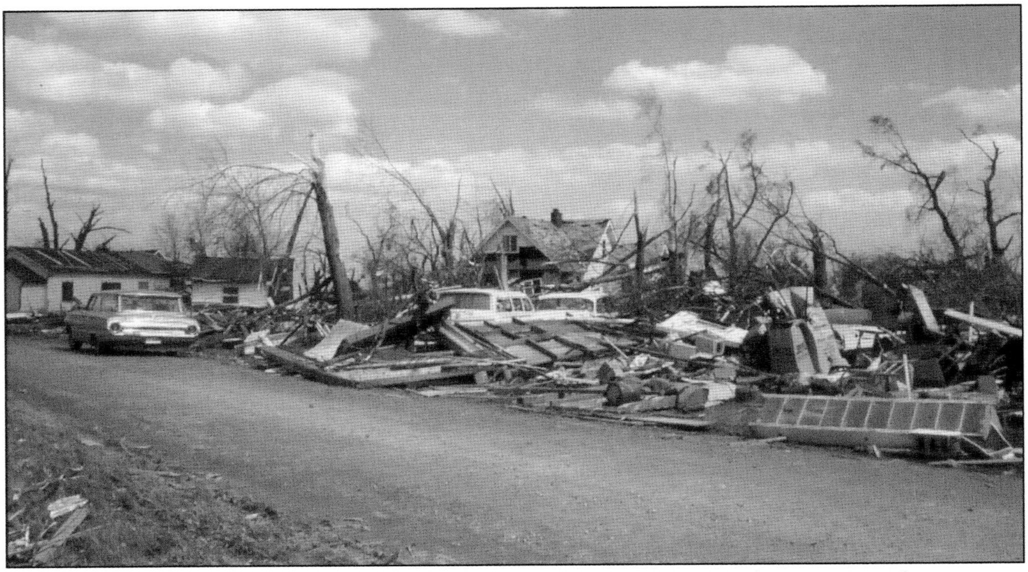

The First Fighter Wing, stationed at Selfridge Air Force Base, set up a disaster control point near 21 Mile Road and Jefferson Avenue. Their prime objective was to assist service personnel and their families in tornado-salvaging operations. The unit had over 100 men available and used all kinds of equipment to assist in the area. They were centered at Lou's Lounge on Jefferson Avenue and commanded by Col. Caleb Moberly and Capt. Max Hoyt. The base housing was right in the area where the tornado had gone through. The first volunteers on the scene were members of the Macomb CBers Club. Within minutes of the tornado's passing, they had an emergency communications system set up and operating. Club president Vince L. Cuker created a citizens band station control center a mile south of the disaster area, and according the *Monitor-Leader*, "Messages were relayed to it from inside the area and from it to the Sheriff's department, Civil Defense offices in both Mt. Clemens and Detroit, and the utility companies." Stationed at the Green School, they also assisted in transporting portable power units and floodlights from Utica and Selfridge Air Force Base.

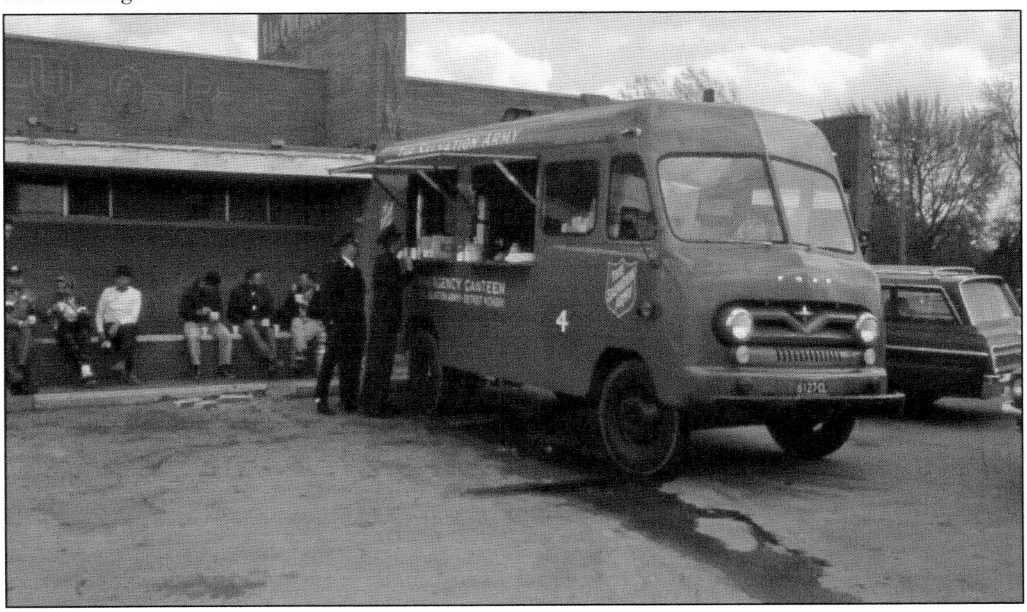

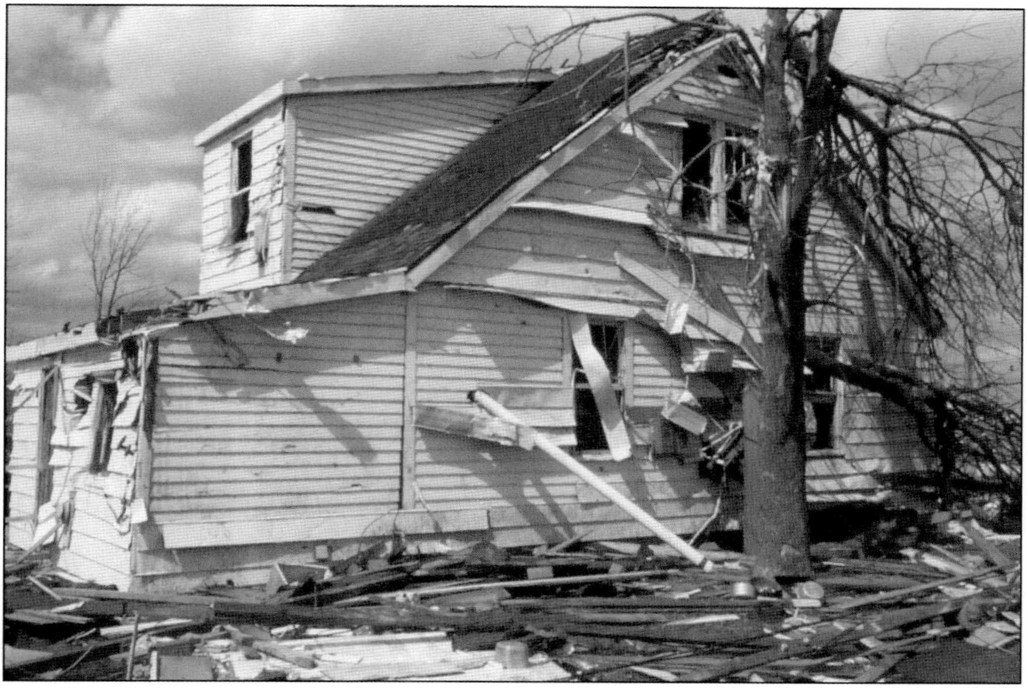

Many buildings' roofs had caved in. It was long considered the deadliest tornado in Michigan in the 20th century, later judged to be at least an F5 with winds over 200 mph—one of few to ever touch down in the state. To Eileen Koch, who had witnessed two other tornadoes in her home state of Kansas, this tornado was different because it hung so low to the ground and the sky was so black. Surrounding areas had violent thunderstorms and golf-ball-sized hail.

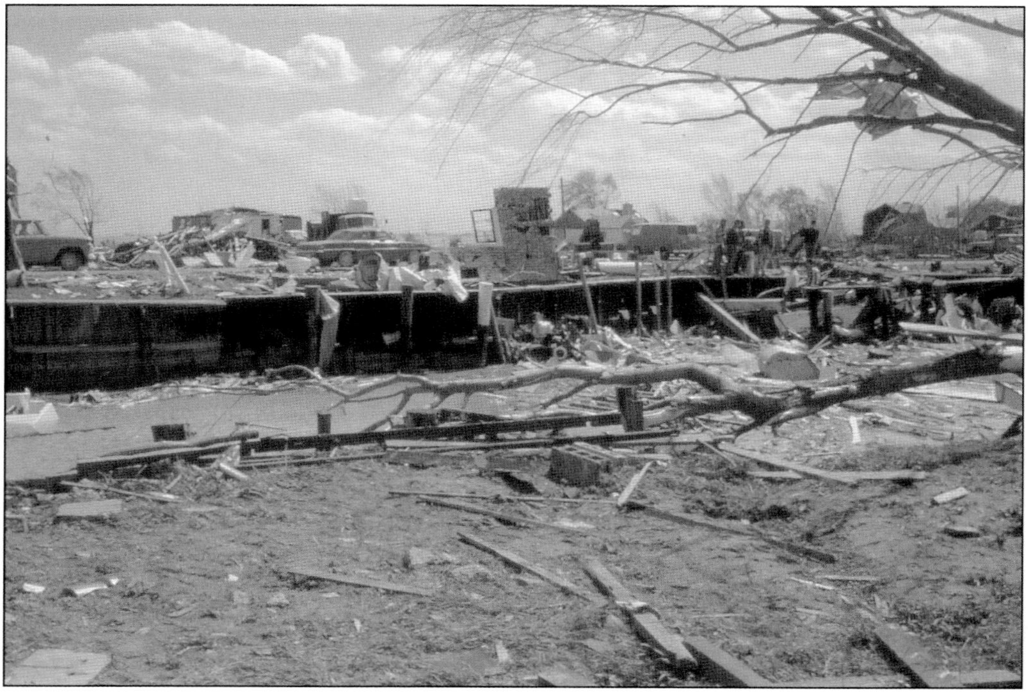

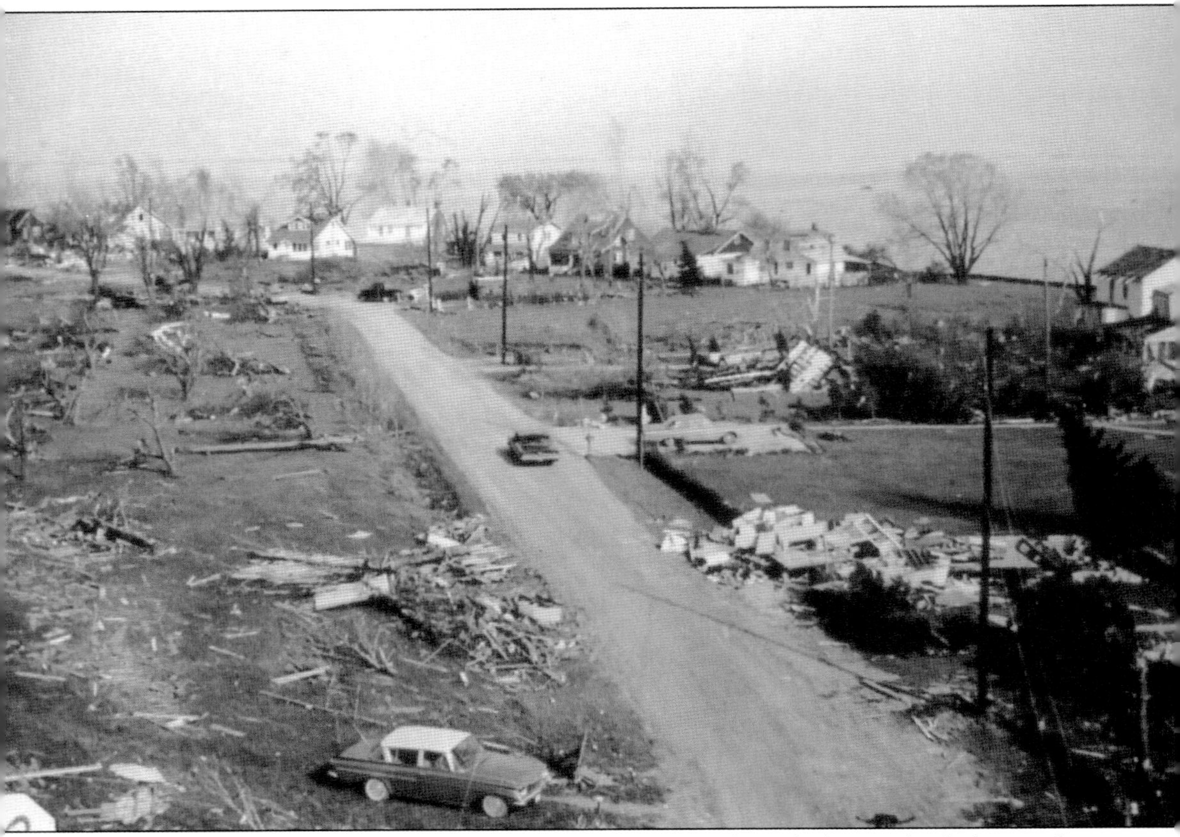

Other strange occurrences included a two-by-four driven through the trunk of a large oak tree, as well as another incident of a dollar bill stuck in a tree. A duck-hunting jacket with the license still on the back, a high-school graduation certificate, and some bonds were found in Canada. A 1962 Rambler was stripped nearly to the frame; it had been picked up and hurled 150 feet into the underbrush, and its wheels sunk into the ground almost out of sight. It took a long time for a few men to dig out from under of a pile of lumber what they thought was a baby, but luckily it turned out to be a life-sized baby doll. In another incident, what was thought to be a crying baby was found to be a lost lamb bleating. There were still a few farms in the two-mile tornado disaster area, and consequently livestock running free was another complication.

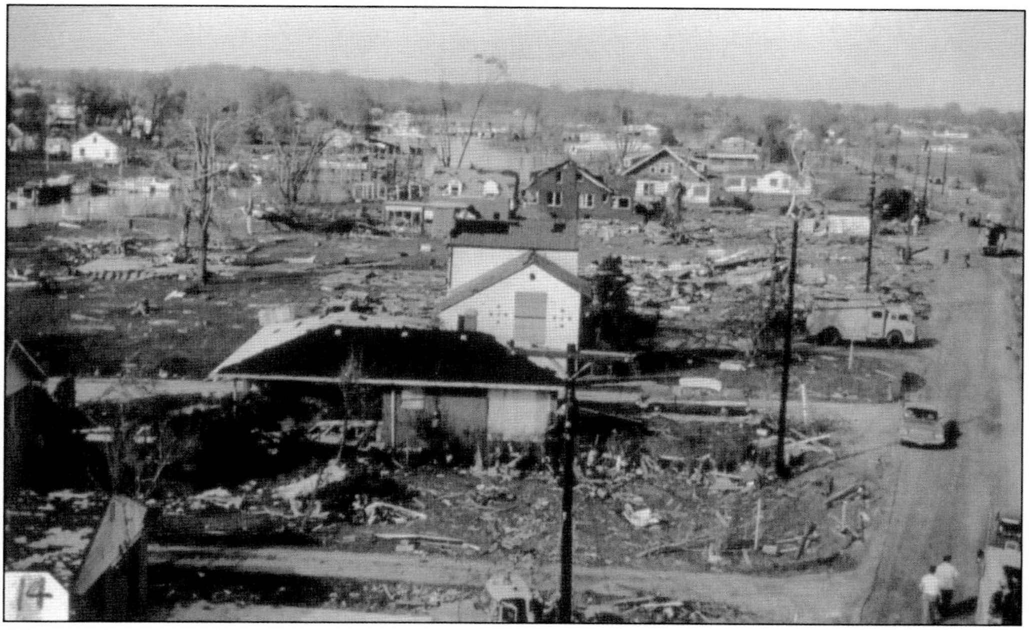

About 150 National Guardsmen stayed in the disaster area for a week. Not long after they first arrived, public announcement trucks with loudspeakers went through the streets instructing people to go to Selfridge Air Force Base, where temporary housing was being set up. They requested that only authorized disaster people remain. People drove or hitched rides to the air base. The blinking lights and sirens of emergency vehicles could be heard throughout the night as emergency crews worked, and they continued into the next day searching for survivors in the rubble. Gov. George Romney visited the disaster area three times. He also made trips to the local hospitals that all housed tornado victims. The most losses by a family were the Sancrants, who lost Wanda Jo, age 36, her 4-month-old son David Joseph, 18-month-old daughter Tina Marie, and her daughter from a previous marriage, 8-year-old Nannette Louise Rigg. Their bodies were flown to their hometown of Fort Worth, Texas, to be buried. Five-year-old Sabrina Sancrant and her sister Sara, as well as their father, Airman First Class Clarence Sancrant, survived.

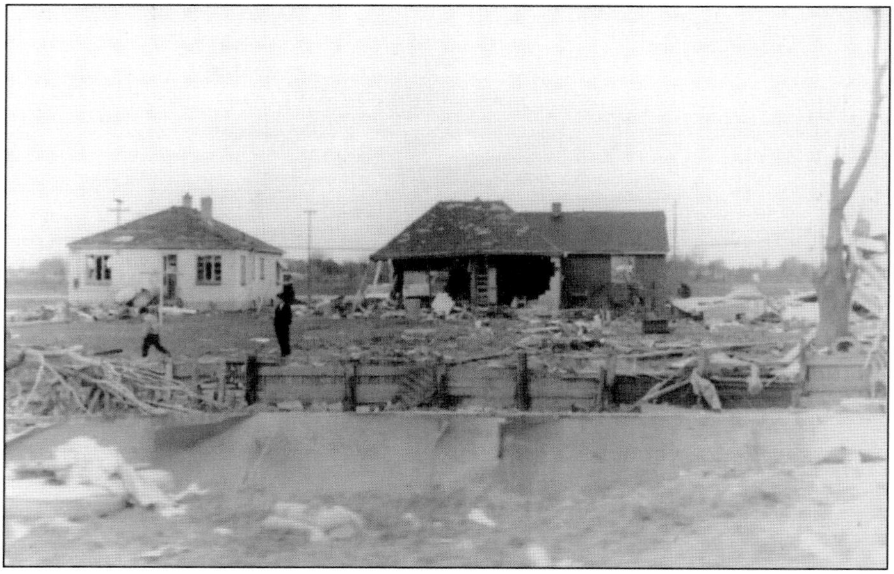

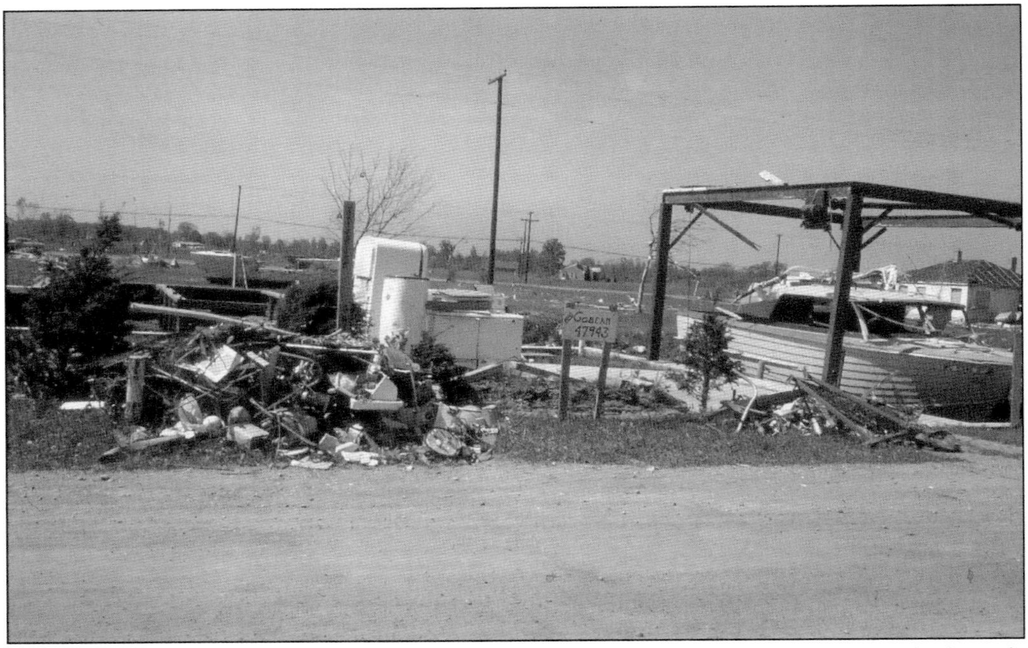

Agencies that stepped in with assistance were the Small Business Administration, which made long-term, low-interest loans available to businesses and homeowners to rebuild. Two Macomb County members of the state legislature introduced legislation to provide between $1 million and $2 million in no-interest loans to assist with rebuilding in the area. A Tornado Disaster Fund was started and over $200,000 was eventually raised to be used to help victims of uninsured losses. Some of the largest contributors included the New Baltimore Community Chest, Manufacturers National Bank, Kowalski Sausage Company, Catholic Kolping Park, the National Bank of Mt. Clemens, and the Mt. Clemens Lions Club.

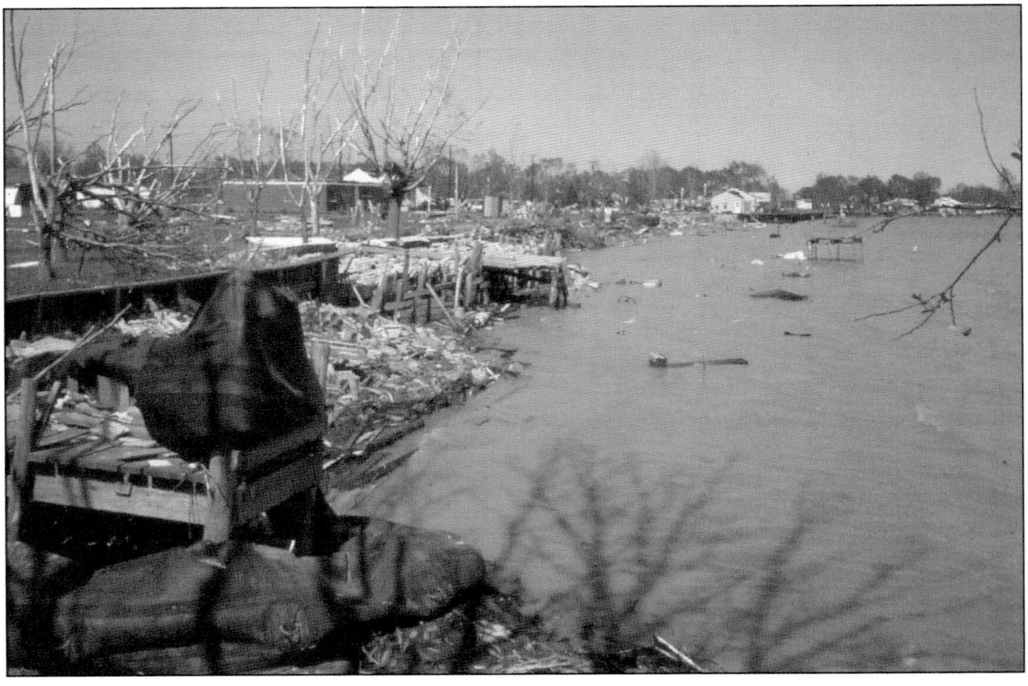

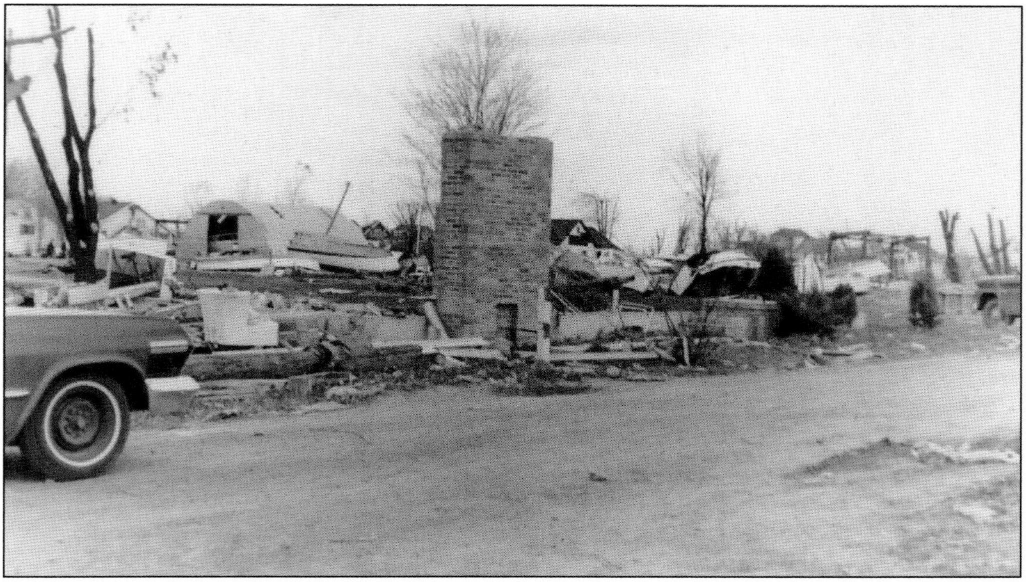

In many instances, only chimneys remained of what were structures. Another tornado-related problem was the fact that many houses in the area still had their own water supply in the form of wells. These wells were considered contaminated after the disaster, and residents were warned to boil all of their water. During the two-week period, inoculations against typhoid were given by the county health department at Green School, which also served as the lost and found and a communications center while students of the school went to nearby Chesterfield Elementary. Many insurance companies, as well as the Insurance Information Institute, established temporary quarters within the area. State insurance officials directly contacted tornado patients as to the extent of their insurance coverage. After securing permission from landowners, the township began bulldozing lots where houses were completely destroyed.

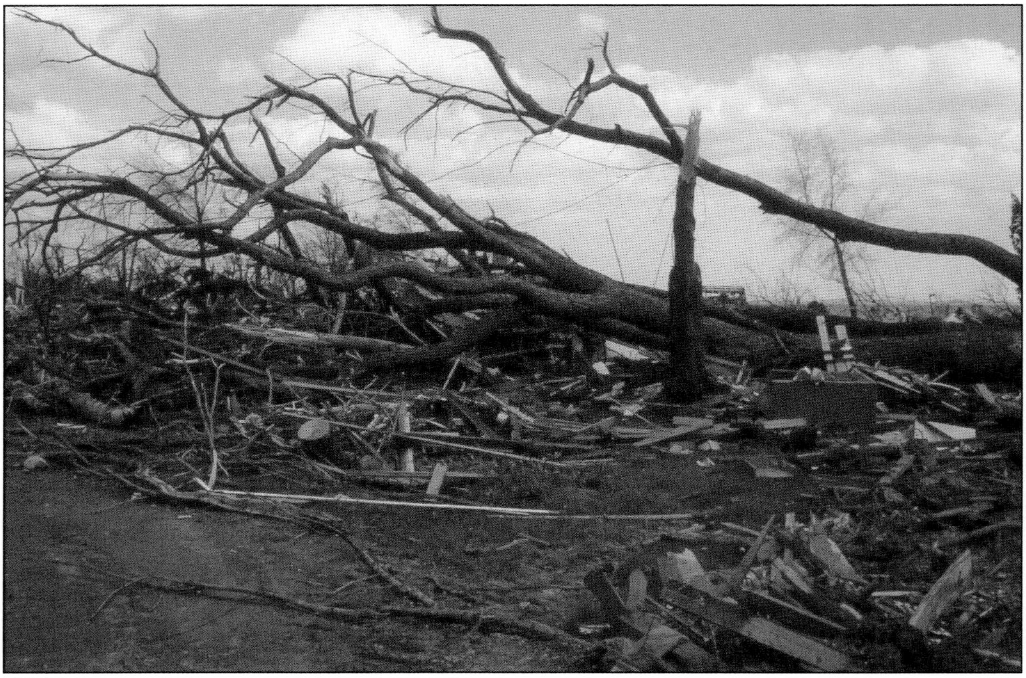

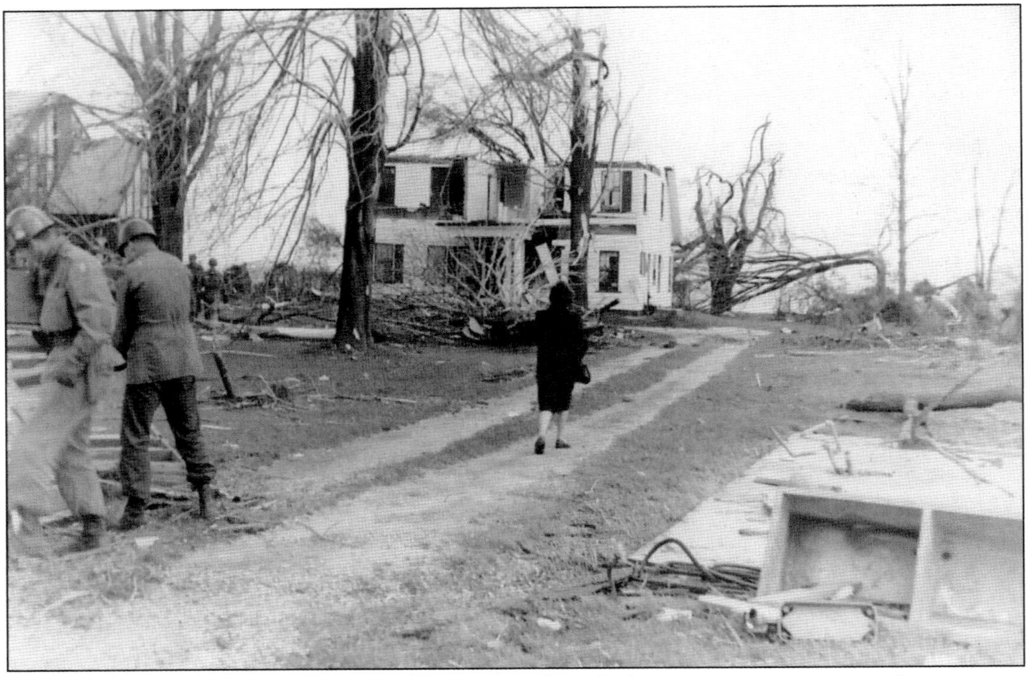

The Red Cross arrived immediately and began providing clothes and, in some cases, cash to victims. It later offered assistance with the rebuilding of homes and replacement of damaged furniture. The Salvation Army also came immediately and began providing food and coffee to the disaster workers and victims. As the Red Cross worked on settling the homeless into temporary quarters, it had a lot of help from the local residents. For instance, George W. Prichs of the Medea Hotel in Mt. Clemens, a structure that once stood where the present county administration building is, offered 40 rooms for the homeless. When it came to pets, the Michigan Humane Society found and successfully returned at least 33 dogs and cats to their owners. The society searched for and rescued many animals and even managed to rescue a goat trapped under a tree.

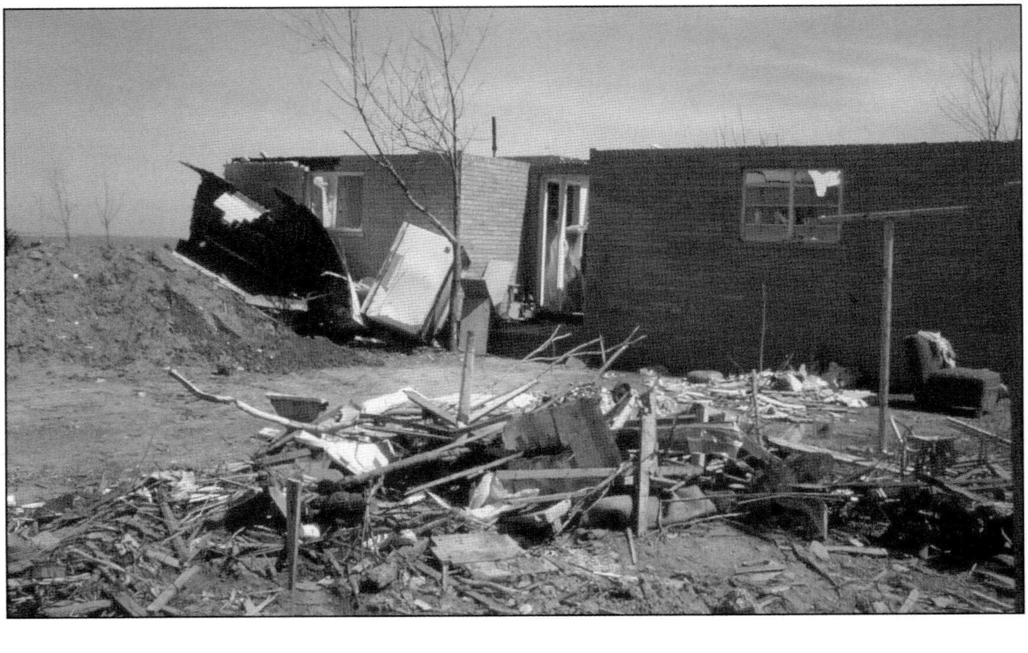

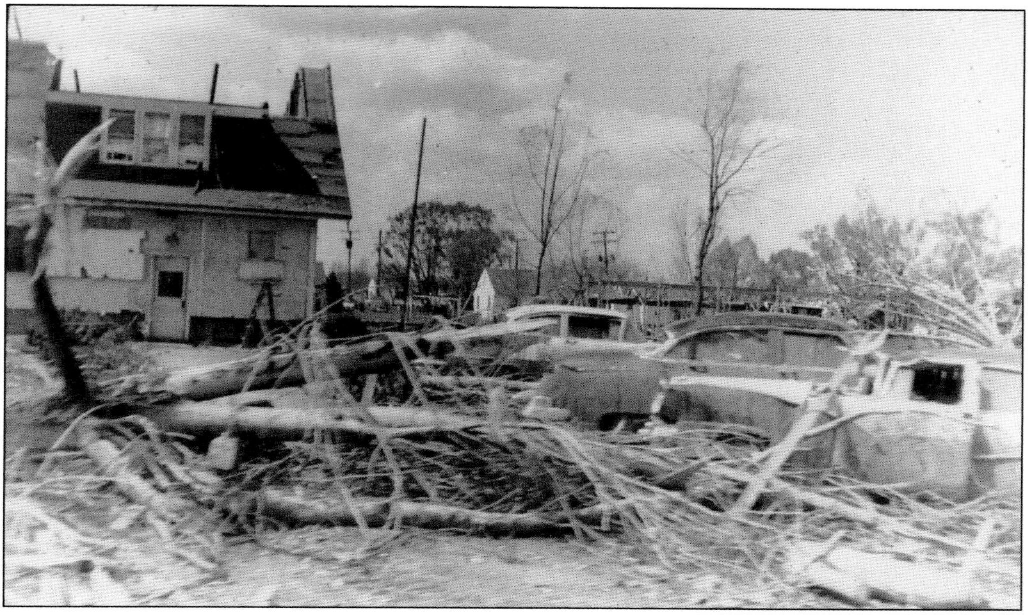

News articles of the day noted that close to 1,000 people were left homeless. In the immediate aftermath of the tornado, people in the area walked around in a state of shock. They wandered through debris-strewn streets and the rubble of their homes wondering what had just happened. For most who witnessed the tornado, it would be tough to think of a more terrifying time in their lives. One strange and uplifting occurrence in the aftermath was when Roseville Police found a baby they had been searching for—floating on a boat in the canal—unharmed.

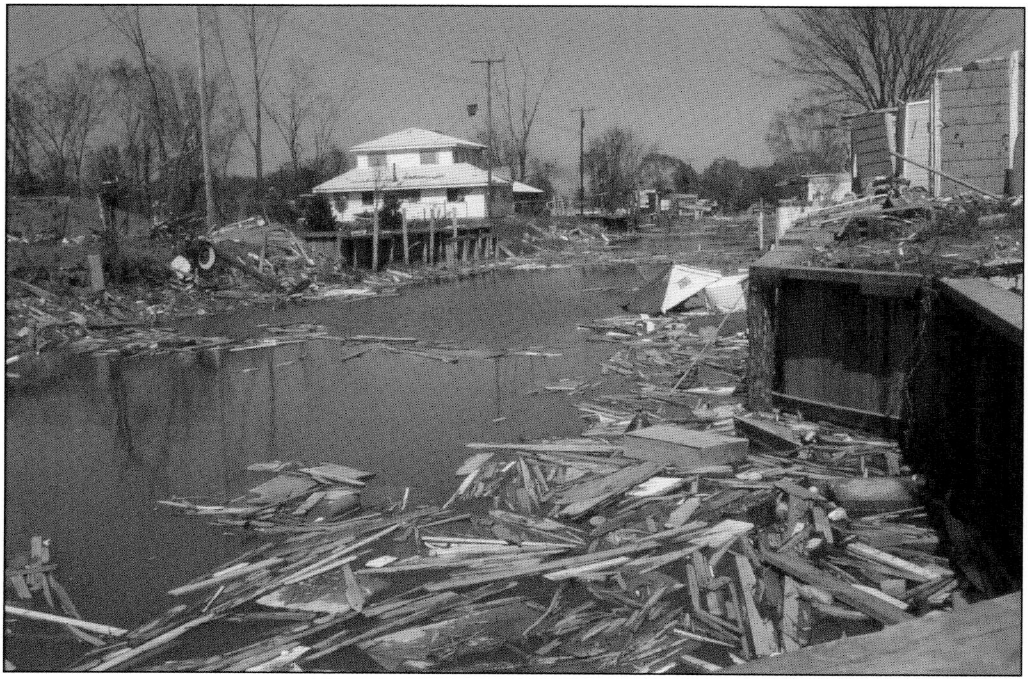

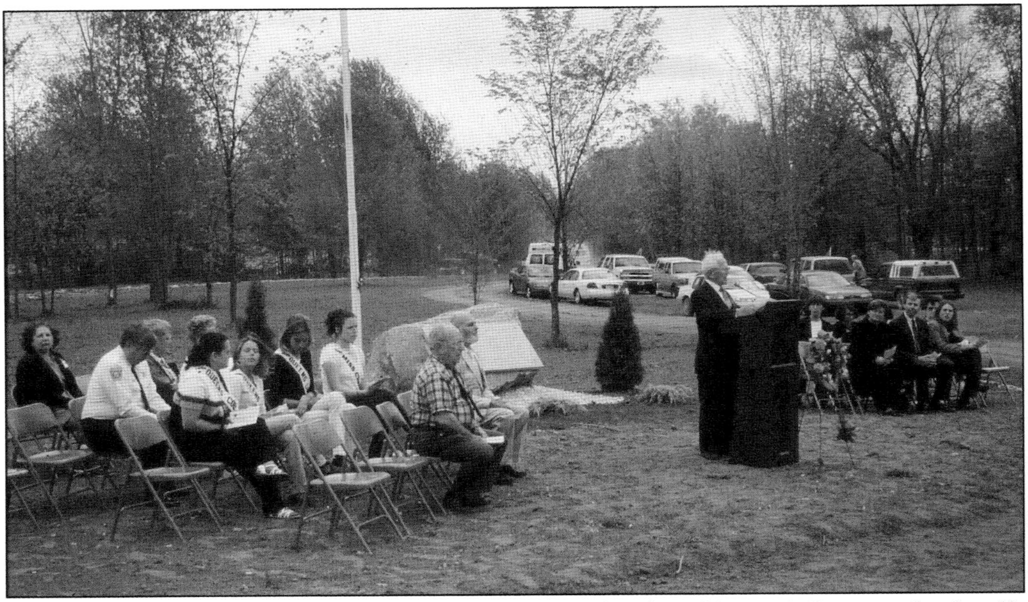

The alarm was first sounded by the Macomb County Civil Defense Unit at 4:42 p.m. to the sheriff's department, signaling that the tornado had been sighted in the region but had not touched down yet. Before getting to Chesterfield at 4:49 p.m., it briefly touched down in Pontiac Township at the intersection of Joslyn Road and Interstate 75. The tornado also briefly touched down in Port Huron after it hit Chesterfield. The people of Chesterfield dedicated a plaque to the victims of the tragedy. Many township, county, and state dignitaries were present at the ceremony.

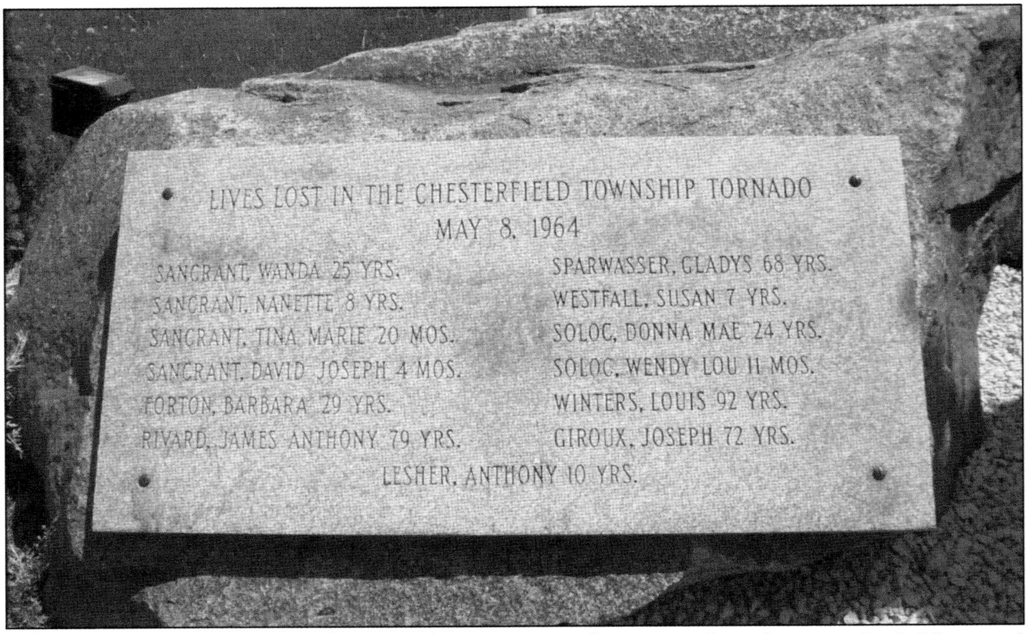

The plaque commemorating the tornado victims was later moved to the township's Historical Village. An initial dollar estimate of the tornado damage was $3,610,693, of which $2,233,825 was covered by insurance, for a net loss of $1,377,138. The damage estimate was put together three days after the tornado and did not even take into account all of the insurance information. (Tornado photographs courtesy of Bob Mack, Keith Weisgerber, and the Kraft Family.)

Six

Growth of Community and Government

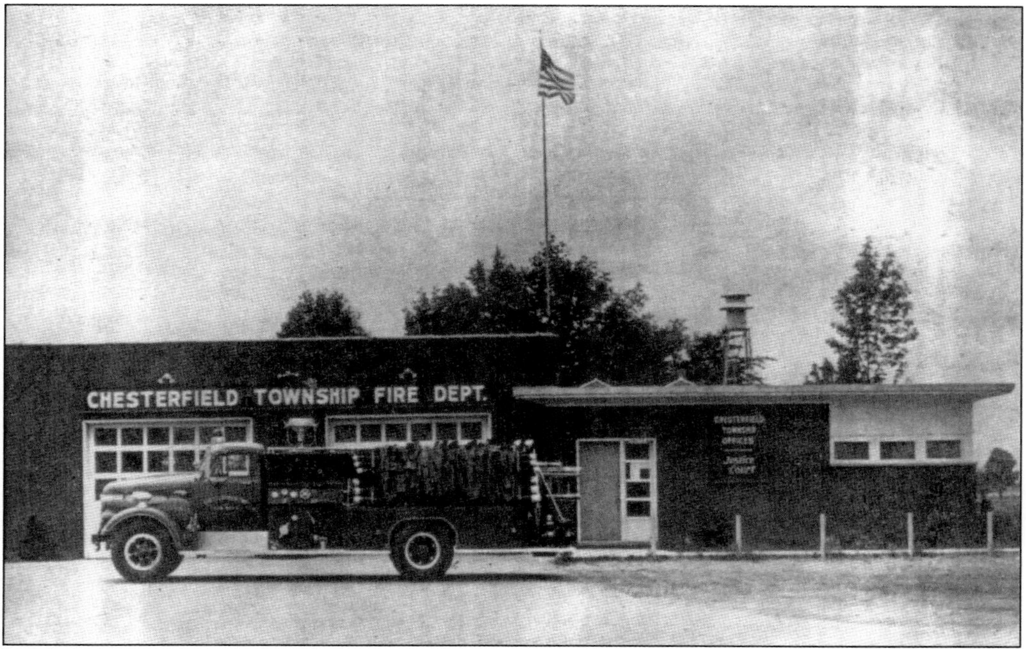

Pictured is the first Chesterfield Fire Station, built in 1954. Up to that year, if there was a fire in Chesterfield Township, the New Baltimore or New Haven Volunteer Fire Department would have been summoned. In January 1954, a meeting was called in Chesterfield Township, where it was decided to form a Chesterfield Fire Department.

YOUR FIRE DEPARTMENT

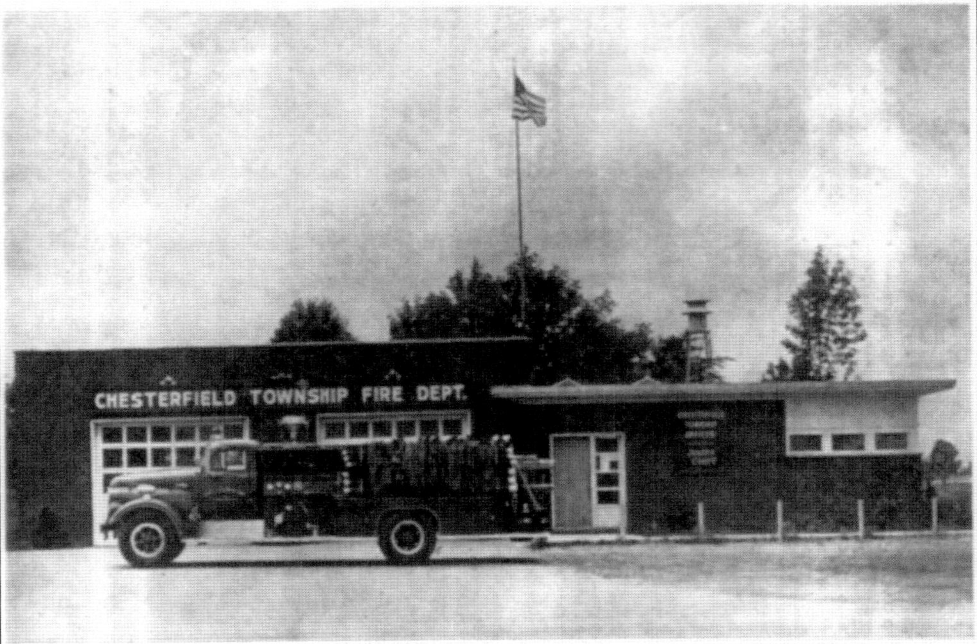

The Chesterfield Township Fire Department was founded at a regular business meeting of the Chesterfield Township Board in July 1954. At this meeting, it was decided that Chesterfield Township had developed to the stage where it could adequately support and maintain its own Fire Department. If it were manned by volunteers.

Prior to this time the Fire departments of New Baltimore and New Haven were under contract to Chesterfield Township.

The members of the Township Board at this period were: Keith Bovenschen, supervisor; Carl Brandenburg, Treasurer; Leo Blakaly, clerk; Phil Green and George Haase, trustees.

Residents of the Township who were interested in becoming volunteer members of the Chesterfield Township Fire Department were asked to attend a meeting with the Township Board. The response was large enough to assure the Township Board that a fire department could be adequately manned.

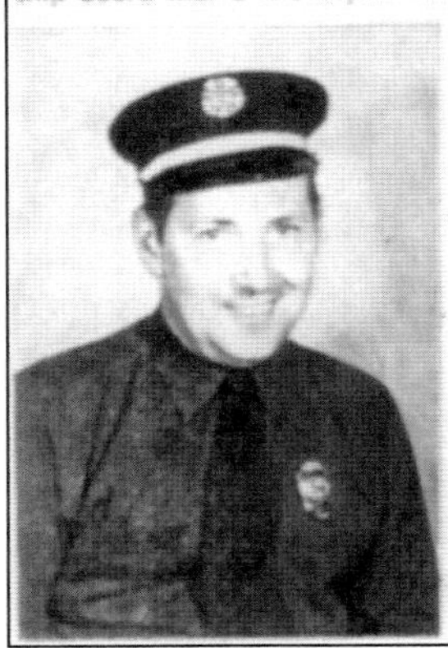

Training of the volunteers was the next step and this was done by Assistant Chief George Chapple of the Port Huron Fire Department working through the University of Michigan Extension Service. Training classes were held each week for 16 weeks.

In December 1954, the Constitution and By-Laws of the Chesterfield Township Fire Department were approved and signed by the Township Board.

A G.M.C. truck was purchased to provide a chassis to mount the body and equipment built by Firemaster Inc.

Since the original purchase, a portable generator, resuscitator and other miscellaneous equipment has been purchased by members of the Fire Department.

The Department now has thirty-one active

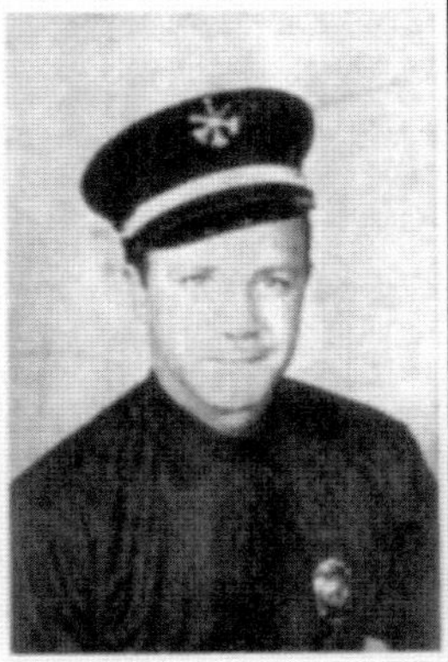

To help establish the fire department, fundraising was undertaken. First, a letter was sent to all residents asking for donations. Following this action, raffles were held, auctions of donated items were mounted, and organizations such as the Chesterfield Lions were solicited for donations. To ensure a sizable crowd would attend one of the fundraisers, a house was moved to the first fire headquarters at Gratiot Avenue and Chesterfield Street. The house was burned in the field behind the station, and the new fire department put it out. Fundraising was successful, and Chesterfield soon had fire trucks and equipment. A water tanker was also purchased for use on the north side of the township, where there were no fire hydrants. (Courtesy of Trinity Archives.)

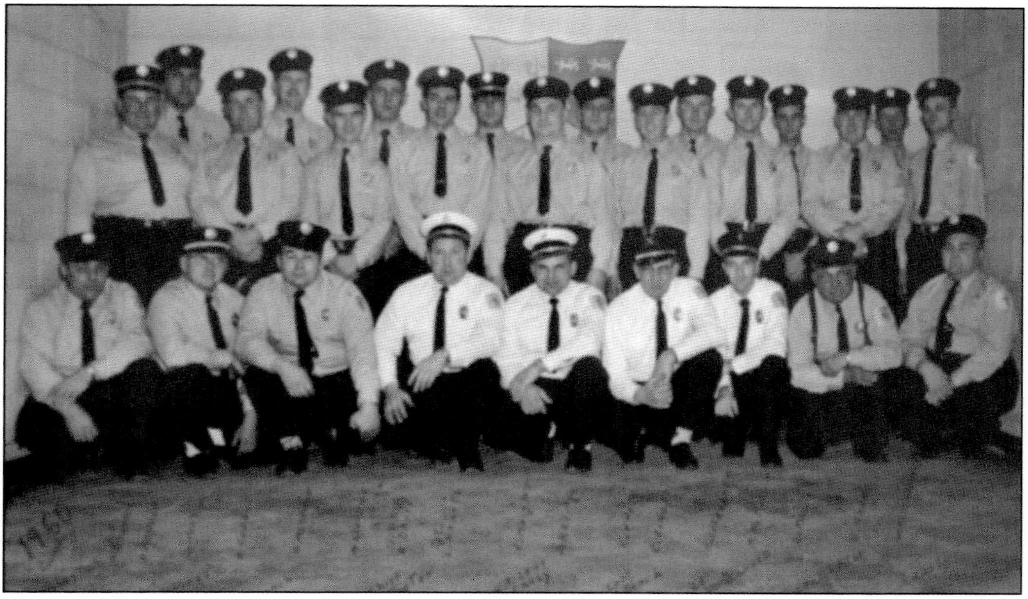

At first there were about 30 volunteers, and these men were trained to become the first fire department. They established bylaws and appointed Frank Robinson, who had worked on the Selfridge Air Base Fire Department, as the first fire chief. After six months assistant chief George Furton took over as fire chief. (Both, courtesy of Trinity Archives.)

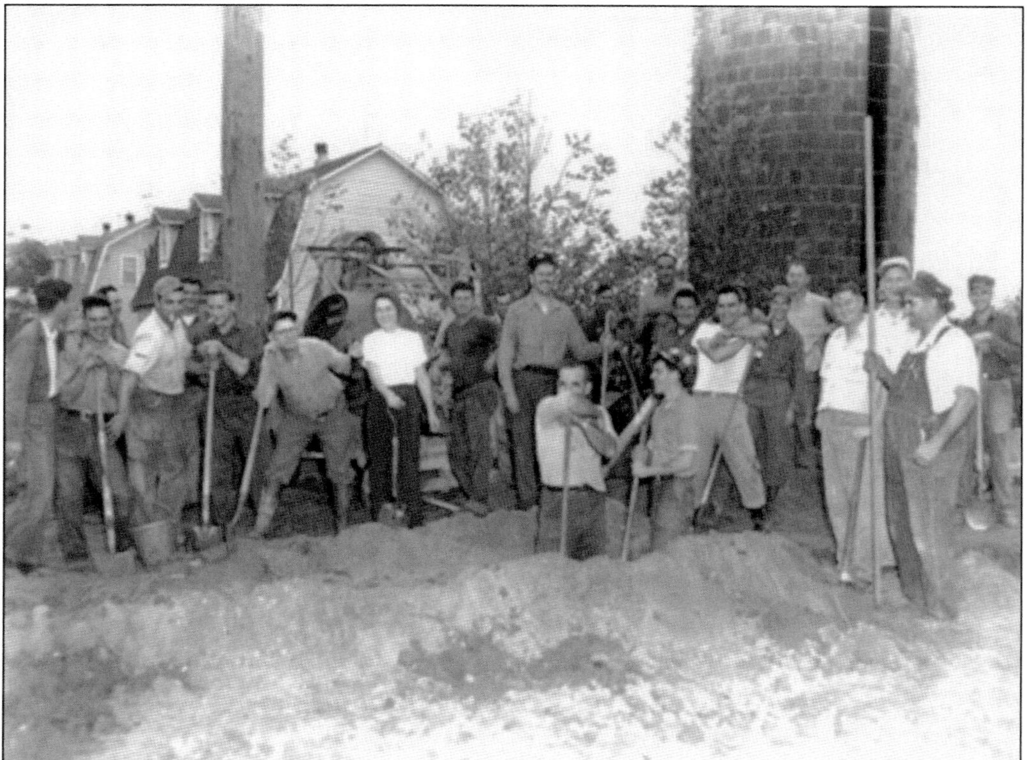

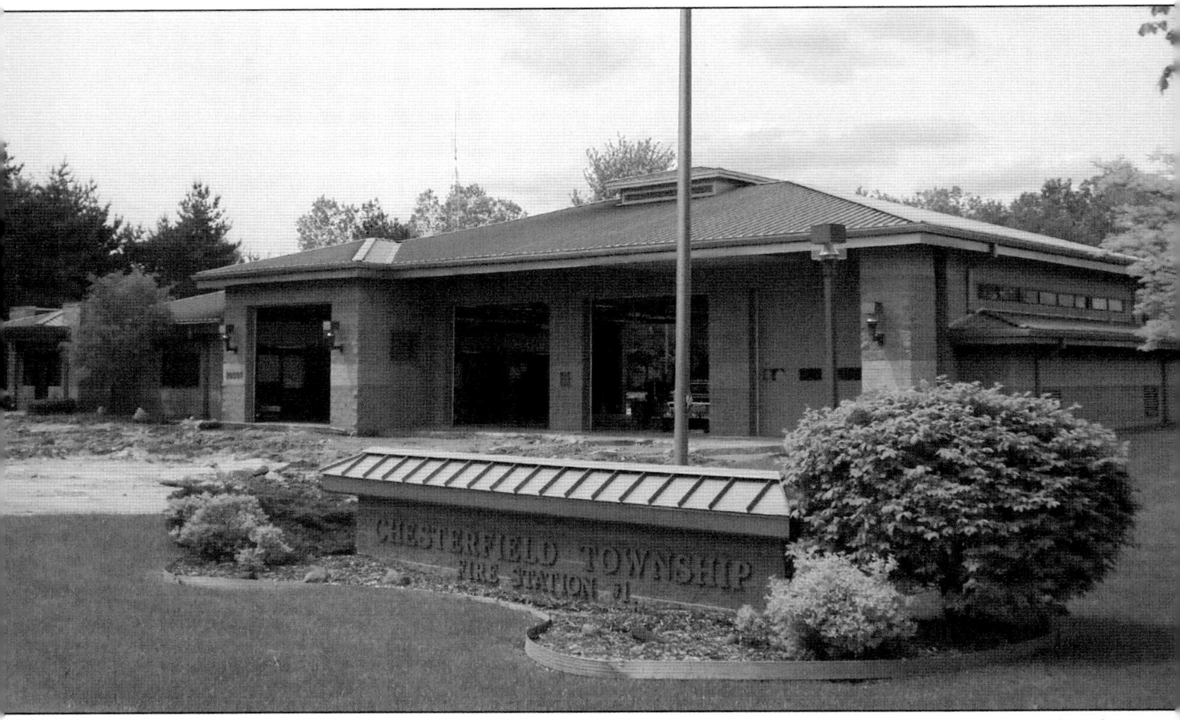

The first Chesterfield Fire Department was formed in 1954. Other early developments for the department were the addition of a ladies auxiliary and a mutual aid pact with surrounding communities to help each other put out fires. In 1973, a second fire station was added on Jefferson Avenue. In 1992, the first station on Gratiot Avenue was replaced with one on 22 Mile Road near Gratiot Avenue, and in 2004 a station was added on 23 Mile Road at Baker Street. (Courtesy of Tracy Antrikin.)

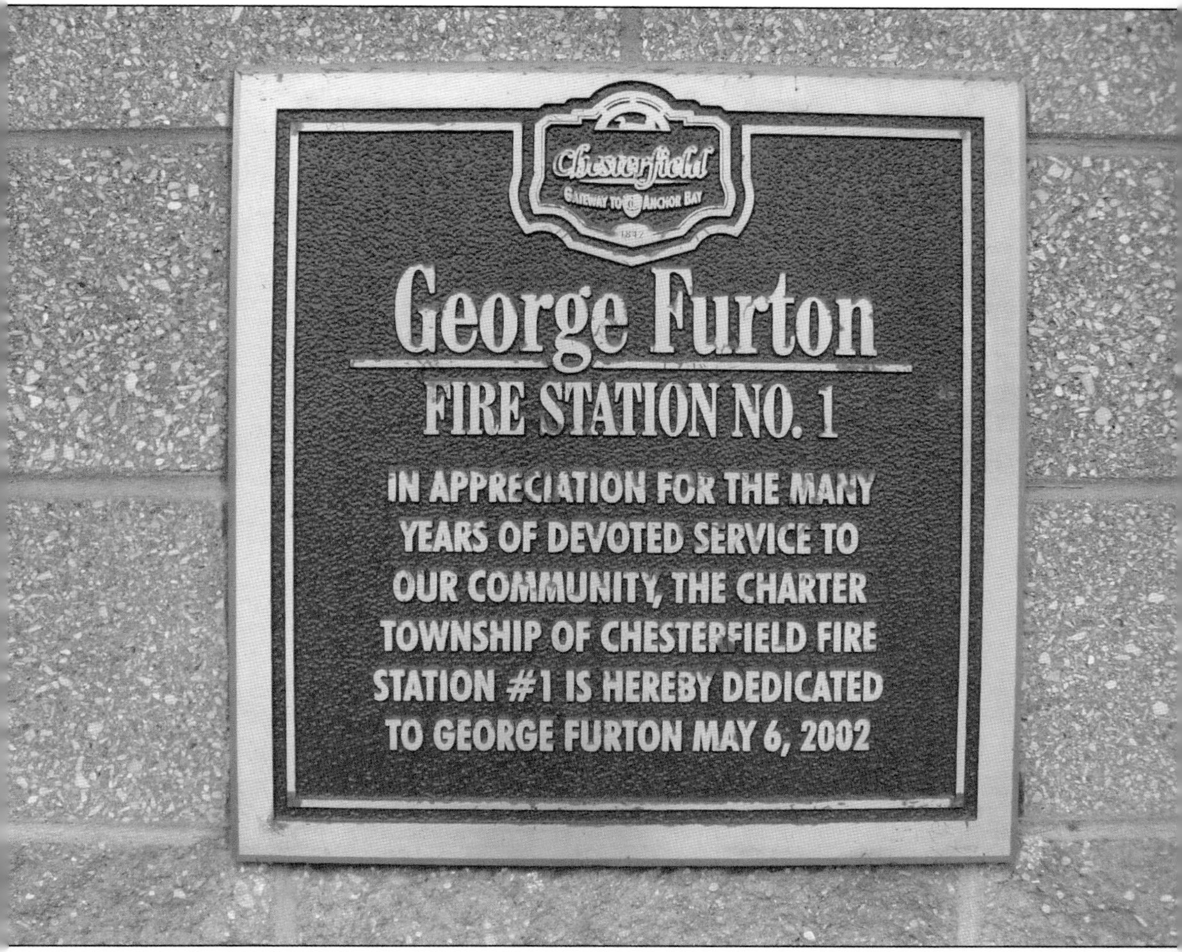

A plaque on the first fire department house honors George Furton. In the early days, firemen would use a "phone fan-out" to notify everyone in the department about a fire. The calls would first go to five people, who would each phone others, who would then phone others, and so on. Today, the fire department has about 50 employees, including paramedics and perhaps a Dalmatian or two. (Courtesy of Tracy Antrikin.)

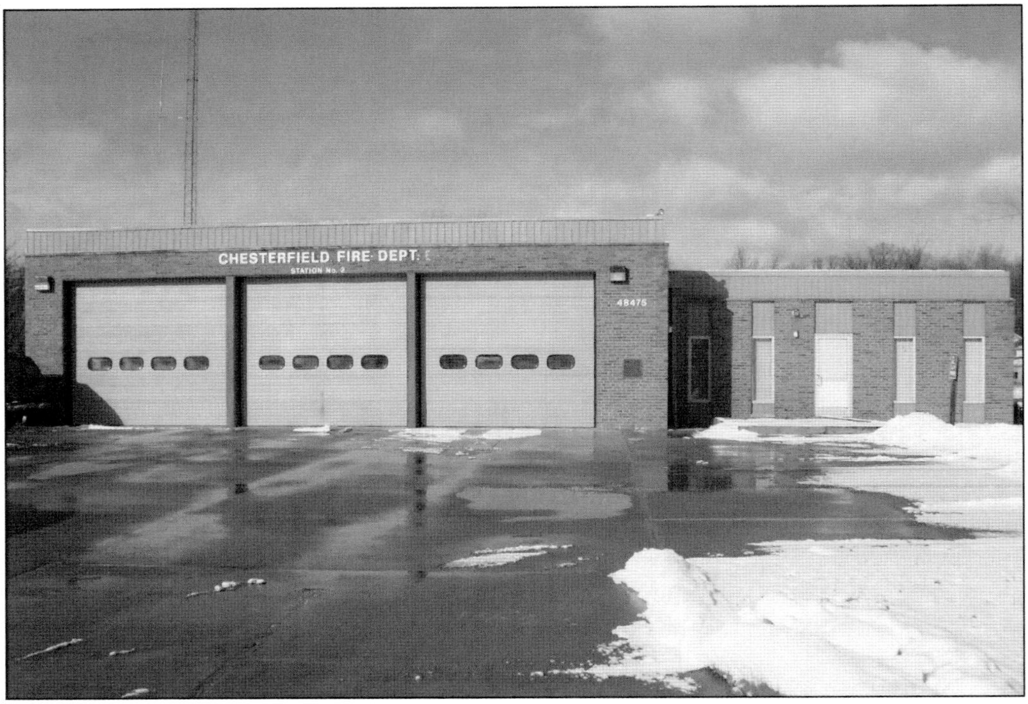

These contemporary photographs show the modern Chesterfield Fire Department building during a quiet moment in a winter setting but always at the ready to respond when needed.

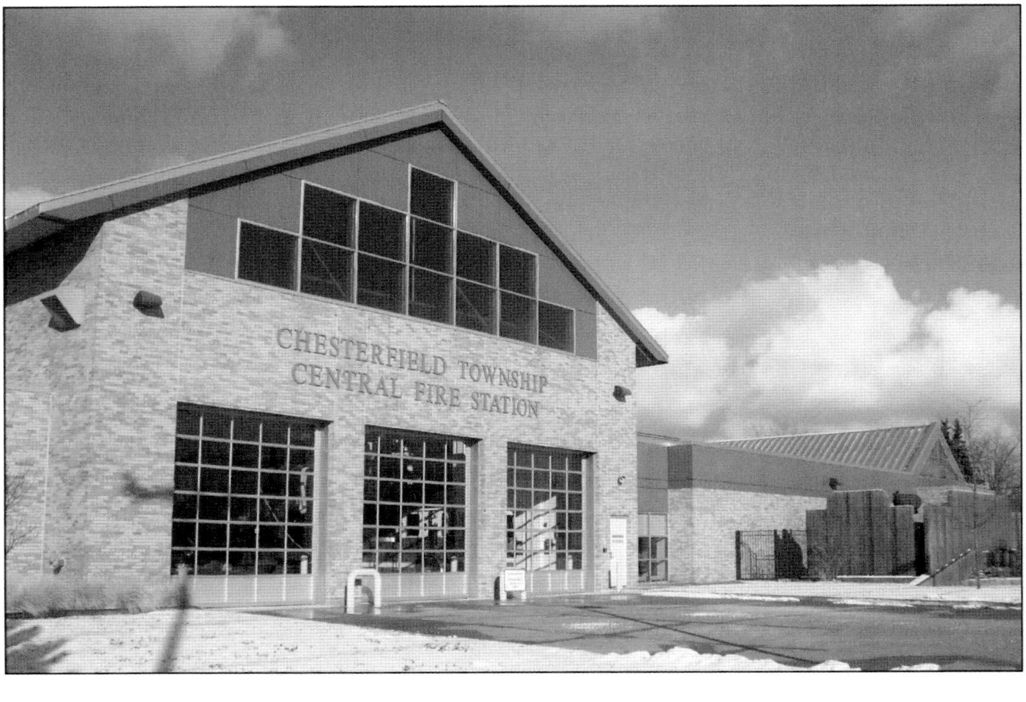

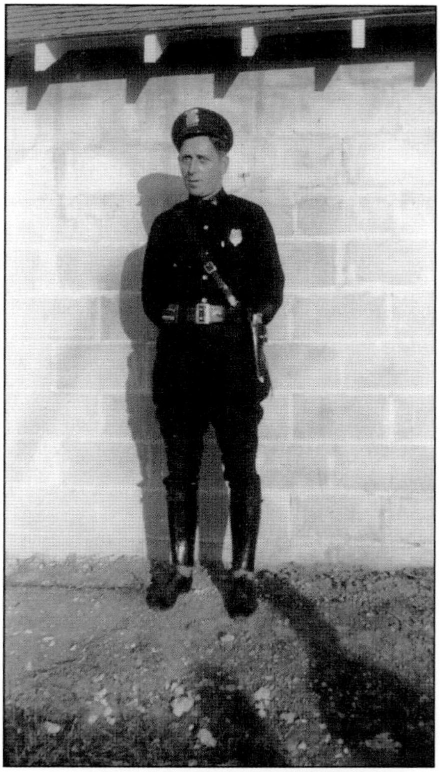

As a rural community for most of its days, Chesterfield had little crime and small need for a large police force. Pictured at right is Orrin Kraft, the constable for Chesterfield Township who worked in his mother's store, Kraft's Korner Market, when he was young. Below, Constables Russell Pipe (with sunglasses) and William Middleton were two of the four police officers who served Chesterfield until the early 1960s. (Right, courtesy of Kraft family; below, the Trinity Archives.)

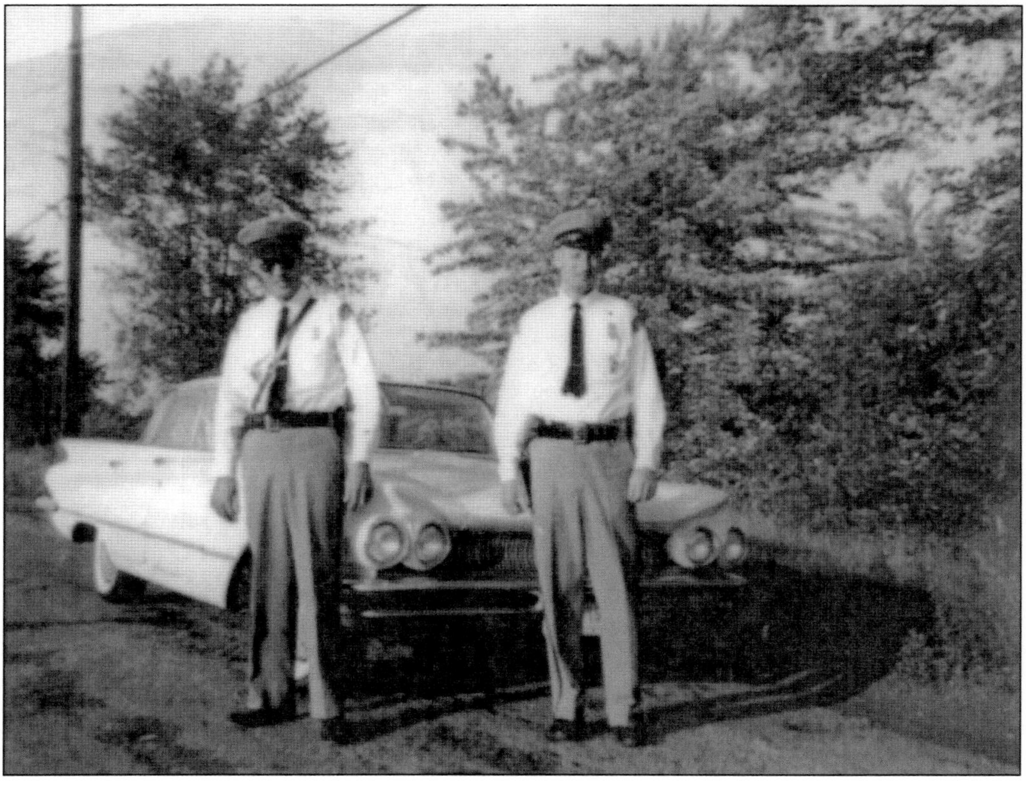

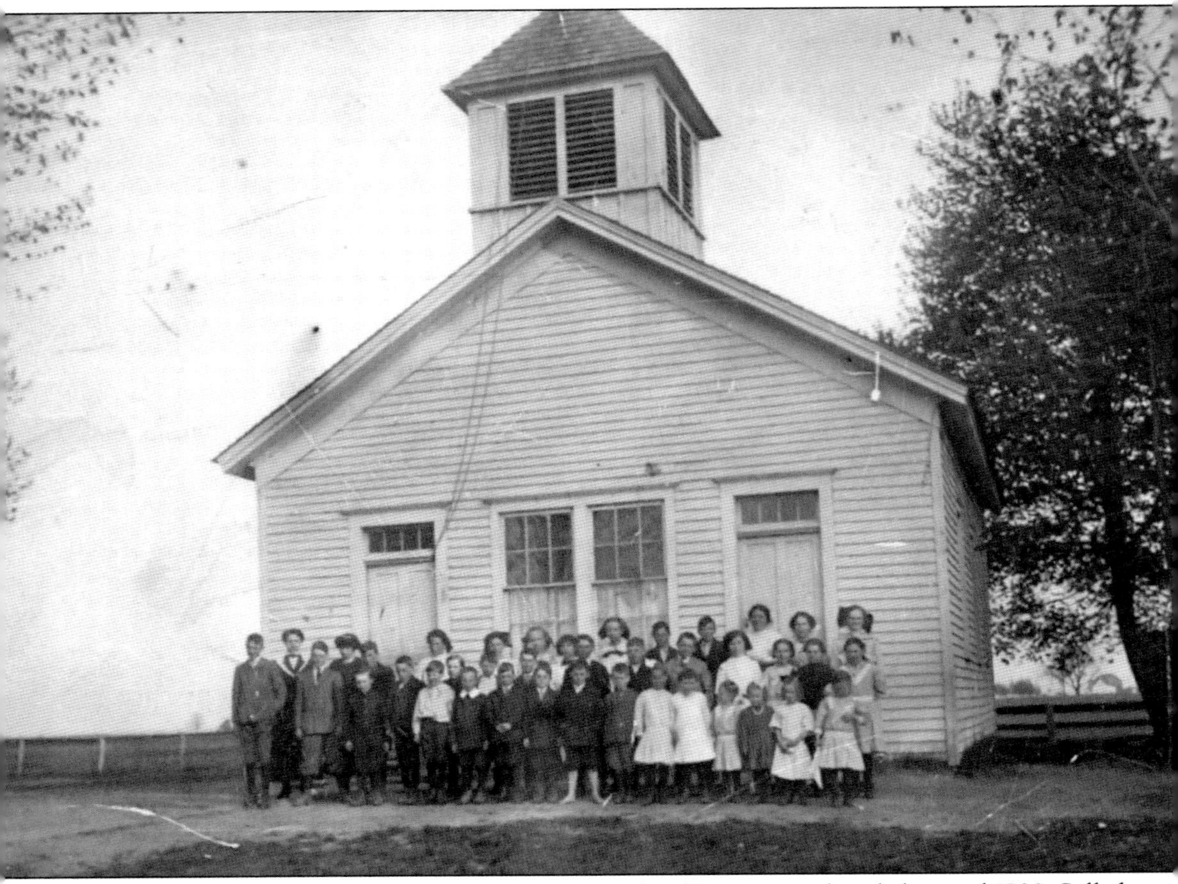

One of the original schools in the L'Anse Creuse School District was founded around 1900. Called the Green School, it must have been light in weight, as it was picked up more than once and moved down the street by the French settlers who felt it should be closer to them. It was picked up and moved from the corner of Cotton and Sugarbush Roads to halfway between Cotton and Hall Roads on Sugarbush Road. The next day, it was moved back by the Green family. This back and forth movement continued until a court ordered that the school was to remain at what is now the intersection of Sugarbush and Graham Roads. (Courtesy of Green School Archives.)

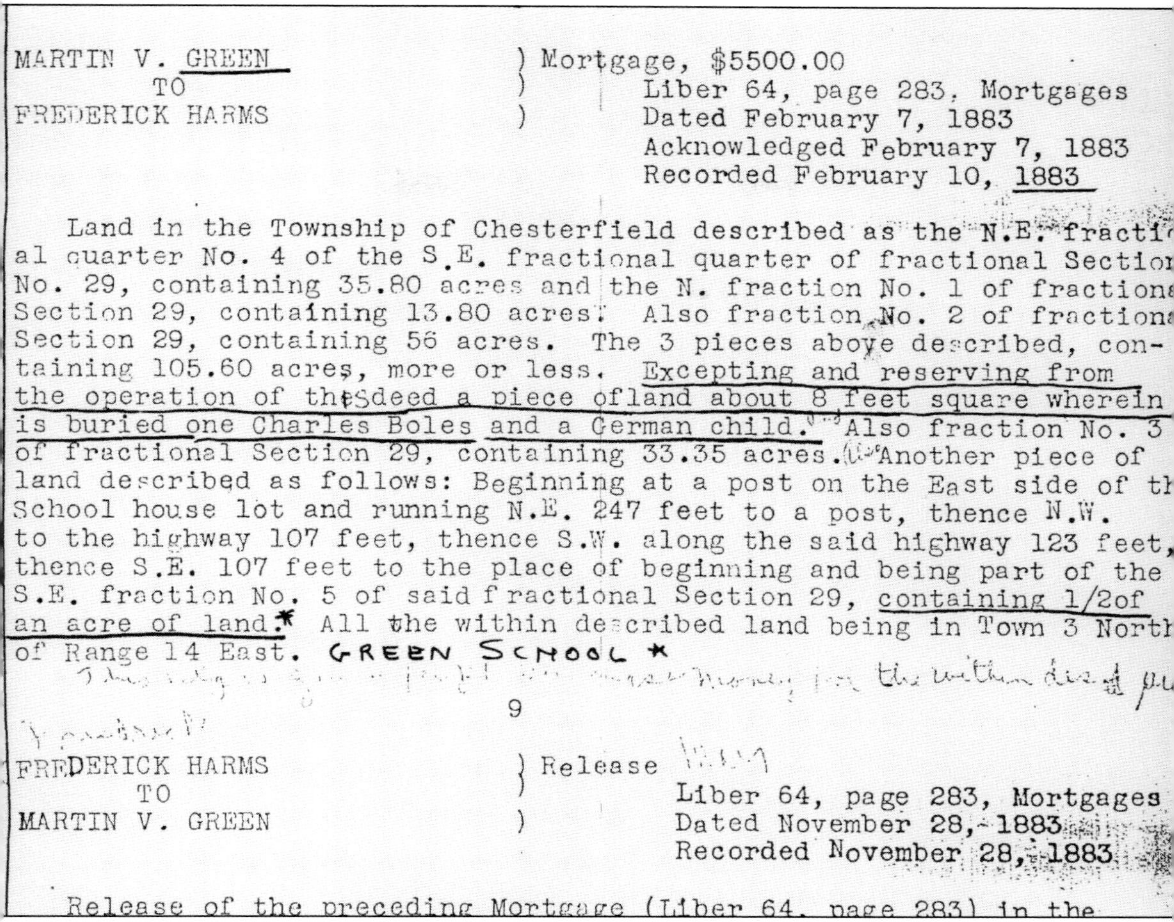

MARTIN V. GREEN) Mortgage, $5500.00
TO) Liber 64, page 283, Mortgages
FREDERICK HARMS) Dated February 7, 1883
Acknowledged February 7, 1883
Recorded February 10, 1883

Land in the Township of Chesterfield described as the N.E. fracti-al quarter No. 4 of the S.E. fractional quarter of fractional Section No. 29, containing 35.80 acres and the N. fraction No. 1 of fractional Section 29, containing 13.80 acres. Also fraction No. 2 of fractional Section 29, containing 56 acres. The 3 pieces above described, containing 105.60 acres, more or less. Excepting and reserving from the operation of this deed a piece of land about 8 feet square wherein is buried one Charles Boles and a German child. Also fraction No. 3 of fractional Section 29, containing 33.35 acres. Another piece of land described as follows: Beginning at a post on the East side of the School house lot and running N.E. 247 feet to a post, thence N.W. to the highway 107 feet, thence S.W. along the said highway 123 feet, thence S.E. 107 feet to the place of beginning and being part of the S.E. fraction No. 5 of said fractional Section 29, containing 1/2 of an acre of land.* All the within described land being in Town 3 North of Range 14 East. GREEN SCHOOL *

9

FREDERICK HARMS) Release
TO) Liber 64, page 283, Mortgages
MARTIN V. GREEN) Dated November 28, 1883
Recorded November 28, 1883

Release of the preceding Mortgage (Liber 64, page 283) in the

The school was built at a cost of $1,400, and operating expenses per year totaled $384, including the teacher's salary. Twenty-seven students attended this one-room schoolhouse that held first through eighth grades until 1929, when it was torn down and replaced by a newer structure at a cost of $30,000. The new building had six rooms with six teachers, a cafeteria, administration offices, and two buses serving it. The Green School was built on the site where Edward Green first found Native American skulls on his property. Green would mount the skulls on fence posts around his farm. The townspeople, alarmed by the scene, held a special meeting to request the skulls be removed (which they were). Marie Quine, born in 1904, lived across the street from the Green School and remembered spending recess and lunch breaks at the school in the backyard, digging for Native American relics such as swords and arrowheads. (Courtesy of Green School Archives.)

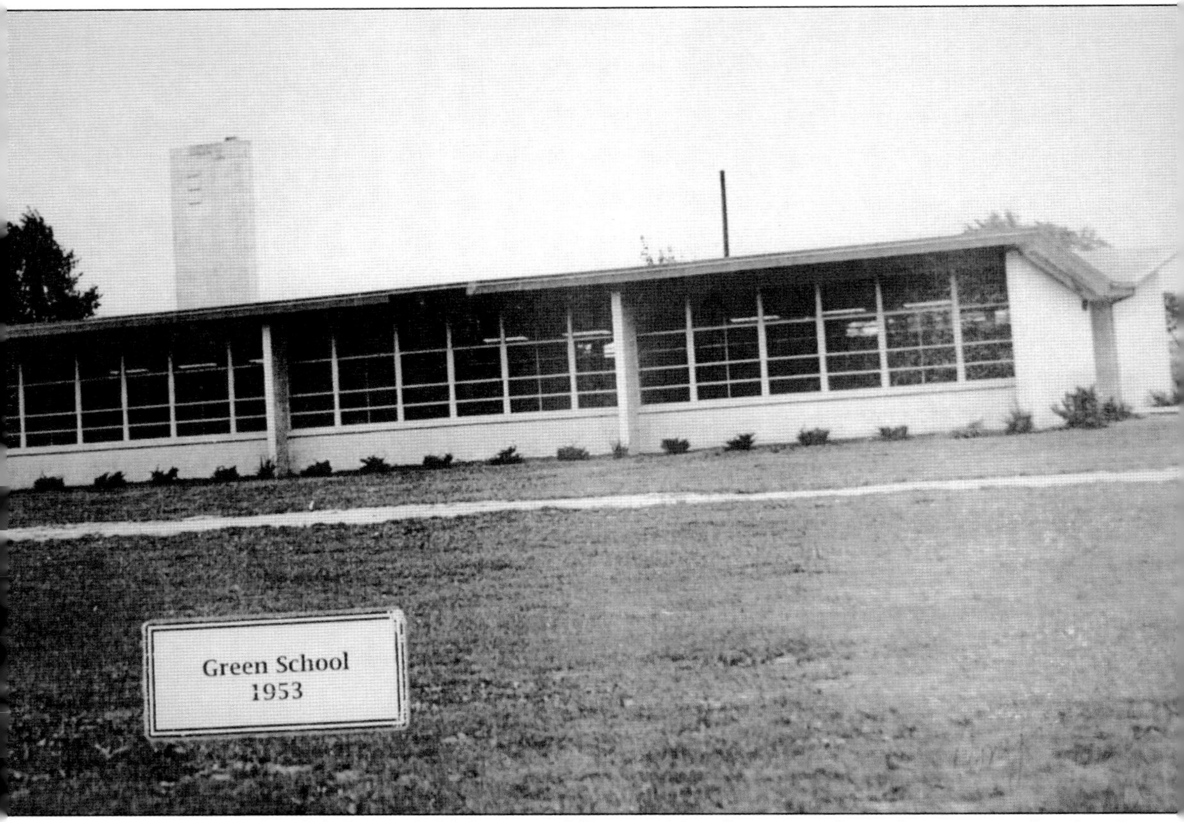

The Green School (Chesterfield Fractional District No. 6) remained an elementary school and part of the L'Anse Creuse School District, one of three school districts located in the township (the other two being Anchor Bay and New Haven). The Weller School (Chesterfield Fractional District No. 1) became part of the Anchor Bay School District, as well as the Chapel School (Chesterfield Fractional District No. 2), which was at 51200 Washington Street at Green Street in New Baltimore. The Old Town Hall School (Chesterfield Fractional District No. 3) was at Maria and Alfred Streets in New Baltimore, and the Salt River School (Chesterfield Fractional District No. 4) was located on 23 Mile Road by the Salt River. (Courtesy of Green School archives.)

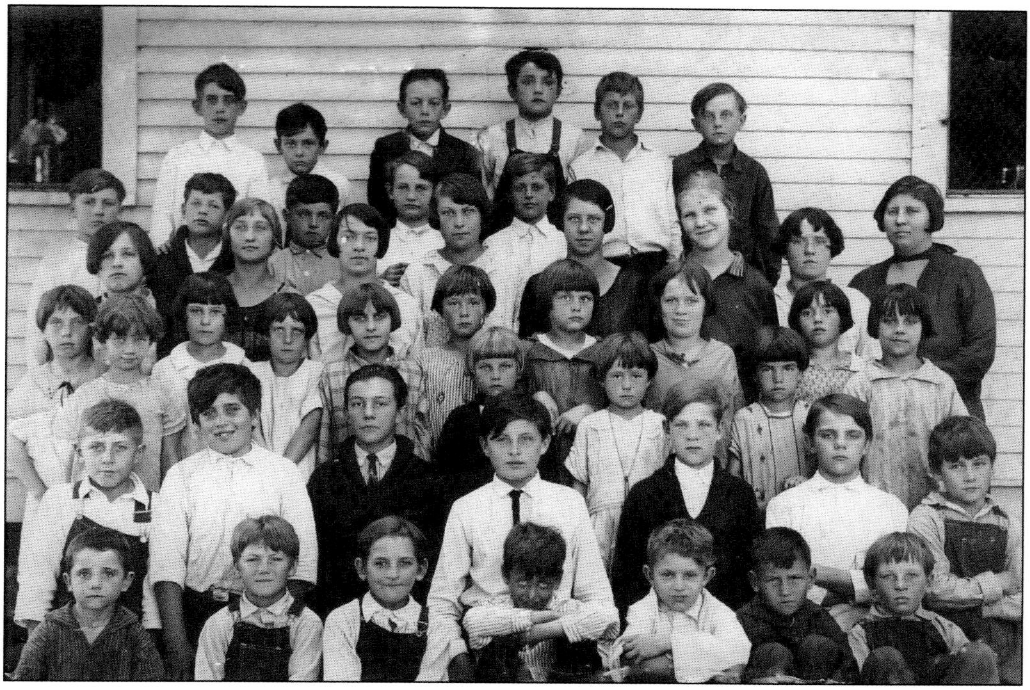

Students from the early days of Green School pose in the photograph above. Pictured below is the Green School as it appears in the 21st century. Other schools in Chesterfield included the Burdon School (also called the Log Cabin School and Chesterfield Fractional District No. 5), located at 25 Mile and Burdon Roads. The original structure was built in 1859 on an area that is now a golf course. That school was replaced by one built across the street at the corner of 25 Mile and Burdon Roads in 1904 (officially 34880 Arnold Road). Another school, the Brooks School (also known as Chesterfield Fractional District No. 7), was at 36795 Marine City Highway. These schools became part of the Anchor Bay School District. They were all one-room schoolhouses and encompassed grades one through eight. (Both, courtesy of Green School archives.)

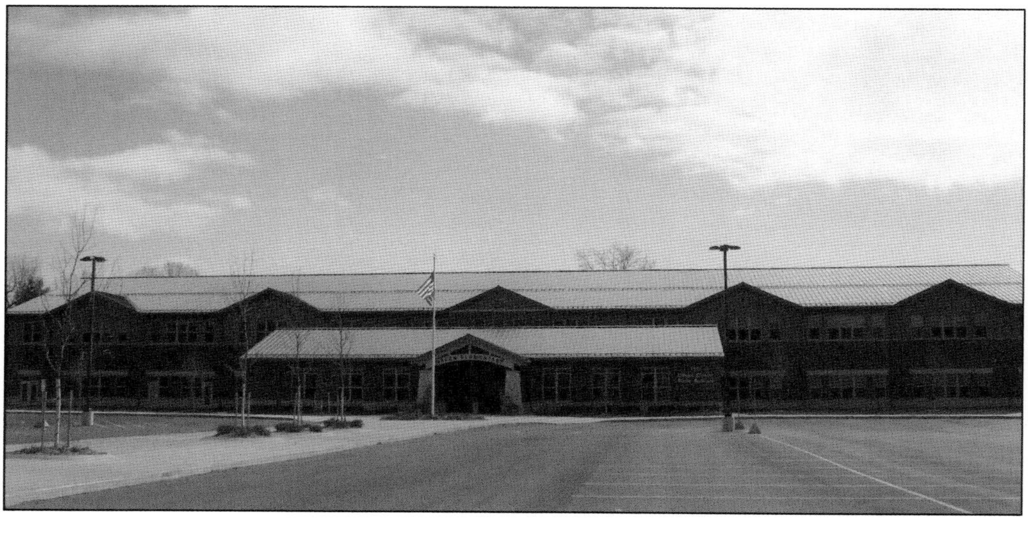

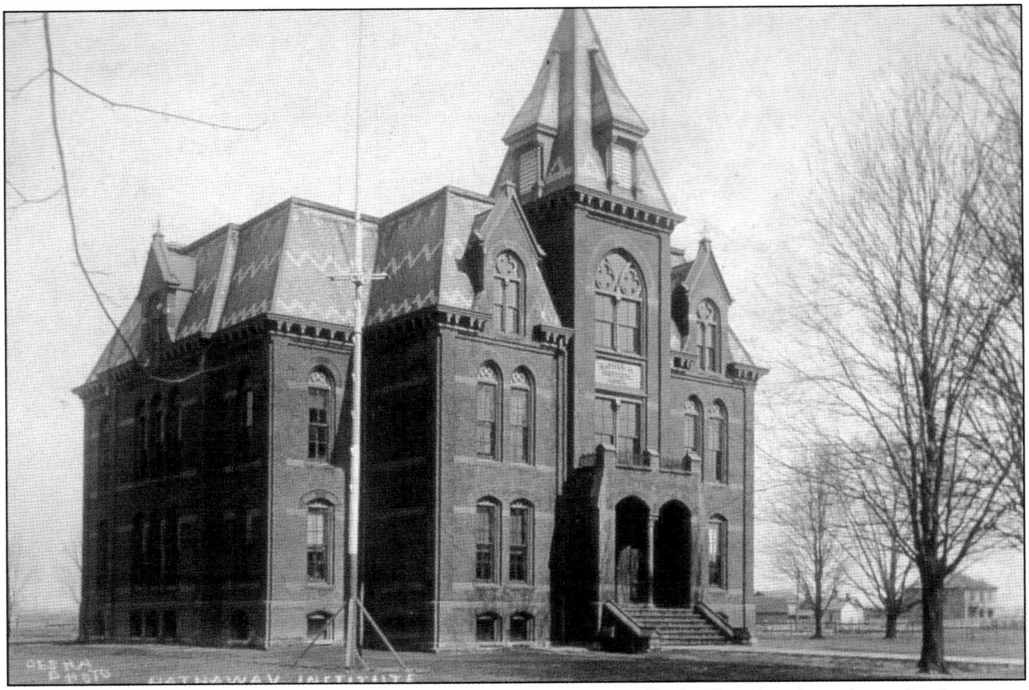

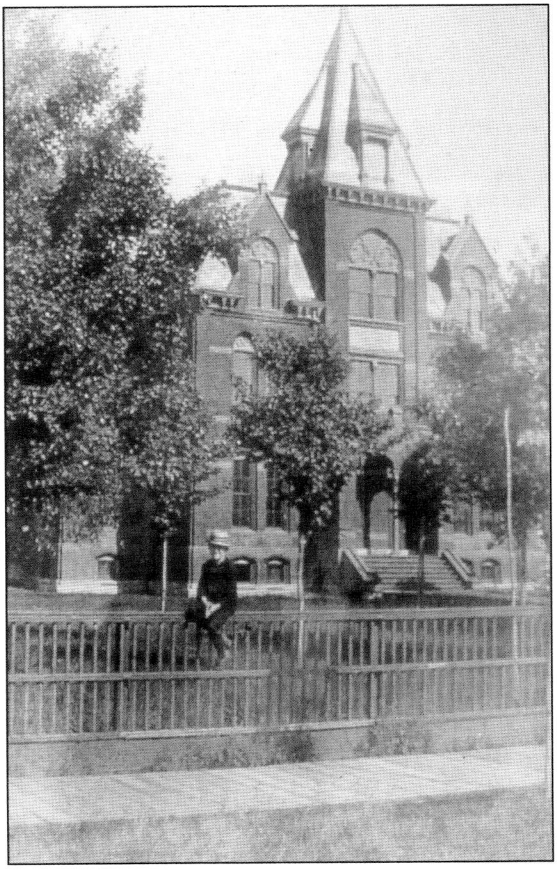

Initially, high school students had to go to Mt. Clemens for high school until 1876, when the Hathaway Institute in New Baltimore was built on land donated by Gilbert Hathaway, one of the area's business tycoons. He owned a stave factory, a commercial dock, and a shipping business. Gilbert willed $15,000 to the city to build a school when he died in 1871. After prolonged litigation, the school was eventually built during 1875 and 1876 for a total cost of $22,000, which is what the fund had grown to after litigation. The institute once trained future teachers. The Hathaway Institute was torn down in 1970, and the municipal offices for New Baltimore were built where it once stood.

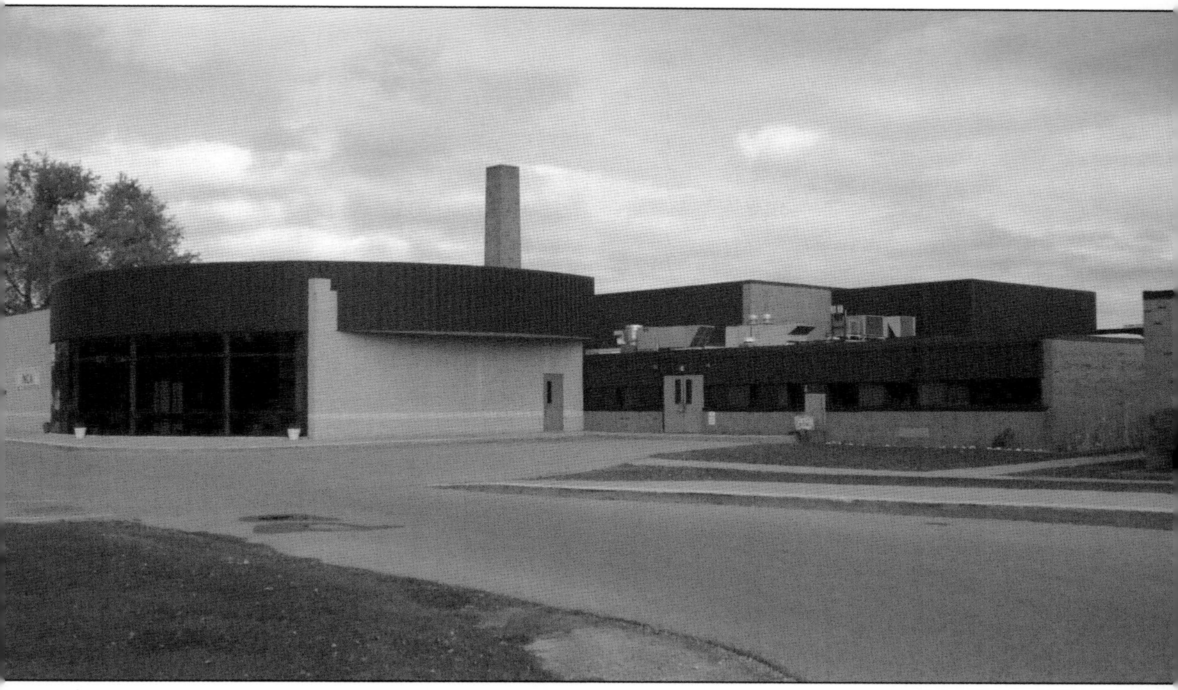

When the first new school since the Hathaway Institute was built, the school district was renamed the Anchor Bay Rural Agricultural Schools, and the new building on Washington Street was called Anchor Bay High School. Later, the district was named the New Baltimore Public Schools and, finally, the Anchor Bay School District. This building is now the Lighthouse Elementary School. It has been remodeled many times and now includes an Olympic-sized swimming pool.

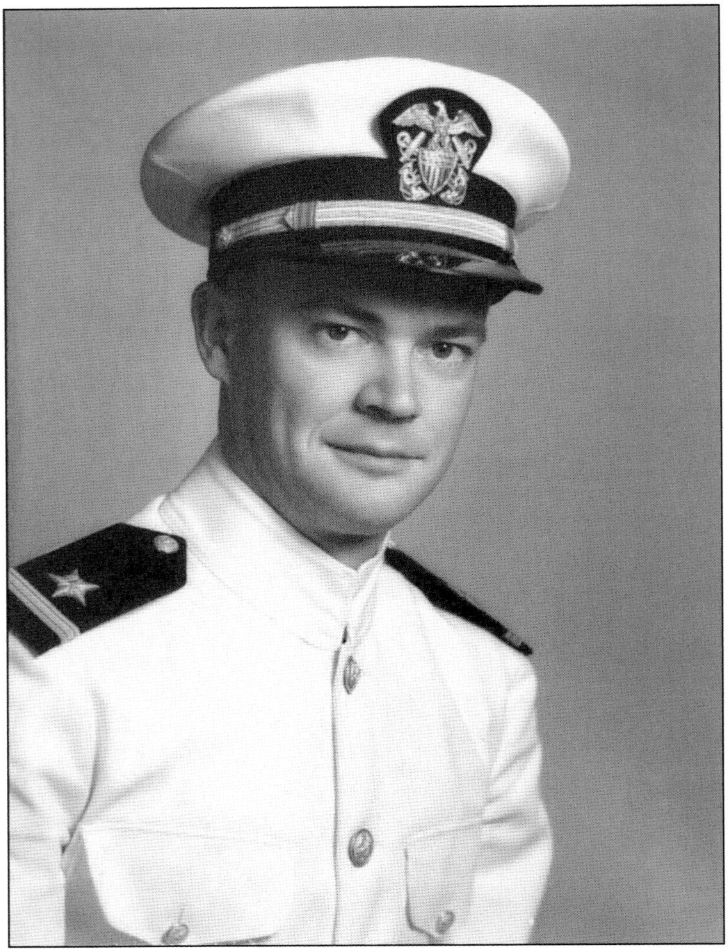

The Anchor Bay School District was consolidated in the mid-1950s. Anchor Bay Elementary was built in 1956 on Ashley Street near Bedford Street. In 1960, Anchor Bay School District built the Dean A. Naldrett Elementary School, named for the superintendent of schools (left) who helped organize the school district. Dean A. Naldrett also happens to be the author's father. (Both, courtesy of Trinity Archives.)

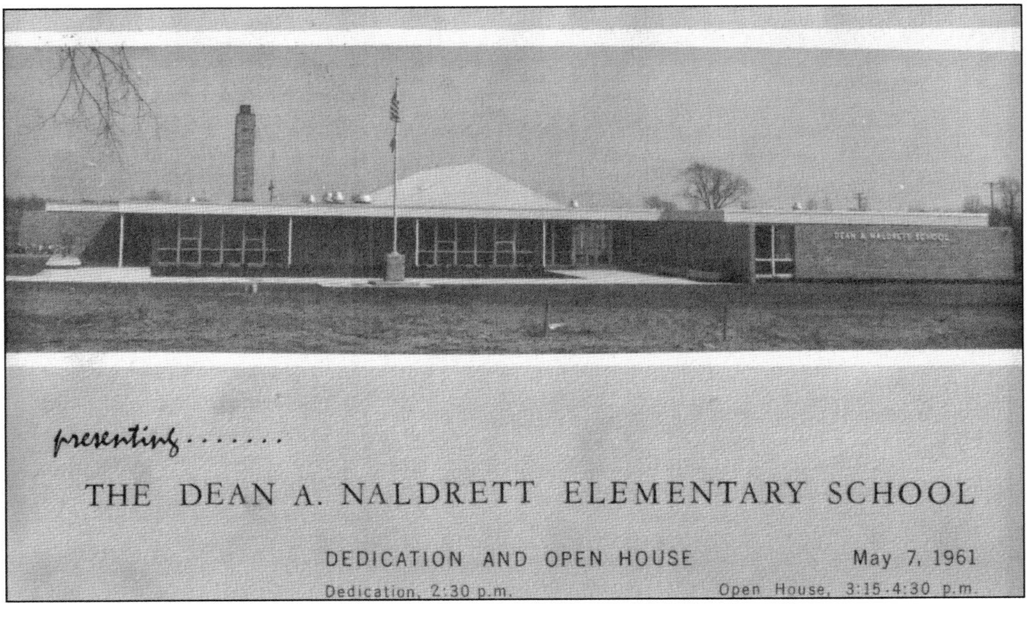

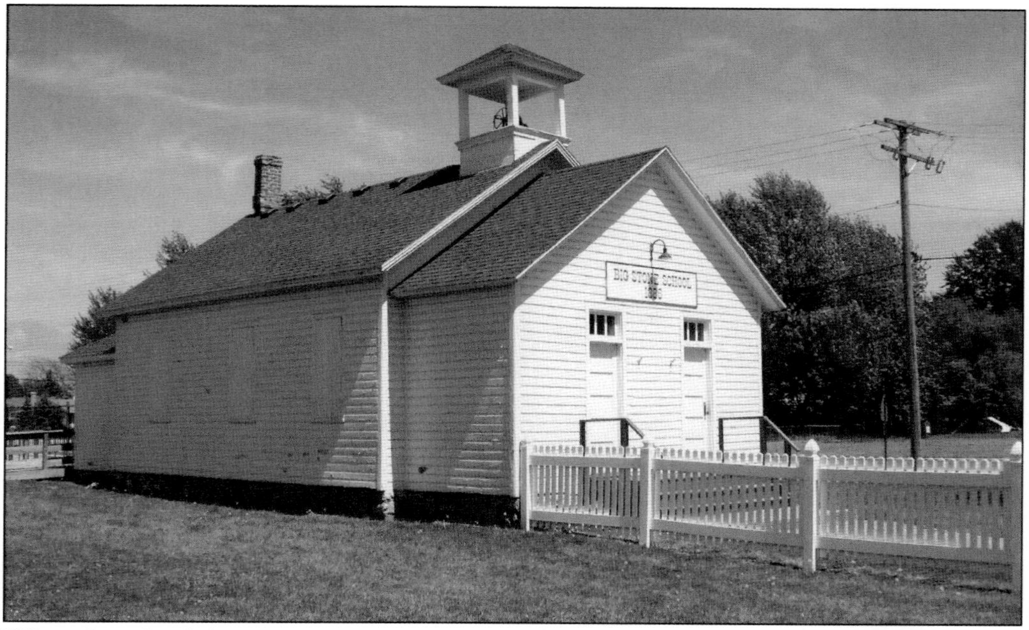

When the school district came into possession of the school known as the Big Stone School (named for, believe it or not, the nearby big stone), Dean Naldrett arranged to have it moved to the area behind the high school on Washington Street (minus the stone). It was used for storage for about 30 years before being restored by the Big Stone School Committee and moved to the front of the property. (Courtesy of Trinity Archives.)

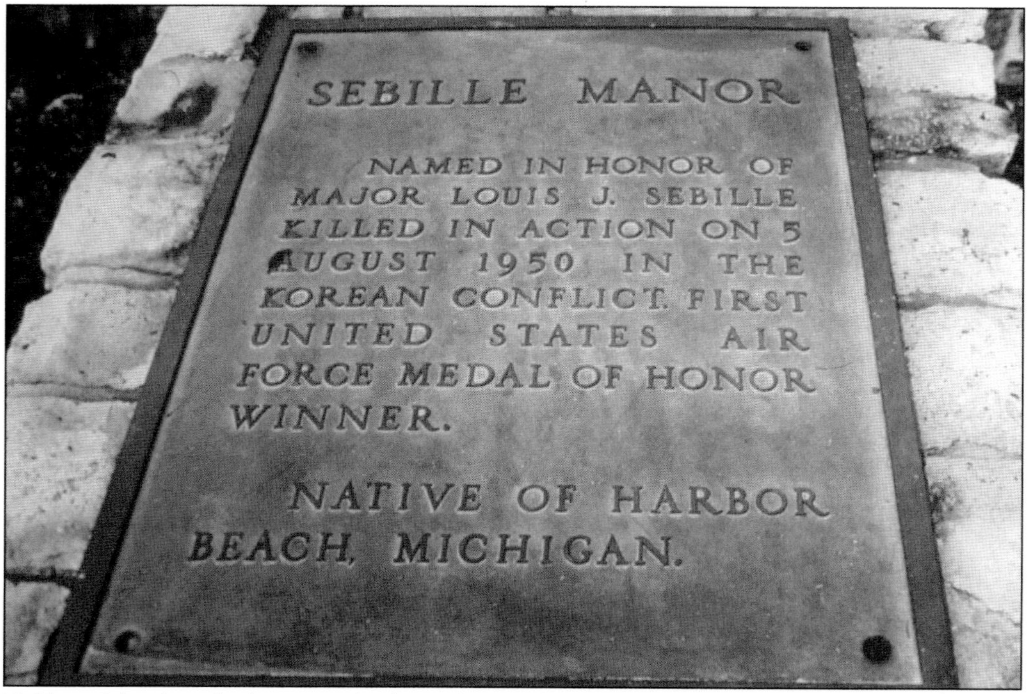

Naldrett School was built on Sugarbush Road across from Sebille Manor, which was the base housing for Selfridge Air Force Base. Sebille Manor, also known as Capehart, closed in 2008. It was named for Maj. Louis J. Sebille who was killed in action in the Korean Conflict in August 1950.

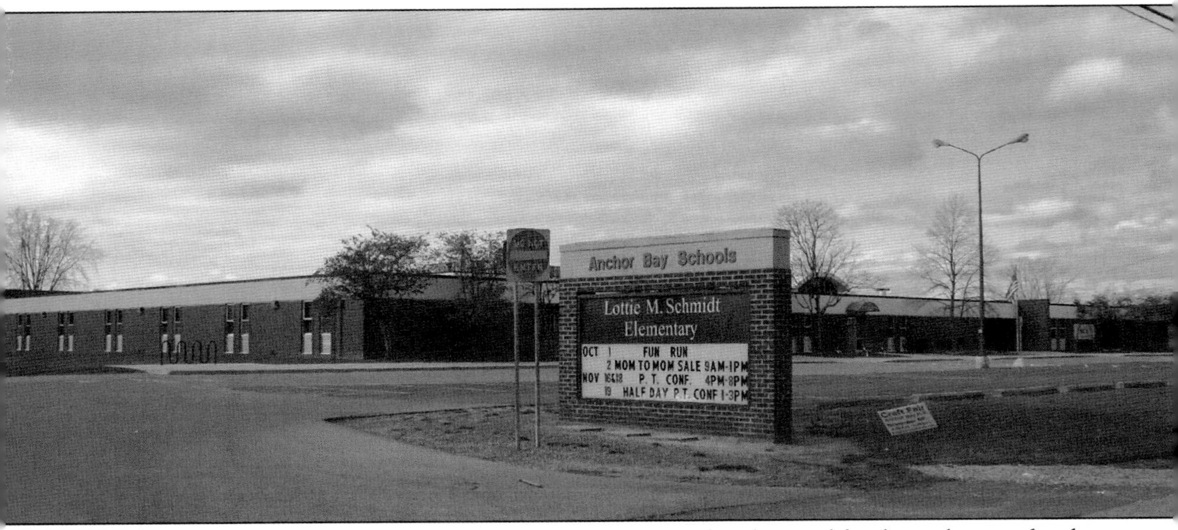

In 1971, Lottie M. Schmidt Elementary School was erected and named for the real estate developer who donated the land. Lottie M. Schmidt was the developer of Chesterfield's most private subdivision, Lottivue. Constructed on lakefront property with two man-made canals, the exclusive, private subdivision shows how far Chesterfield has come since the Great Depression when one could make a down payment on a canal lot in Anchor Bay with 25 live chickens or a small load of used lumber. Lottie was a teacher who sold real estate in the summer. Her first development, Anchor Bay Shores, right off Jefferson Avenue, was erected during the Great Depression, and it took years to sell all the lots. Later developments were Anchor Bay Harbor and Anchor Bay Gardens. They were located on Forton and Mallard Streets. Her most ambitious project was Lottivue, which was named in her honor when she died in 1956. When Lottivue sites were first offered in 1957, unimproved canal sites were sold for as low as $2,700. Since then, homes in Lottivue have sold from $500,000 to $1 million.

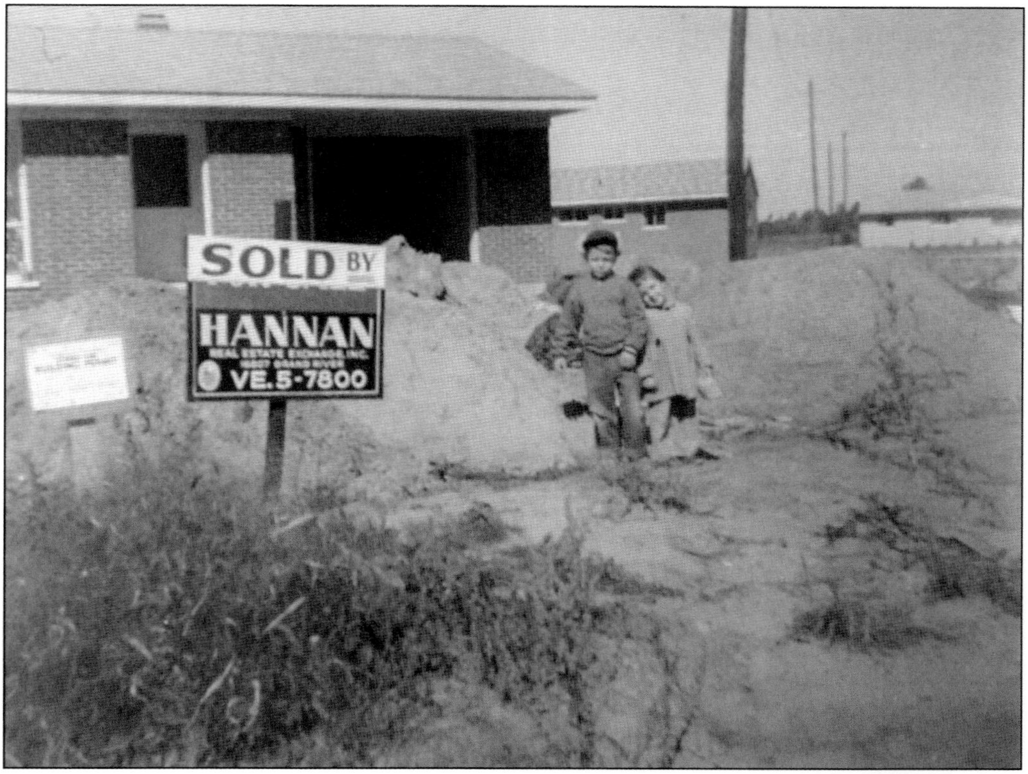

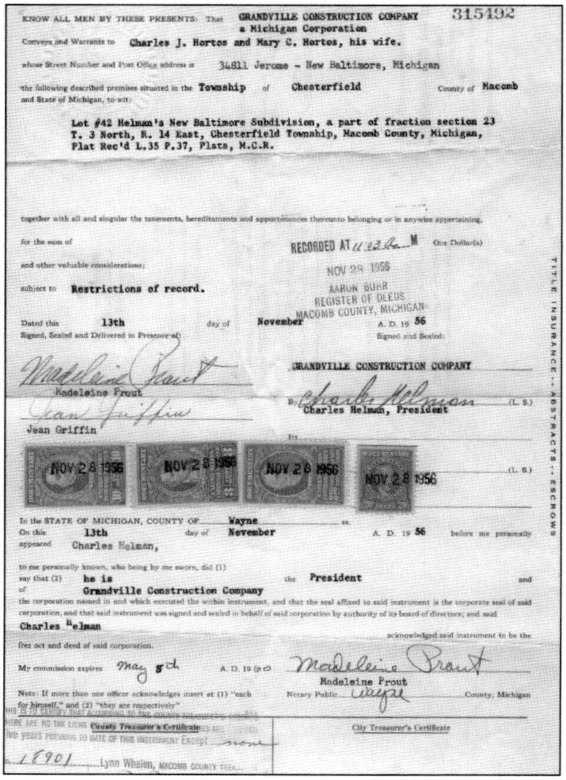

KNOW ALL MEN BY THESE PRESENTS: That GRANDVILLE CONSTRUCTION COMPANY a Michigan Corporation 315492

Conveys and Warrants to Charles J. Hortos and Mary C. Hortos, his wife.

whose Street Number and Post Office address is 34811 Jerome - New Baltimore, Michigan

the following described premises situated in the Township of Chesterfield County of Macomb and State of Michigan, to-wit:

Lot #42 Helman's New Baltimore Subdivision, a part of fraction section 23 T. 3 North, R. 14 East, Chesterfield Township, Macomb County, Michigan, Plat Rec'd L.35 P.37, Plats, M.C.R.

together with all and singular the tenements, hereditaments and appurtenances thereunto belonging or in anywise appertaining,

for the sum of One Dollar(s)

RECORDED AT 11:03 a. M
NOV 28 1956
AARON BURR
REGISTER OF DEEDS
MACOMB COUNTY, MICHIGAN

and other valuable considerations;

subject to Restrictions of record.

Dated this 13th day of November A. D. 19 56

Signed, Sealed and Delivered in Presence of: Signed and Sealed:

Madeleine Prout
Madeleine Prout

Jean Griffin
Jean Griffin

GRANDVILLE CONSTRUCTION COMPANY
By Charles Helman (L. S.)
Charles Helman, President
Its
(L. S.)

NOV 28 1956 NOV 28 1956 NOV 28 1956 NOV 28 1956

In the STATE OF MICHIGAN, COUNTY OF Wayne ss.
On this 13th day of November A. D. 19 56 before me personally appeared Charles Helman,
to me personally known, who being by me sworn, did (1) say that (2) he is the President and of Grandville Construction Company the corporation named in and which executed the within instrument, and that the seal affixed to said instrument is the corporate seal of said corporation, and that said instrument was signed and sealed in behalf of said corporation by authority of its board of directors; and said Charles Helman acknowledged said instrument to be the free act and deed of said corporation.

My commission expires May 8th A. D. 19 60

Madeleine Prout
Madeleine Prout
Notary Public Wayne County, Michigan

Note: If more than one officer acknowledges insert at (1) "each for himself," and (2) "they are respectively"

County Treasurer's Certificate | City Treasurer's Certificate

THIS IS TO CERTIFY THAT ACCORDING TO THE COUNTY TREASURER'S RECORDS THERE ARE NO TAX LIENS ... FIVE YEARS PREVIOUS TO DATE OF THIS INSTRUMENT Except none

18901 Lynn Whelen, MACOMB COUNTY TREA...

The first housing development to be known as a subdivision in Chesterfield Township was built in 1957 on Jefferson Avenue at Altman Street. In fact, as it was the only subdivision in the township for years, it was often known simply as "The Subdivision." According to the advertisements, one could get a three- or a four-bedroom house, 60 feet across in front, with an 80-foot lot and a sliding "window wall" that provided access to the backyard. Other amenities included a paneled dining room, a built-in vanity in the master bath, and a "food waste disposer." Built by Grandville Construction Company, prices began at $15,750. The photograph above shows Pat and Jackie Hortos in front of their Jerome Street house. (Both, courtesy of Mary Hortos.)

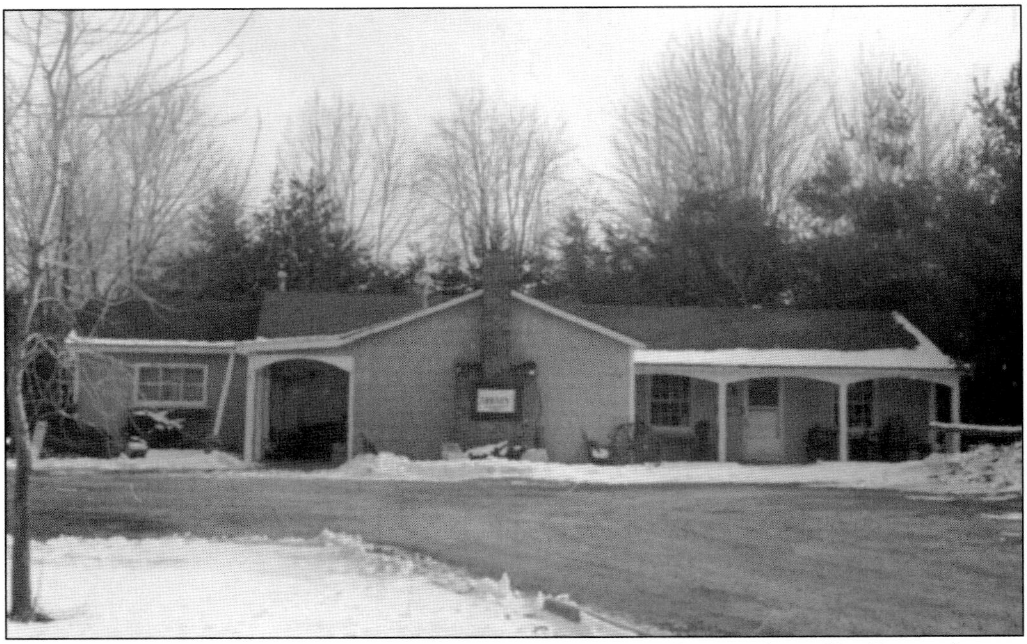

Bernard T. Trinity
NEIGHBORHOOD LIBRARY

47460 SUGAR BUSH RD.
MT. CLEMENS, MICHIGAN

June 16, 1976

Chesterfield Township Board
50177 Gratiot Ave.
Mt. Clemens, Michigan 48043

Dear Members of Chesterfield Township Board;

Listed below are the expenses for the library from Jan. 1, 1975 thru Dec. 31, 1975.

EXPENDITURES

Heating	$272.40	
Electric	73.97	
Telephone	65.26	
Office supplies and expenses	60.26	
Upkeep and decorating	221.27	
New books and papers	6.00	
Repairs or display	52.61	
Outside labor (Saturdays and days off)	232.00	
Total		$983.99

CASH RECEIVED

Chesterfield Township	$585.00	
Overdue fines on books	132.00	
Total		$717.00

I would also like to draw to your attention that prior to 1973 the library was allowed $1825.00 per year for expenses.

It was suggested that I put down the difference between Bernard's salary per two week period and my salary for the same period.

Bernard's gross pay	$209.28	
Ceola's gross pay	171.36	
Difference		$37.92

One other practice I will continue, as with Bernard,

During the 1950s, Bernard and Oceola Trinity established the first library in Chesterfield Township. Because of their love of history, they expanded it to include a museum. The document illustrates that the Trinity Library was successful enough for the township to provide funding. The Trinitys were two of the first historians of the area to display in their museum and write about many of the Native American artifacts discovered in Chesterfield Township. They also had the interior of part of their museum set up like an old general store. (Both, courtesy of Trinity Archives.)

TRINITY PUBLIC LIBRARY and Historical Museum

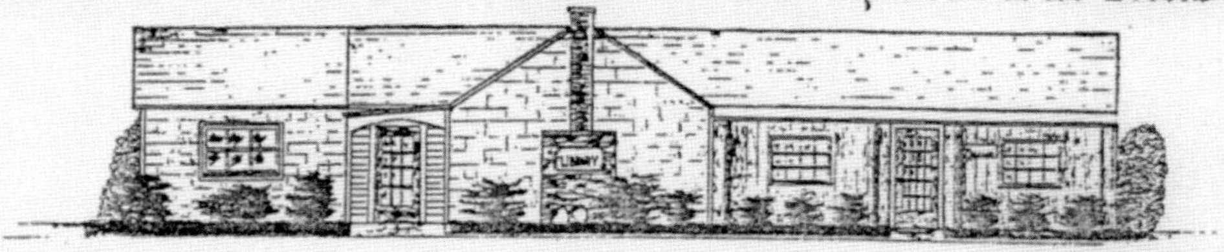

47460 Sugarbush Road · Mt.Clemens, Michigan 48045 · (313) 949-0937

BOOKS CIRCULATED FROM THE TRINITY LIBRARY

Year	Adult Books	Juvenile Books	Miscellaneous
1976	5151	5415	167
1977	5523	8017	196
1978	9024	6791	211
1979	11,835	6822	236
1980	19,153	10,593	260

This document shows the book circulation of Trinity Library in 1976. The official archives of Chesterfield Township, located in the Chesterfield Township Public Library, are called the Trinity Archives in honor of Bernard and Oceola Trinity. So indoctrinated were the citizens of Chesterfield to library service that it was not long before Chesterfield Township, experiencing large growth in the late 1980s and early 1990s, voted in a library millage and established the Chesterfield Township Public Library. Initially located at one of Chesterfield's first official shopping centers, the Premier Center, it won the Michigan State Library Excellence award in 1996 under the directorship of Marion Lusardi. In 2000, the library moved to a larger building closer to the ever-popular crossroads of Gratiot Avenue and 23 Mile Road. (Courtesy of Trinity Archives.)

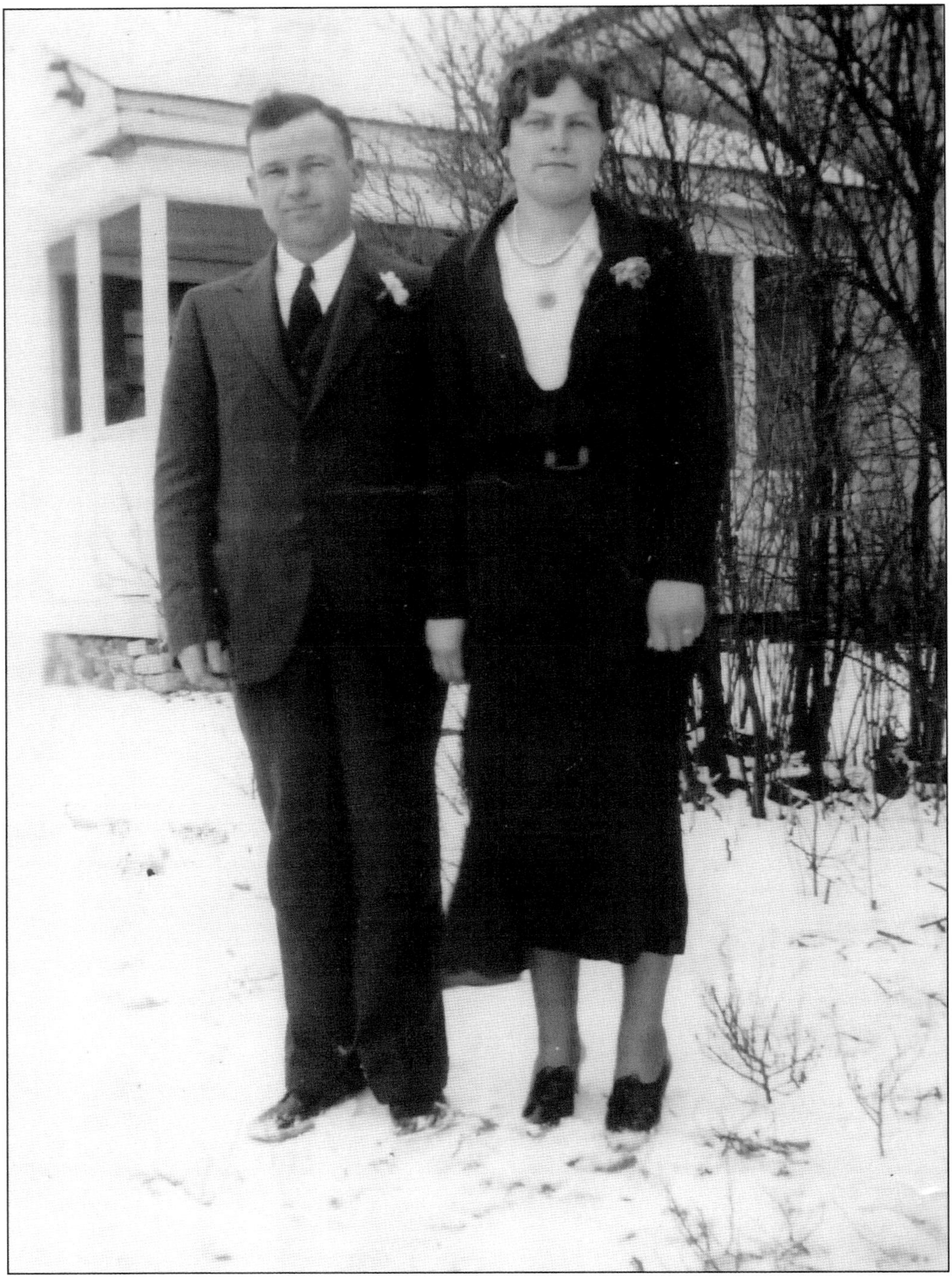

The Rivard family can trace their ancestry back to Nicolas Rivard, who arrived in the area in the 1600s. (The Rivards were with Antoine Cadillac in 1701 when he founded Detroit.) More than 300 years later, members of the Rivard family continue to reside in the Chesterfield area. August L. and Theresa Rivard pose in front of the Rivard farmhouse on their wedding day in January 1935.

Seven

People and Families of Chesterfield Township

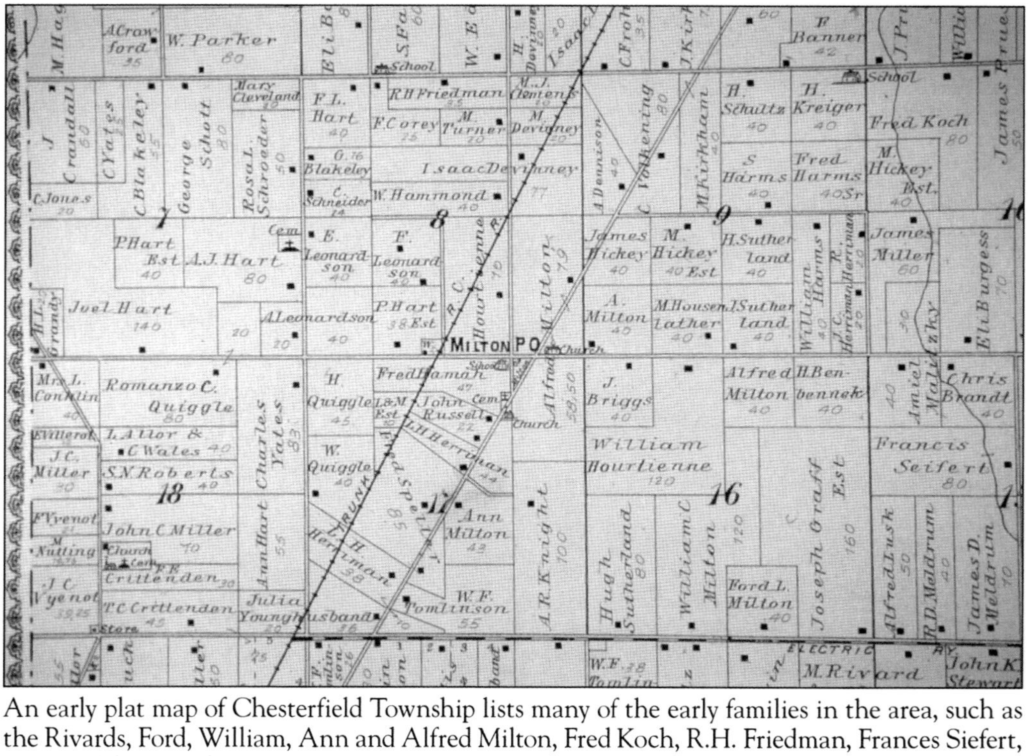

An early plat map of Chesterfield Township lists many of the early families in the area, such as the Rivards, Ford, William, Ann and Alfred Milton, Fred Koch, R.H. Friedman, Frances Siefert, George Schott, and many more.

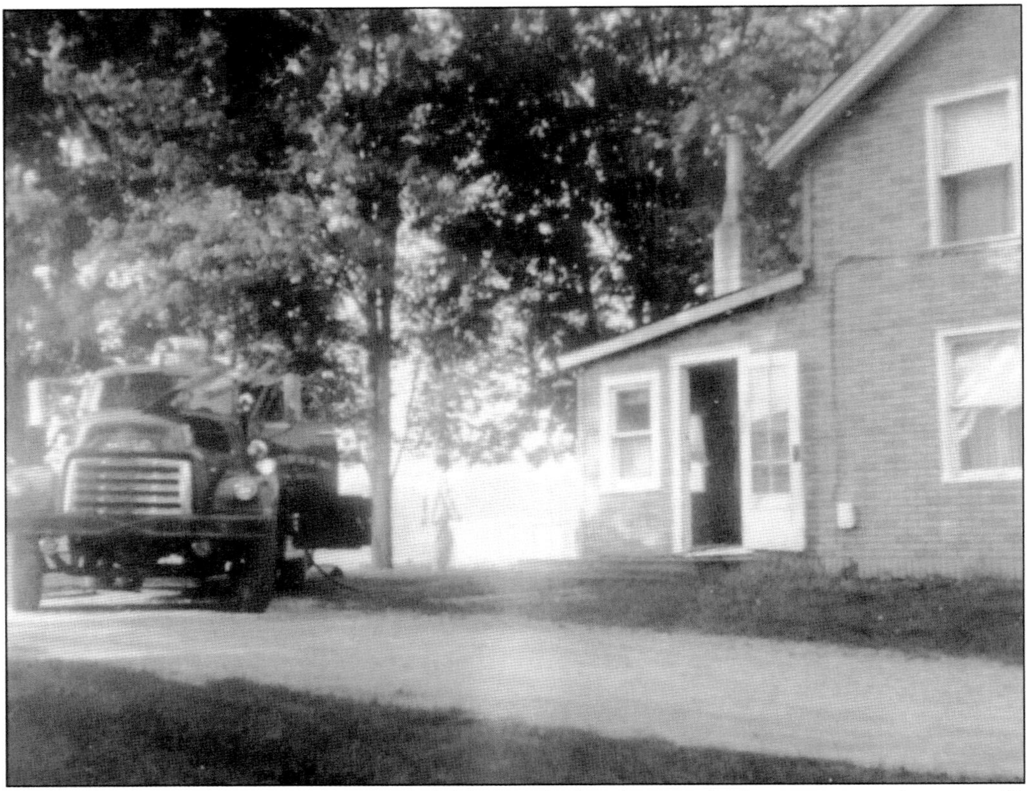

Most of the early dwellings of Chesterfield, mainly farmhouses, had to get water from a well. Pictured above is the William Rivard farmhouse, and below is an image of the family running a waterline from William's house to August Rivard's house from the main water well.

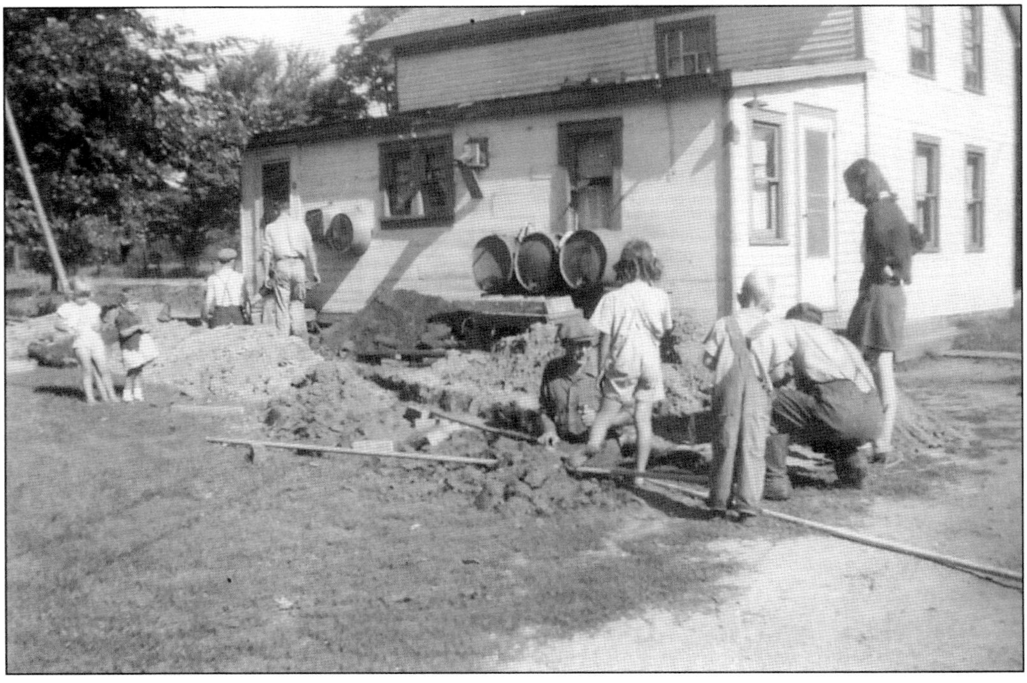

In 1864, Alexander Rivard (1842–1928) had a cooper (barrel making) business at 51718 Washington Avenue called the Rivard Cooper Shop. He was also a wood dealer, using the Perkins Mill for his supplies. August Rivard sold wood and manufactured cement blocks. In the picture above, he is next to a cement block machine that could make one block a minute. In the image below, Rivard speaks to a customer. (Both, courtesy of Roy Rivard.)

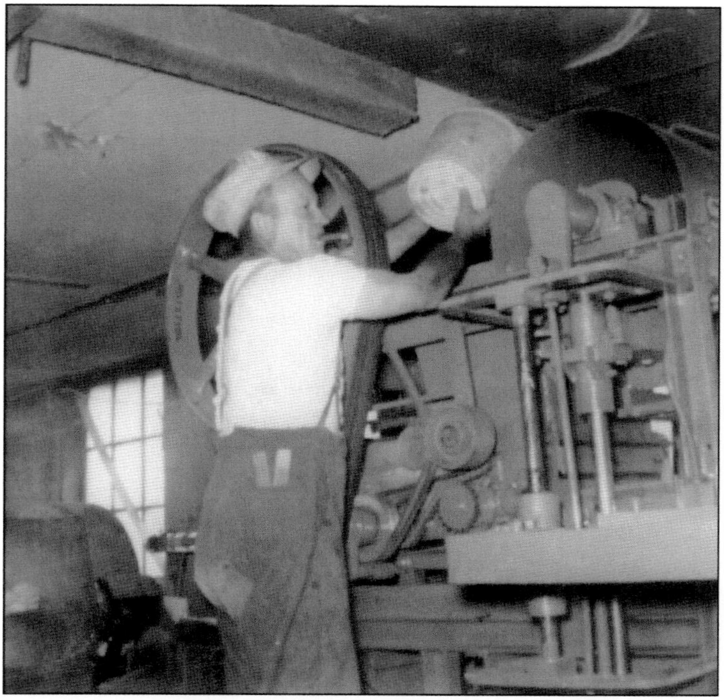

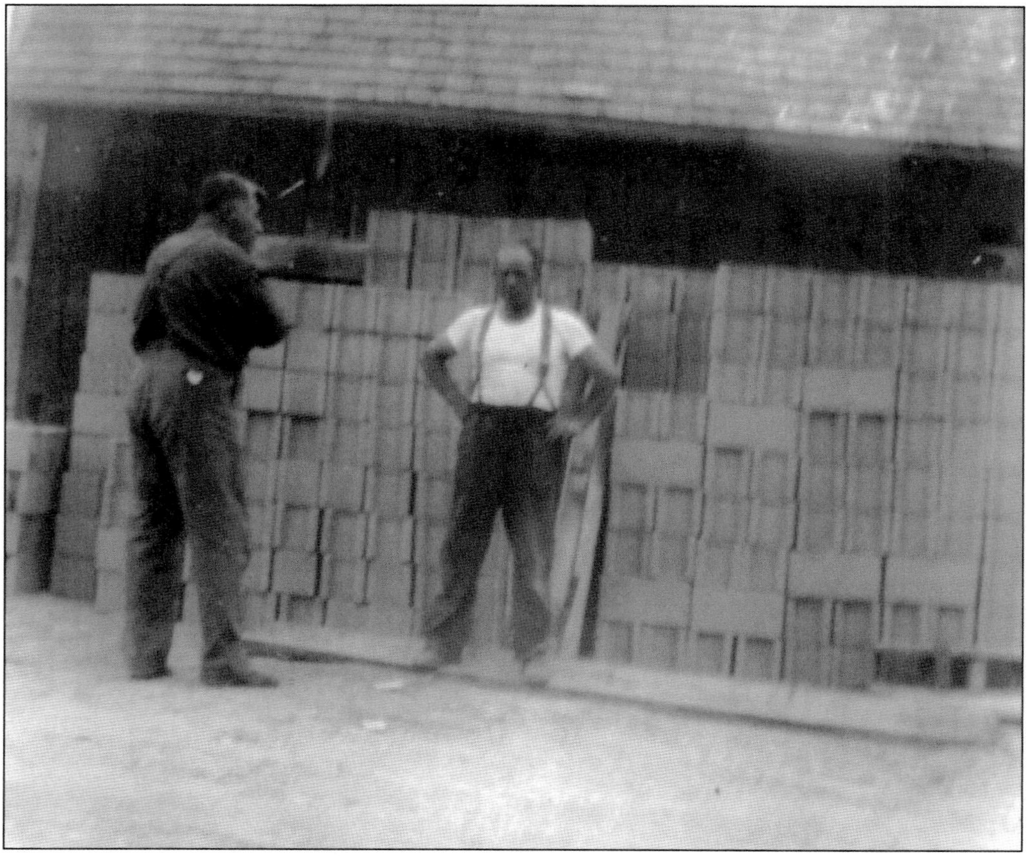

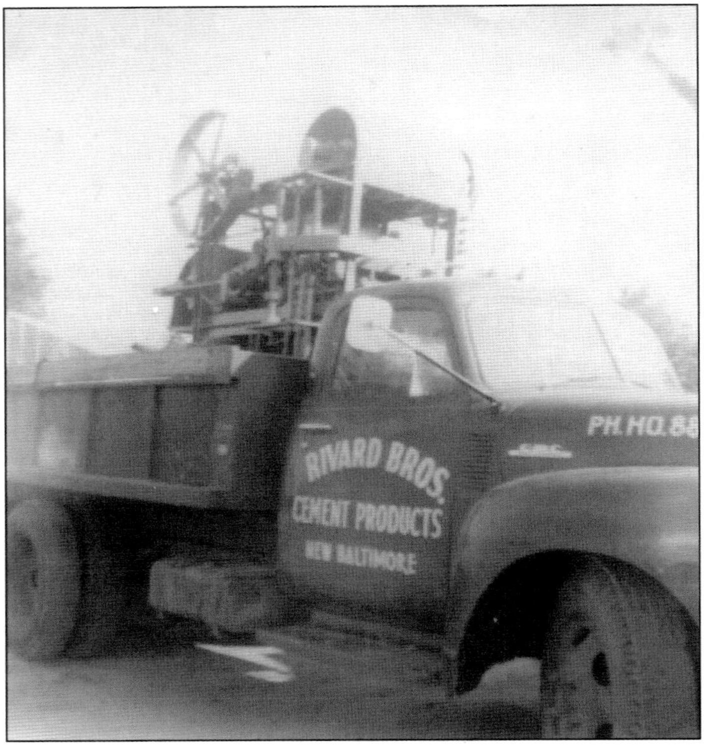

The name of the business, as reflected on the door of the truck, was at first Rivard Bros. It was later changed to August Rivard and Sons. French families like the Rivards were the earliest settlers in Chesterfield. One of the earliest recorded settlements was that of Pierre Yax in 1796 at the mouth of Crapeau Creek. The first purchase of government land was made by Fabian Robertjean on August 20, 1820, in Section 11 of Chesterfield near New Baltimore's Washington Street. (Both, courtesy of Roy Rivard.)

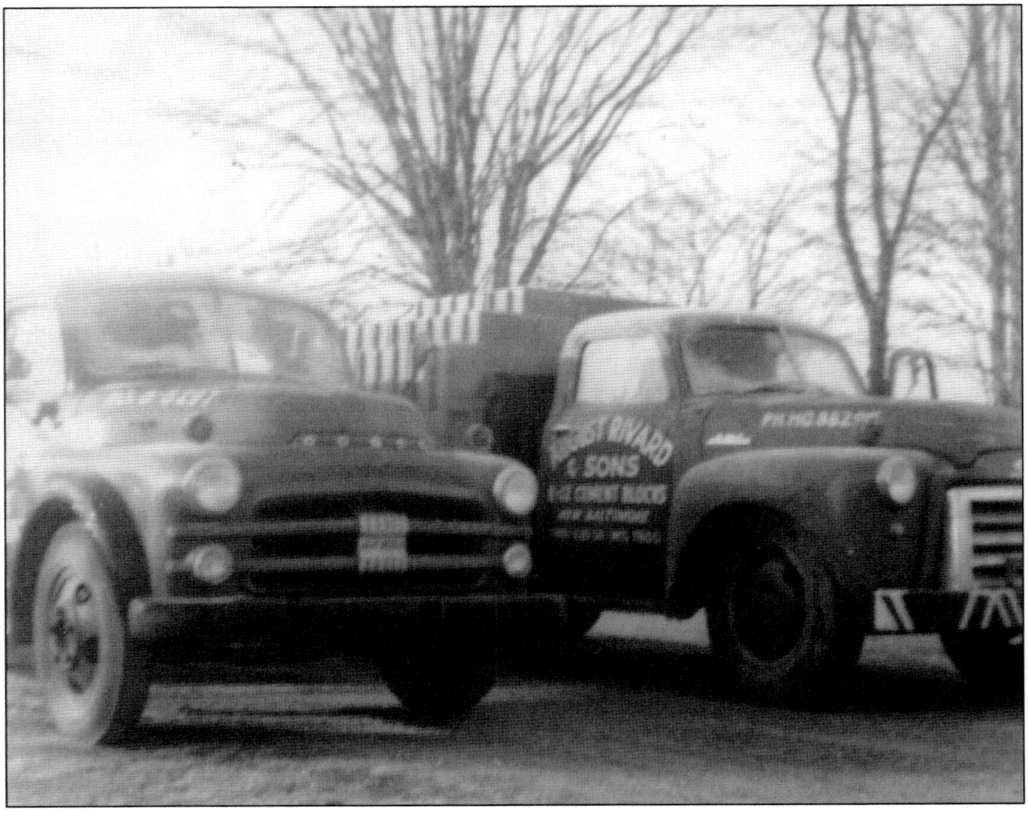

William Rivard is seen at right with his prize chicken, and the photograph below shows cement blocks curing in the sun on the Rivard farm The first actual white settler in Chesterfield was Charles Seer who, along with his grandson Charles Jennar, settled near the Aux Vase River Native American village in 1819. At one time, there was a local French dialect known as Sugar Bush, named for the road. This dialect, also known as "Up River French," was investigated by linguist Dr. Pilling in February 1960. The last main enclave of the dialect, from where Dr. Pilling assembled the vocabulary, was considered to be Chesterfield and nearby Anchorville and Marine City. (Both, courtesy of Roy Rivard.)

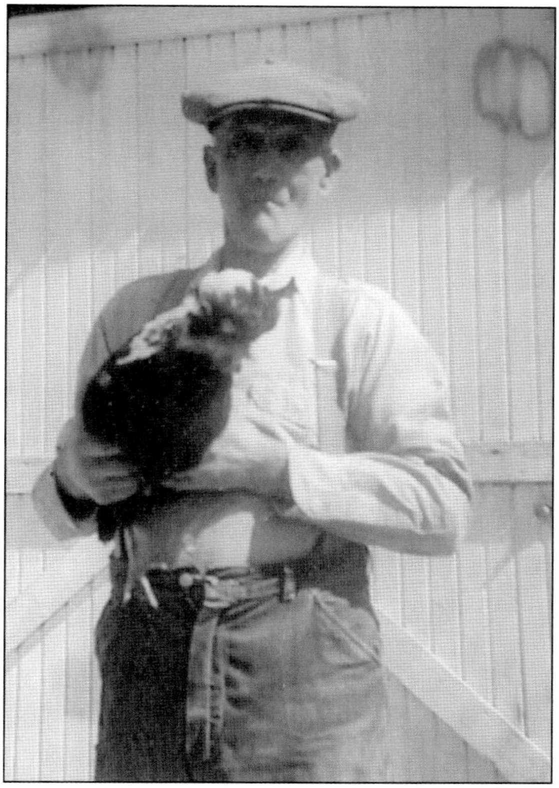

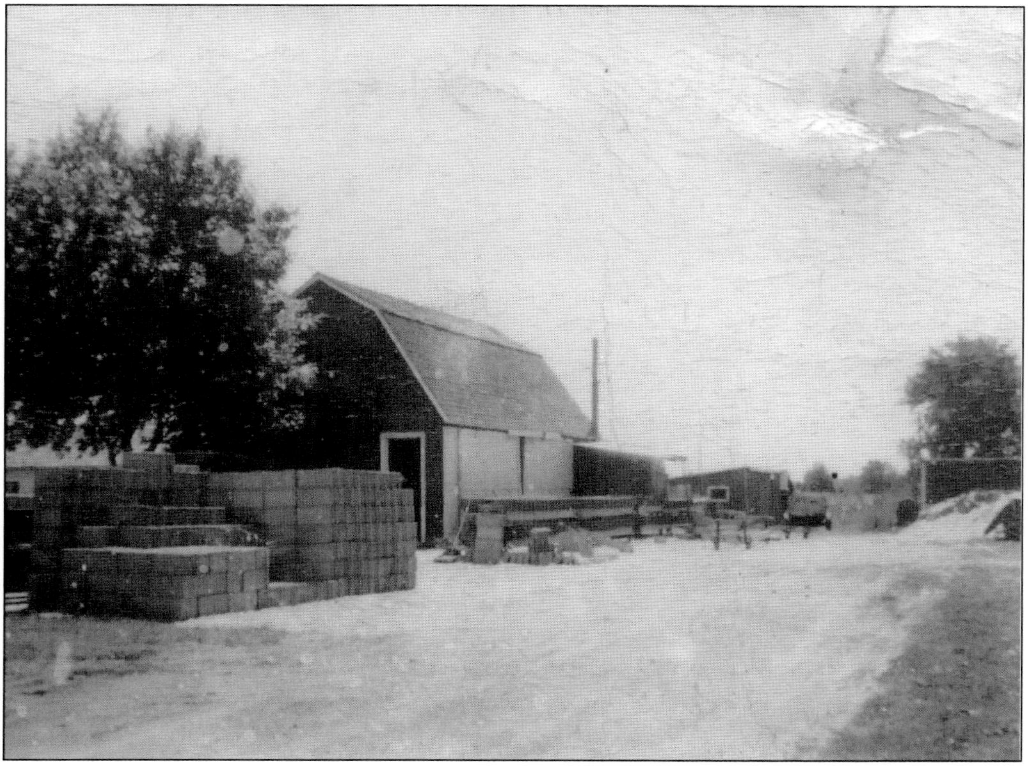

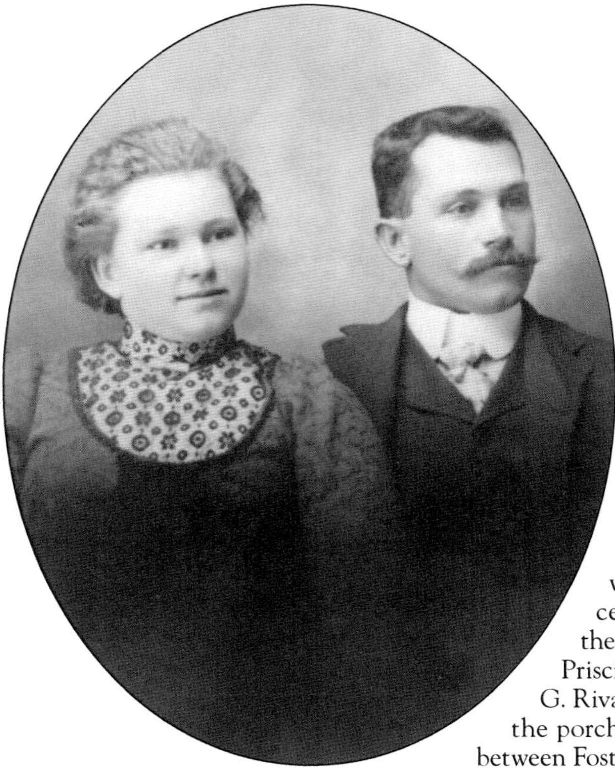

French wedding customs brought over to the New World included firing guns in the air to make noise and having the wedding party walking in a procession, led by a fiddler, to the reception. After the French Revolution and during the reign of Napoleon, the wedding reception was a cause for much celebration and would often last into the wee hours of the morning. At left are Priscilla (Stella) Furton Rivard and William G. Rivard. Below is Stella Rivard standing on the porch at her farmhouse on 23 Mile Road between Foster and Sass Roads.

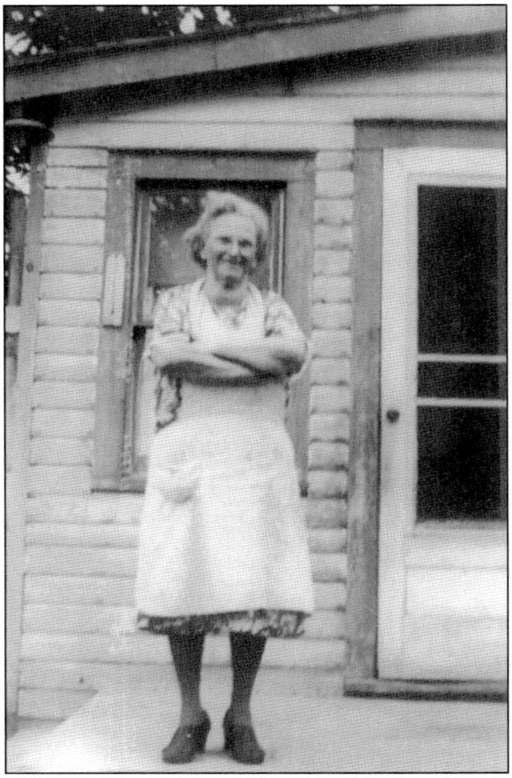

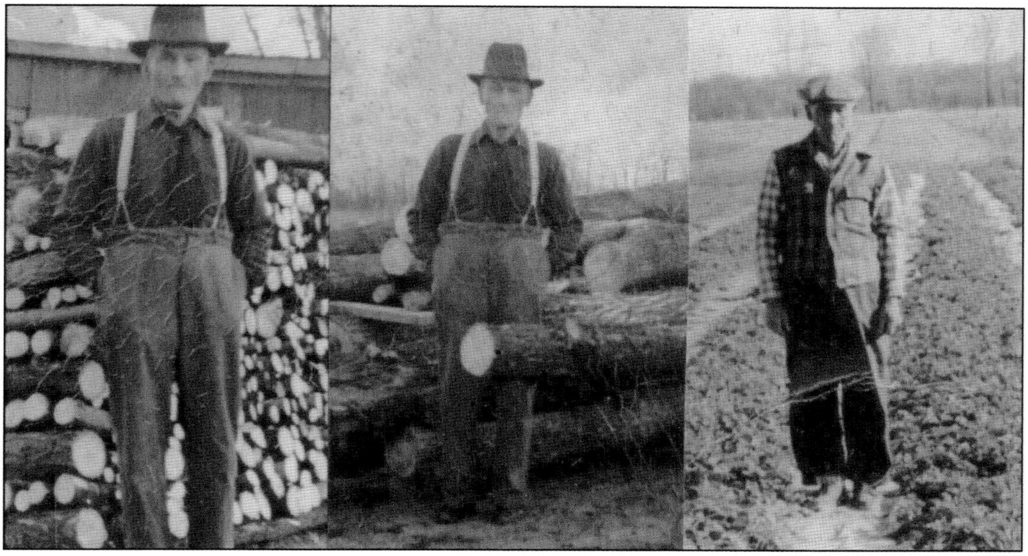

Other customs were brought to the New World by the French pioneers. For instance, during the feast, the bride's garter would be removed (sometimes ceremoniously by a boy going under the table to retrieve it), and then the garter would be cut up and sold to the guests. Above is William Rivard in various shots at work. Below is a Rivard wedding scene.

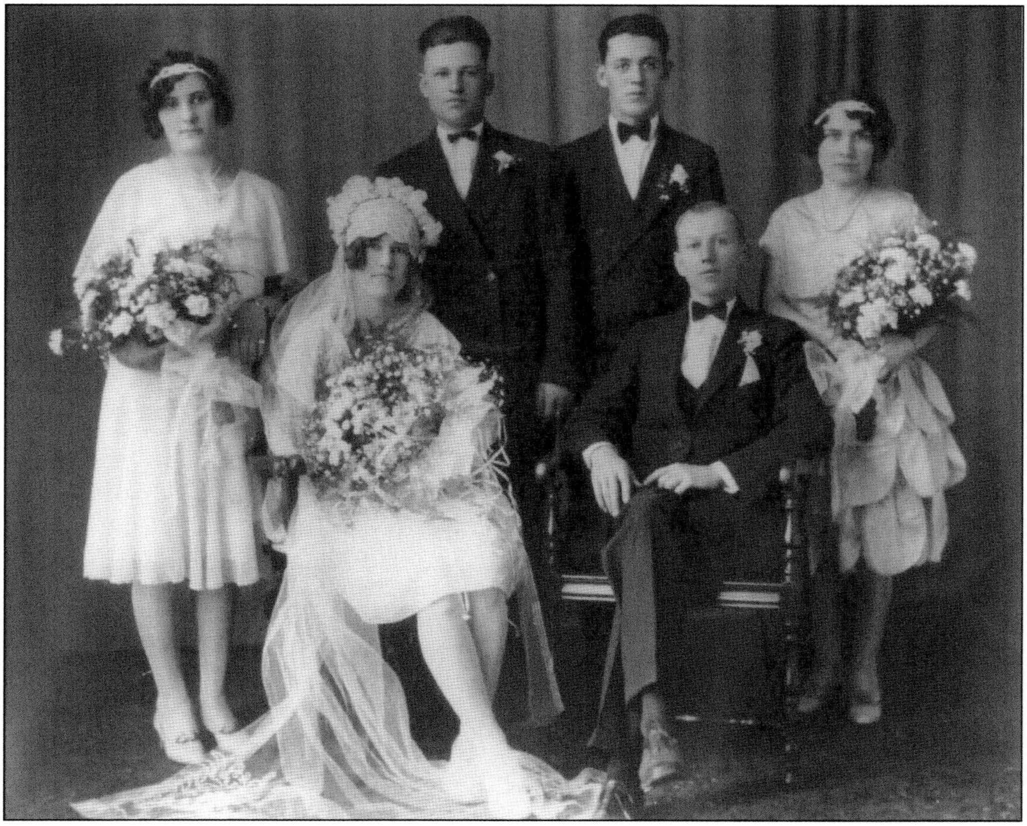

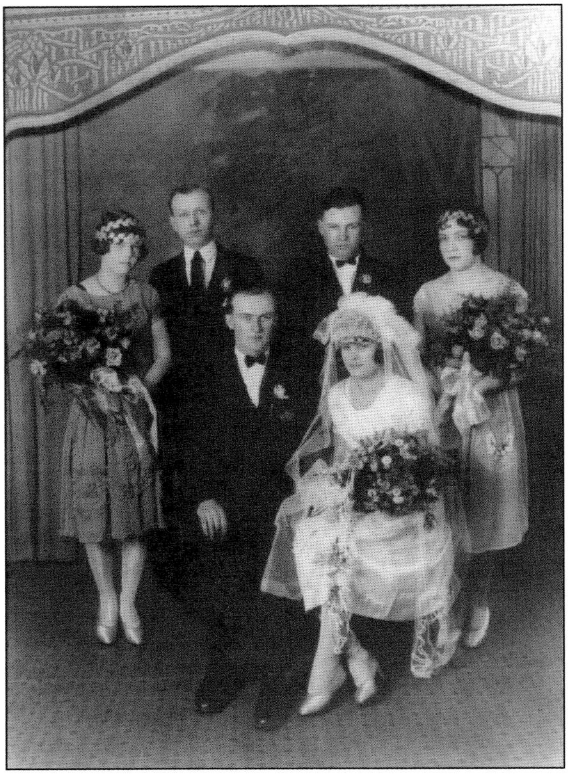

When the couple retired to the wedding room or bedroom, their friends would traditionally invade the room, carrying a chamber pot usually inscribed with "to the bride" and filled with seasoned food and wine to be served to the couple. Throwing confetti at the bride and groom originated in France in the late 19th century and was brought to the New World, where rice and birdseed are also used.

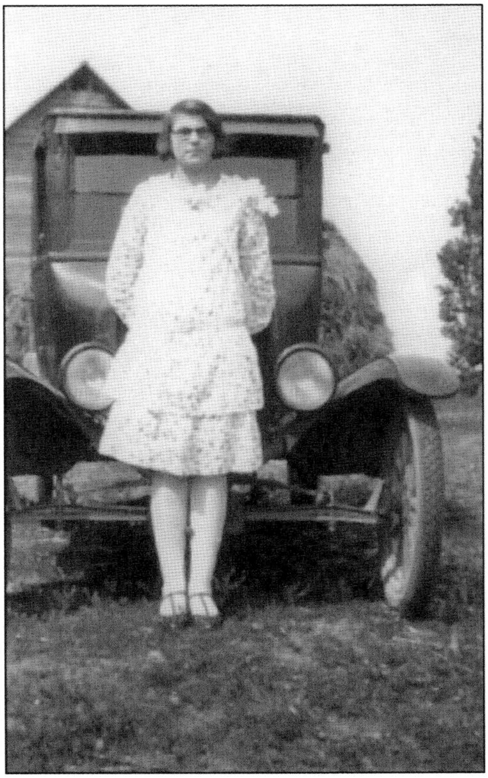

Anna Theresa Klein Rivard, daughter of William Rivard, is pictured standing by the new car that her father purchased before he accidentally backed it into a tree shortly after buying it. After that, he insisted Anna do all the driving.

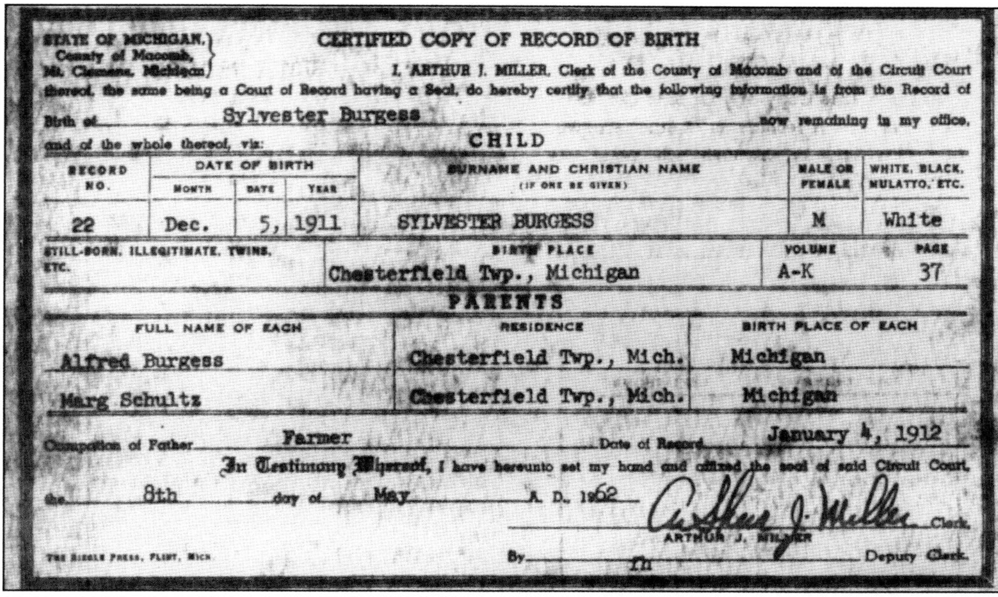
STATE OF MICHIGAN, County of Macomb, Mt. Clemens, Michigan

CERTIFIED COPY OF RECORD OF BIRTH

I, ARTHUR J. MILLER, Clerk of the County of Macomb and of the Circuit Court thereof, the same being a Court of Record having a Seal, do hereby certify that the following information is from the Record of Birth of Sylvester Burgess now remaining in my office, and of the whole thereof, viz:

CHILD

RECORD NO.	DATE OF BIRTH: MONTH	DATE	YEAR	SURNAME AND CHRISTIAN NAME (IF ONE BE GIVEN)	MALE OR FEMALE	WHITE, BLACK, MULATTO, ETC.
22	Dec.	5,	1911	SYLVESTER BURGESS	M	White

STILL-BORN, ILLEGITIMATE, TWINS, ETC.	BIRTH PLACE	VOLUME	PAGE
	Chesterfield Twp., Michigan	A-K	37

PARENTS

FULL NAME OF EACH	RESIDENCE	BIRTH PLACE OF EACH
Alfred Burgess	Chesterfield Twp., Mich.	Michigan
Marg Schultz	Chesterfield Twp., Mich.	Michigan

Occupation of Father Farmer Date of Record January 4, 1912

In Testimony Whereof, I have hereunto set my hand and affixed the seal of said Circuit Court, the 8th day of May A. D., 1962

ARTHUR J. MILLER Clerk.

By Deputy Clerk.

THE BIGELOW PRESS, FLINT, MICH

Most of the original settlers of Chesterfield Township were at first the Native Americans before the French and English came to the area. As time went by, more ethnic groups immigrated to Chesterfield. Loraine DeMuynck, a lifelong resident of Chesterfield Township, descended from the Moerman family who emigrated from Belgium in the early 1900s. Loraine's grandparents came to this country in 1913 and left their three children, Julius, Adrianna, and Suzanne, with a seamstress in Belgium until they were able to settle on a farm. They originally lived in Ohio for a short time before moving to a farm at County Line and Arnold Roads (25 Mile Road) in Chesterfield Township. While living at this location, Loraine's uncle Achille went back to Belgium to retrieve the three children and brought them to Chesterfield, arriving just prior to the start of World War I. The birth certificate above is from 1911, and the Red Star Line passport below is from the 1910 era when the Moerman family immigrated to the United States. (Both, courtesy of Loraine DeMuynck.)

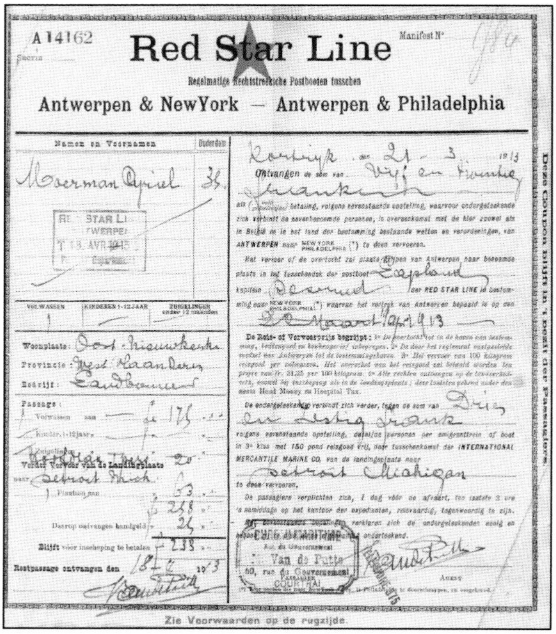
A 14162

Red Star Line

Manifest N°

Regelmatige Rechtstreeksche Postbooten tusschen

Antwerpen & NewYork — Antwerpen & Philadelphia

Namen en Voornamen: Moerman Cyriel — Ouderdom: 38

VOLWASSEN 1 — KINDEREN 1-12 JAAR — ZUIGELINGEN onder 12 maanden

Woonplaats: Oost-Nieuwkerke

Provincie: West Vlaanderen

Bedrijf: Landbouwer

Passage:

Verder Vervoer van de Landingplaats naar Detroit Mich

Daarop ontvangen handgeld

Blijft voor inscheping te betalen

Restpassage ontvangen den

Kortrijk, den 21-3 1913

Ontvangen de som van

Het vervoer of de overtocht zal plaats hebben van Antwerpen naar bestemde plaats in het tusschendek der postboot Lapland

der RED STAR LINE

De Reis- of Vervoerprijs begrijpt:

Head Money en Hospital Tax.

INTERNATIONAL MERCANTILE MARINE CO. van de landingsplaats naar Detroit Michigan te doen vervoeren.

Van de Putte

60, rue du Gouvernement

COURTRAI

Agent

Deze Coupon blijft in 't bezit der Passagiers.

Zie Voorwaarden op de rugzijde

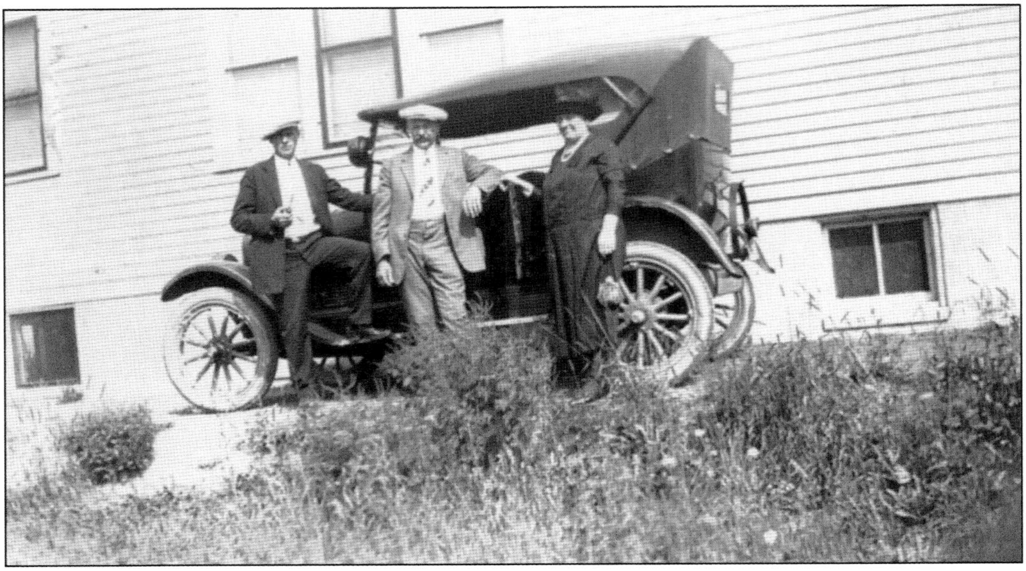

The Moermans lived on the farm on County Line Road and raised sugar beets for about four years. From there, they rented a farm located at the intersection of 24 Mile and Foster Roads in 1918. In the photograph below of the farm, there is an auction going on. The Moermans lived there until Achille was able to get a job working for Henry Ford and moved to Detroit for several years. After that, they rented a farm at 22 Mile and Fairchild Roads in 1934. (Both, courtesy of Loraine DeMuynck.)

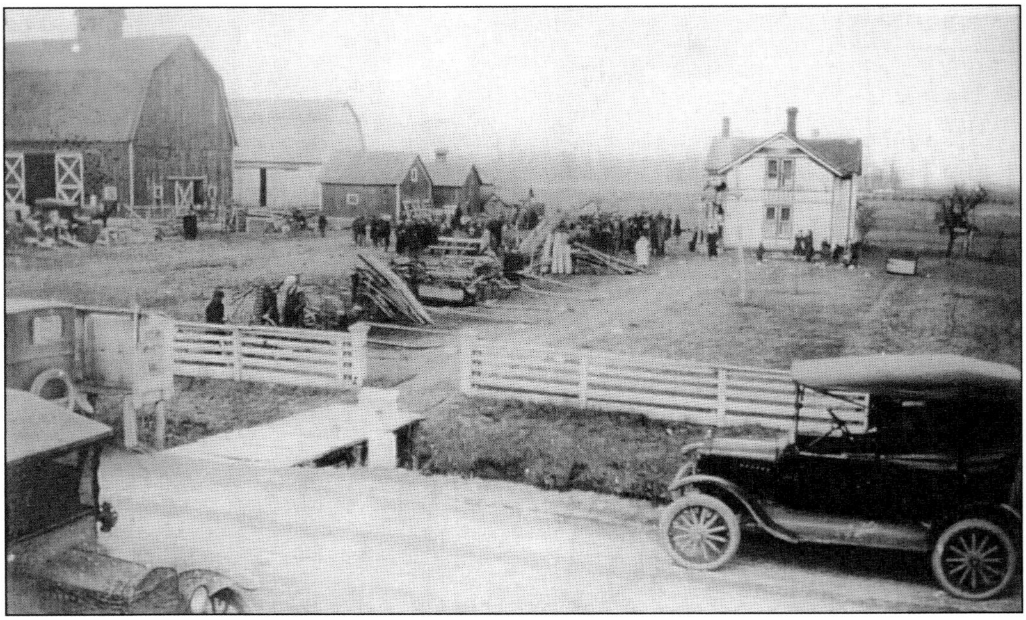

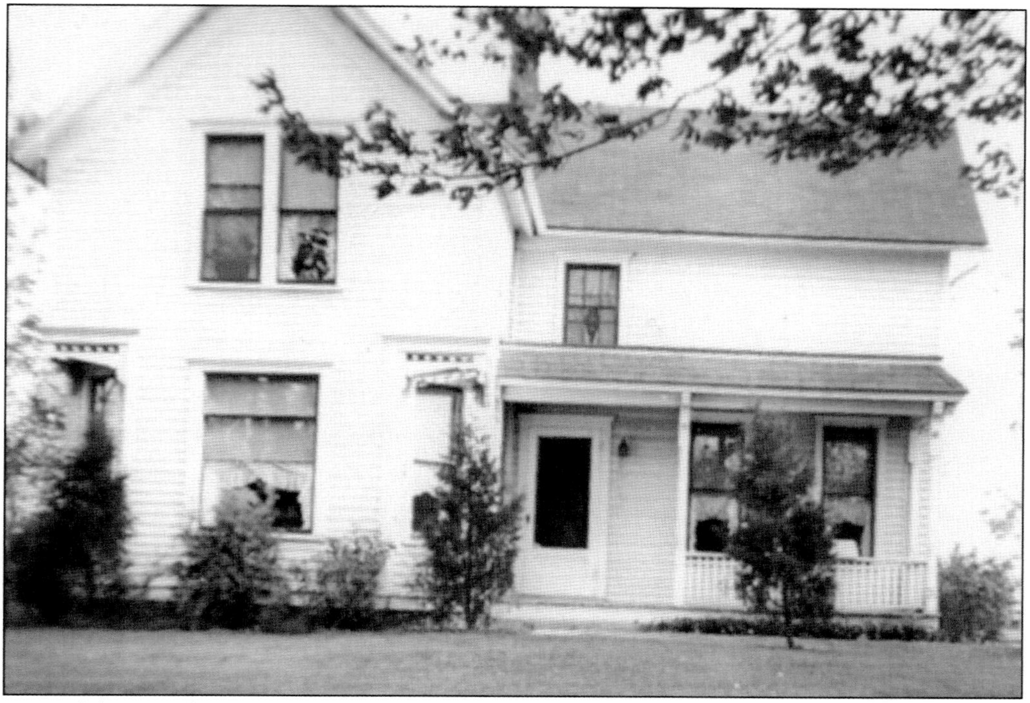

Most of the prior farms were rented or sharecropped, but the Moermans saved and were eventually able to buy a farm on 24 Mile Road just east of the Salt River, where they lived until they were unable to farm anymore. They then bought a small plot on 23 Mile Road. Loraine's mother, Adrianna, married Sylvester Burgess, and they lived in the farmhouse on 24 Mile Road (above). They had a dairy farm from 1939 through 1964 until Sylvester and Adrianna sold the farm and moved to Pointe Lakeview Drive. Their daughter Loraine went to school and graduated from St. Mary's in New Baltimore. Below is the Chesterfield Pump Station, which contains a plaque dedicated to Maurice Demunynck, the first water and sewer superintendent of Chesterfield Township and husband of Loraine.

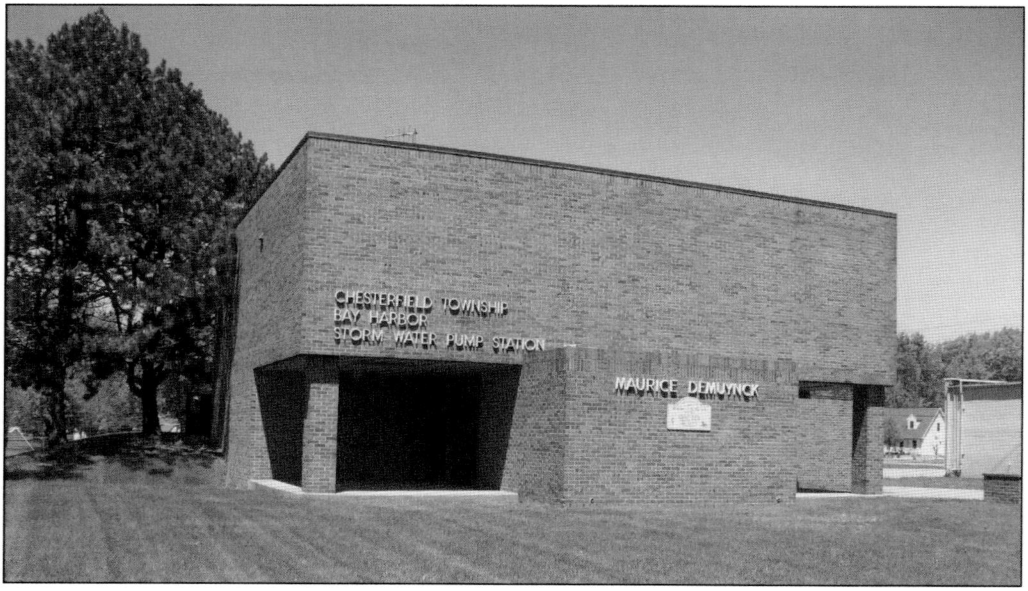

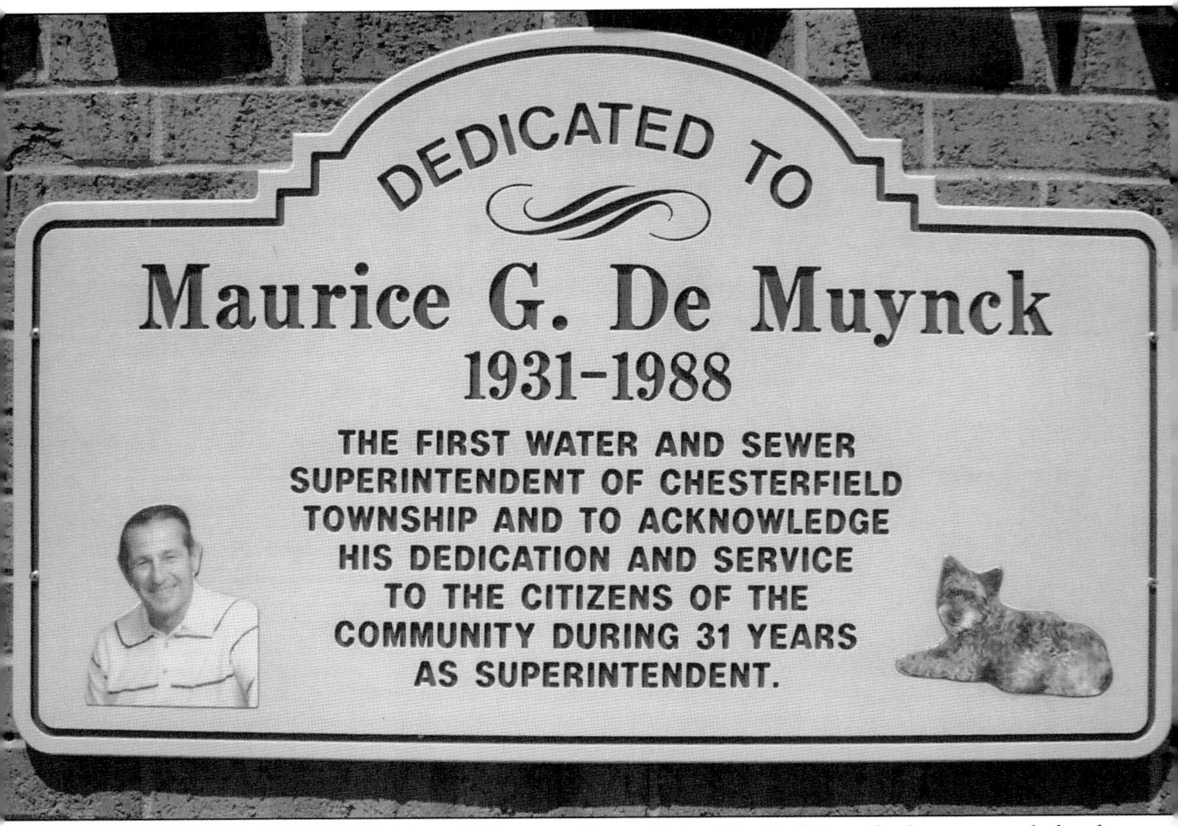

In 1952, Loraine met and married Maurice. He was hired by Carl Brandenburg to work for the first Chesterfield Township Water Department. Maurice worked for Chesterfield for 31 years, during which time Chesterfield received both city water and sewers as the population continued to grow. He was working as the first water sewer department superintendent when he passed away in 1988. Loraine served as trustee on the Chesterfield Township Board of Supervisors from 1992 until 2000. Her son Brian has since served on the board. (Courtesy of Trinity Archives.)

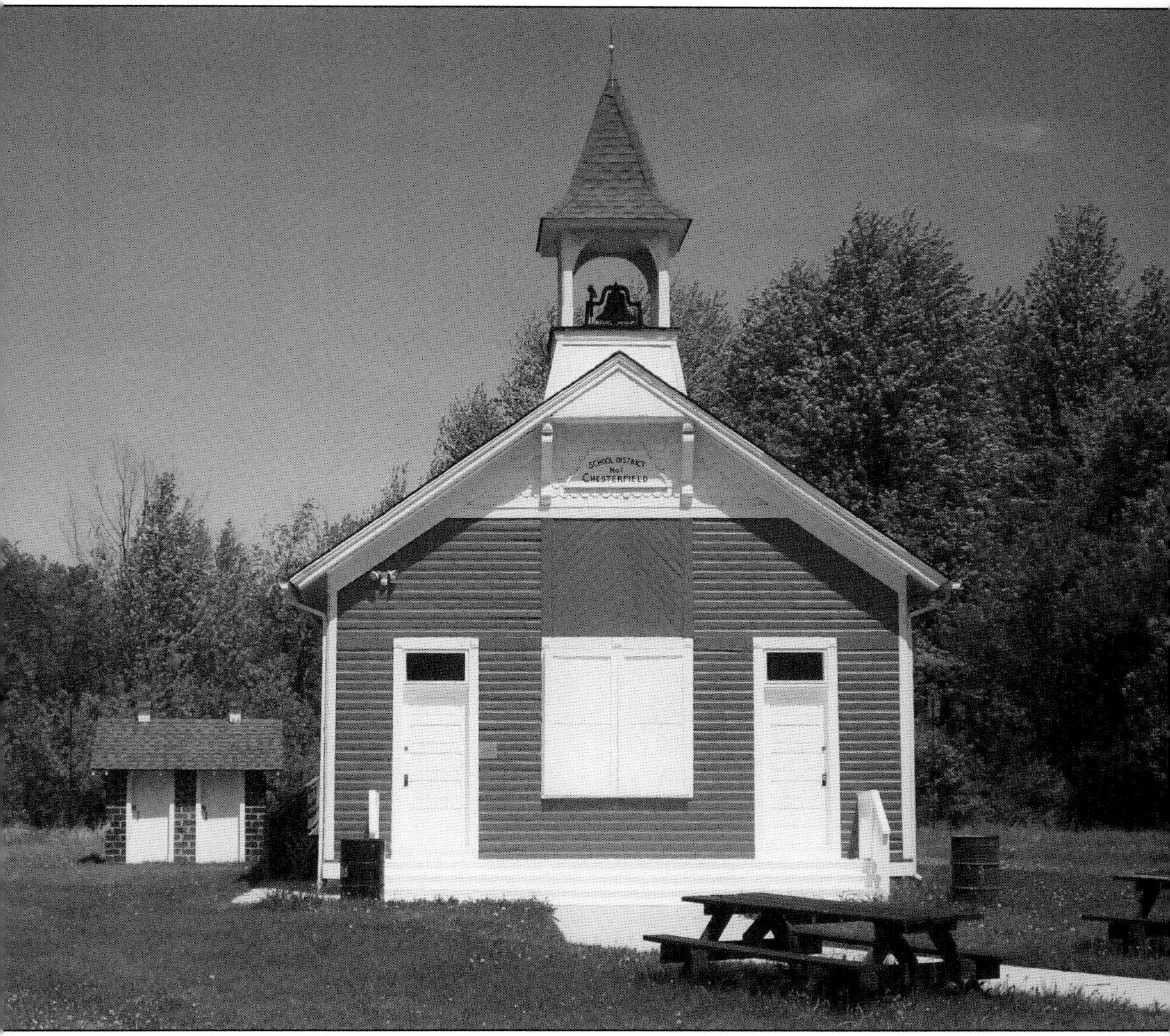

The Chesterfield Township Historical Society was formed in 1993 by George Furton and others. Charter members included Connie Bowles, Merle Davies, Mary Deardon, Mary Hortos, Don and Mary Jane Howitt, Shirley Johnson, Karl Mark Pall, Betty Wogen, and Jan Uglis The historical society started a historical village next to the township hall on Sugarbush Road. In it is the Weller School, moved from its original location at 22 Mile Road and Gratiot Avenue. (Courtesy of Trinity Archives.)

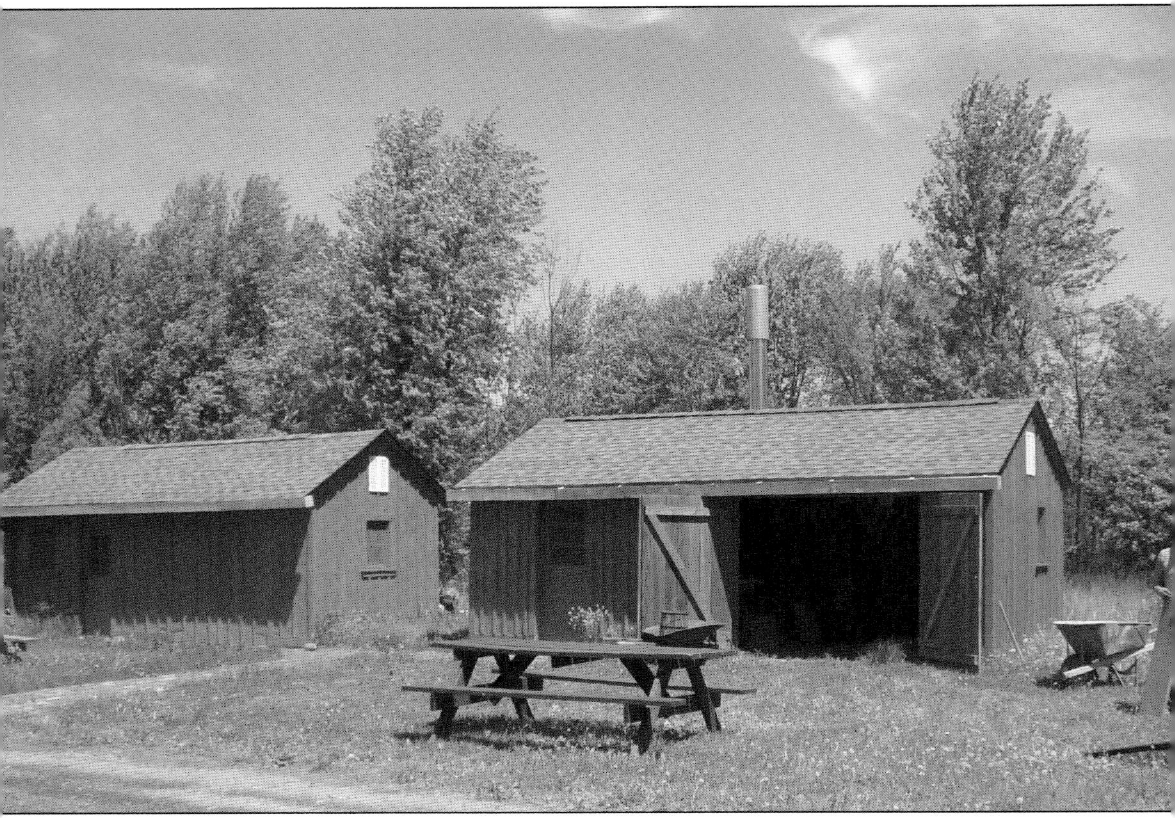

The Chesterfield Historical Village was developed by the Chesterfield Township Historical Society as a way for the local populace to know its history. A couple of the buildings on the property date back to the early days of the township and were originally preserved by Bernard Trinity for his museum. These buildings have since been renovated and repurposed as a cobbler and a blacksmith shop. (Courtesy of Trinity Archives and Deborah Walsh.)

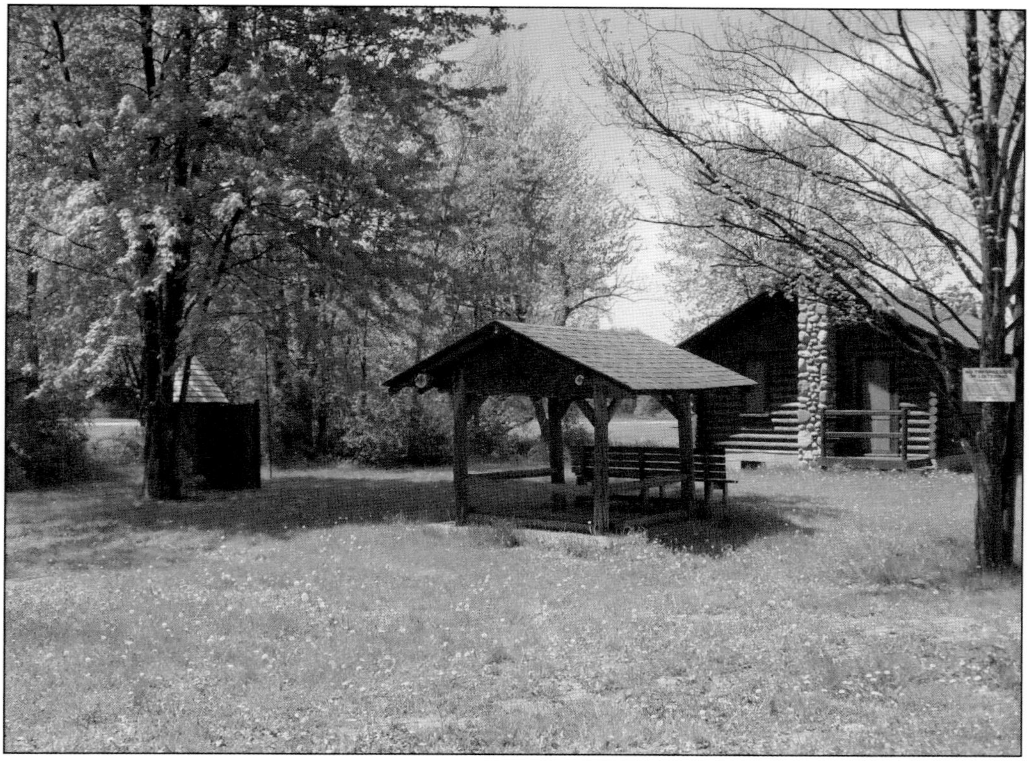

In 2003, a log cabin was discovered in the woods of Washington Township as real estate developers planned to clear some land. They donated it to the Chesterfield Township Historical Society, who had it transported to the historical village. The log cabin also came with a pump house and round outhouse. (Both, courtesy of Trinity Archives and Deborah Walsh.)

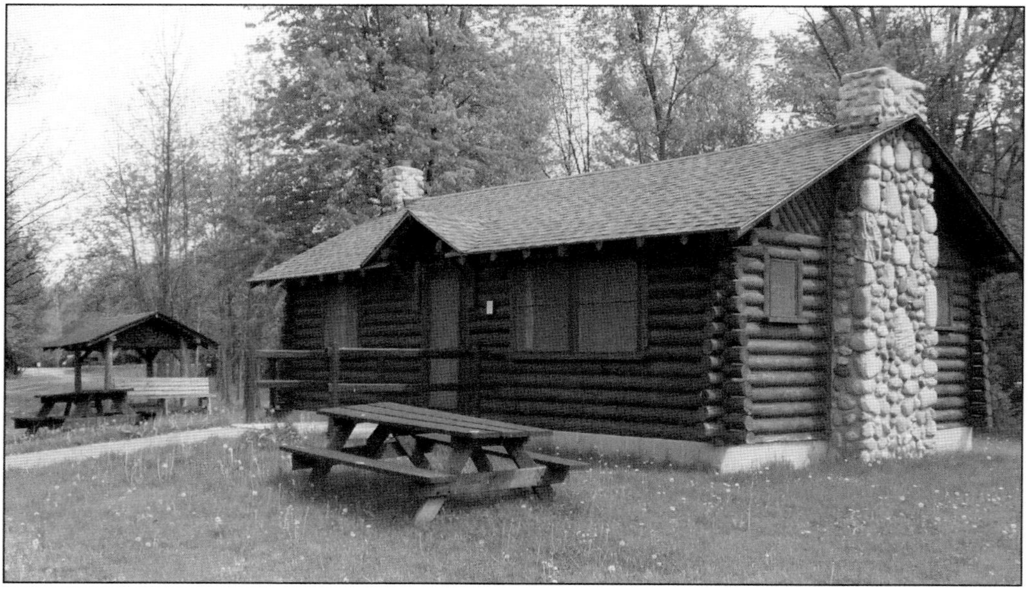

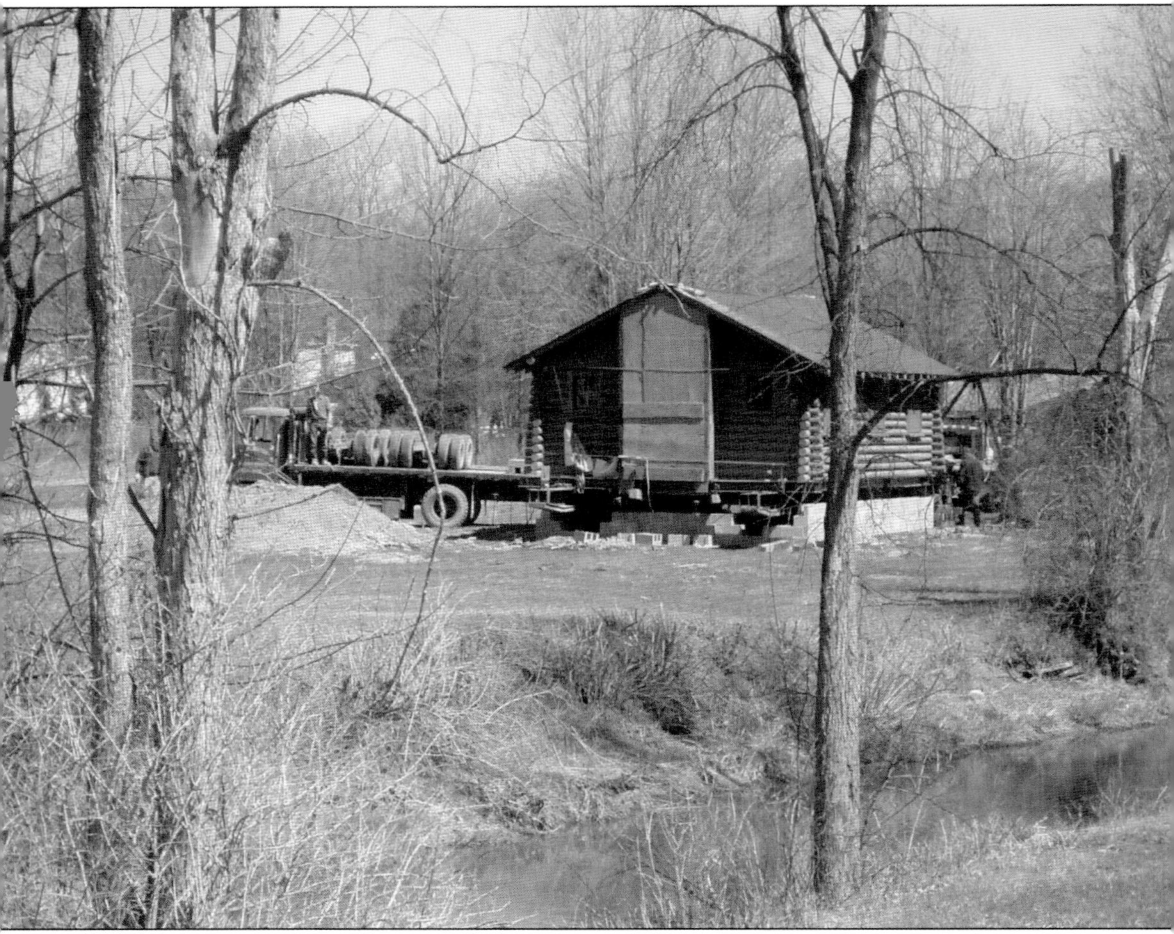

When the log cabin was moved to the village from Washington Township, the trek involved moving telephone wires and other obstacles. Other improvements continue to be made to the historical village. The road leading into the village was recently named for the Deeby Family. George Deeby was instrumental in facilitating the improvements made to the historical village. (Courtesy of Deborah Walsh.)

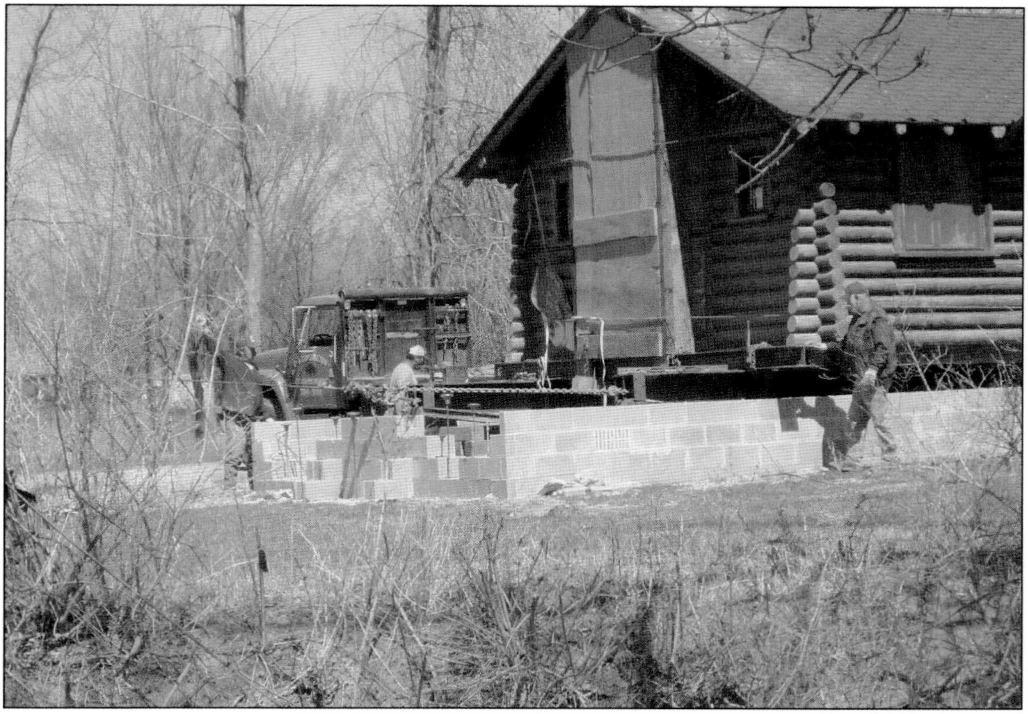

These images show the move of the cabin at various stages. Great care had to be taken not to disturb wires and to prevent damage to the cabin. (Both, courtesy of Deborah Walsh.)

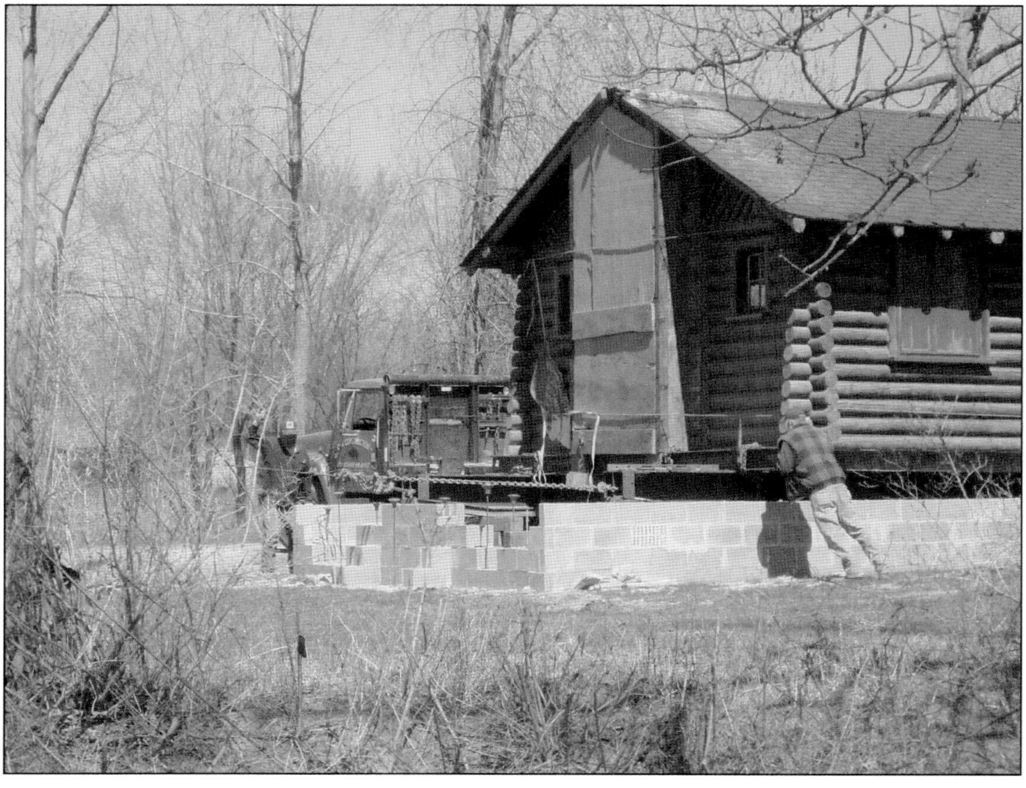

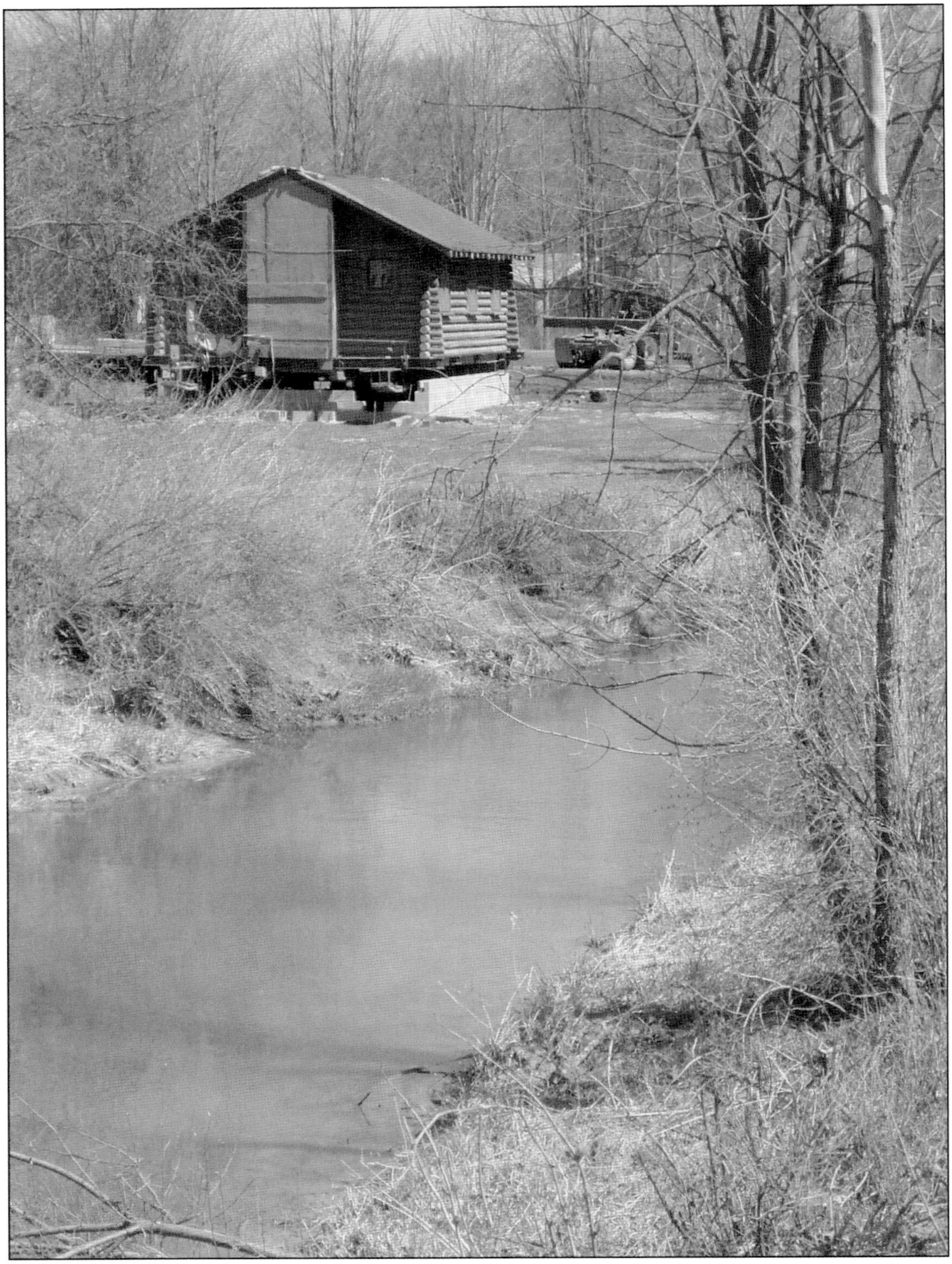

The cabin is very picturesque in its new setting and marks a great success for the Historical Village. (Courtesy of Deborah Walsh.)

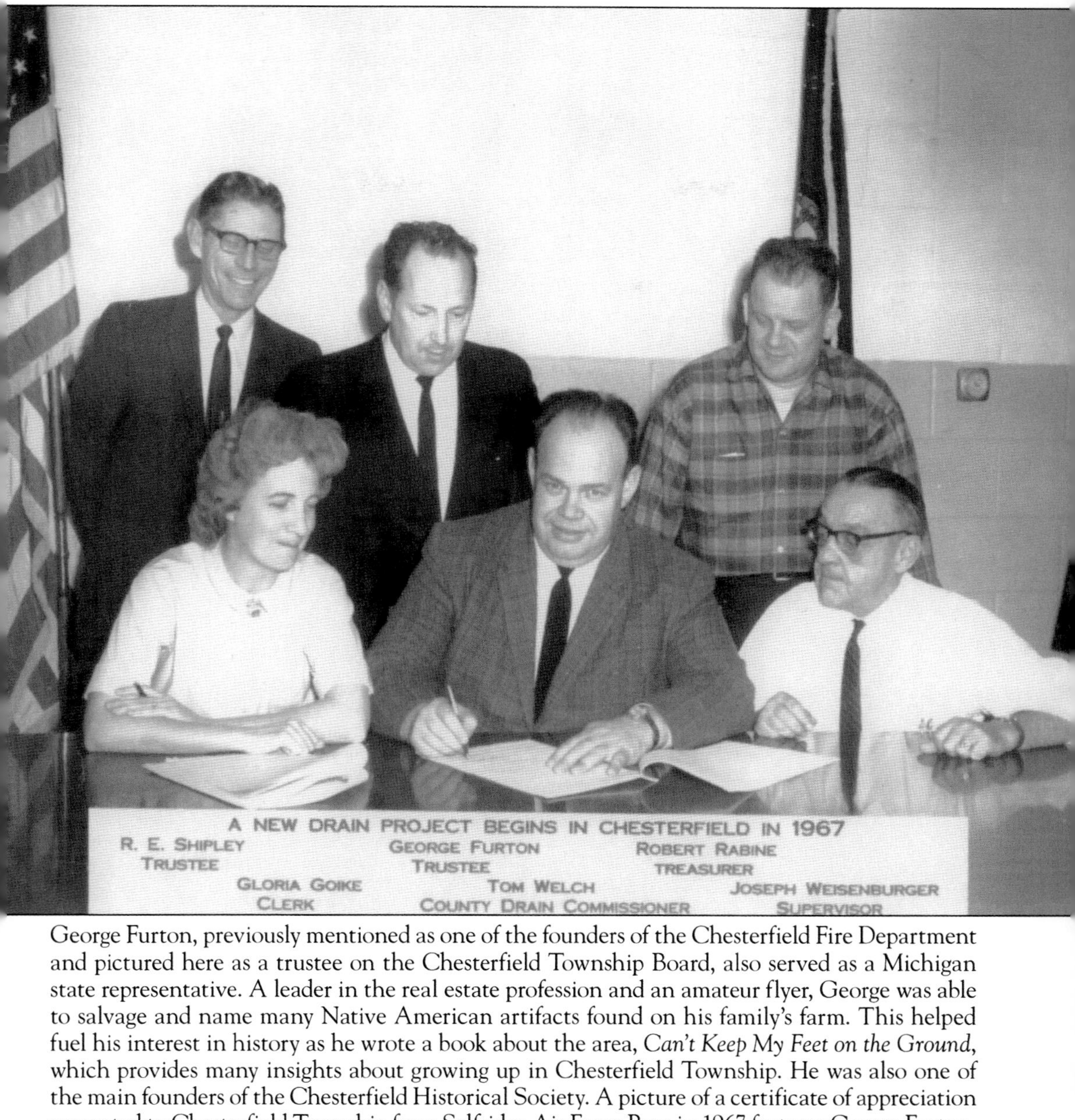

George Furton, previously mentioned as one of the founders of the Chesterfield Fire Department and pictured here as a trustee on the Chesterfield Township Board, also served as a Michigan state representative. A leader in the real estate profession and an amateur flyer, George was able to salvage and name many Native American artifacts found on his family's farm. This helped fuel his interest in history as he wrote a book about the area, *Can't Keep My Feet on the Ground*, which provides many insights about growing up in Chesterfield Township. He was also one of the main founders of the Chesterfield Historical Society. A picture of a certificate of appreciation presented to Chesterfield Township from Selfridge Air Force Base in 1967 features George Furton. (Courtesy of Trinity Archives.)

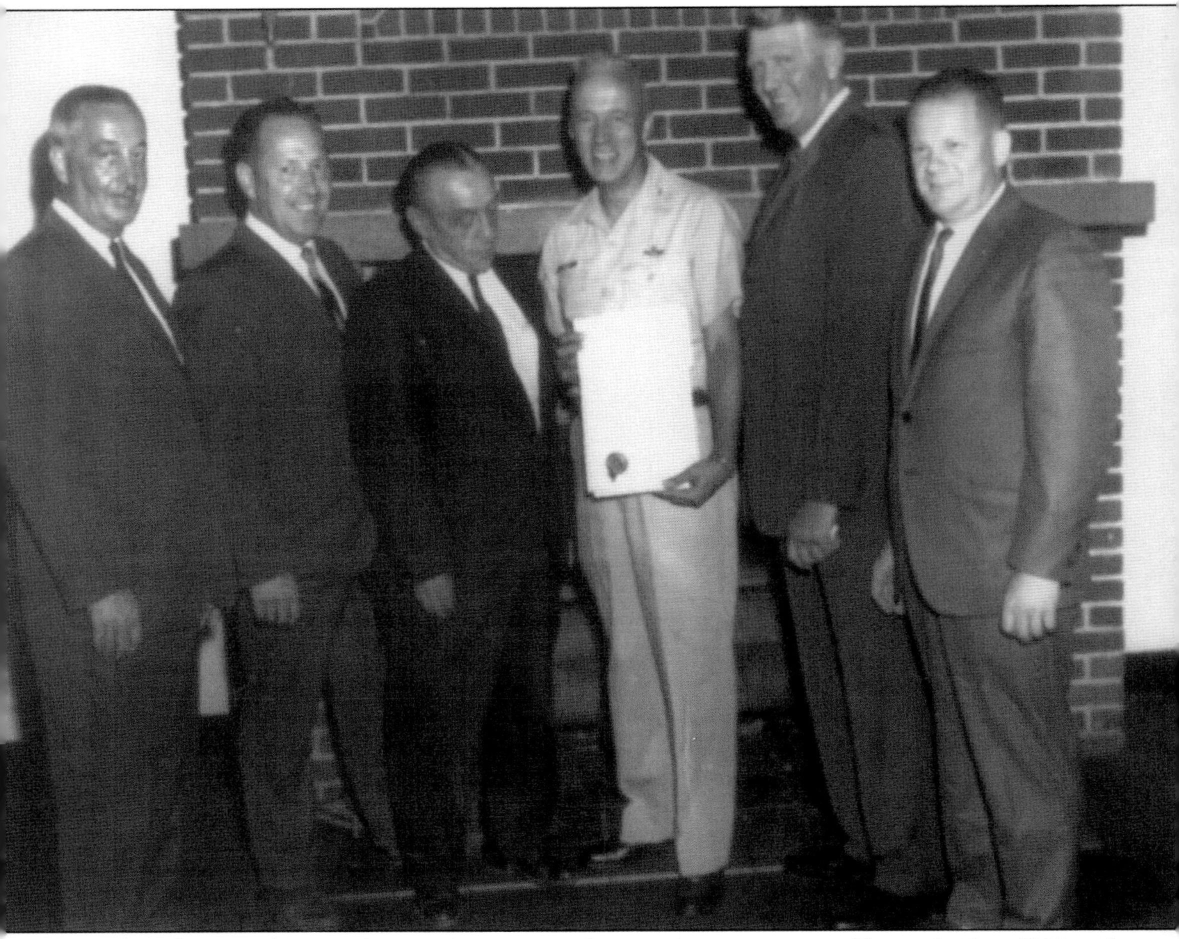

This photograph was taken at the signing of a new drain project in Chesterfield in 1967 with George Furton (second from the left). The past and present supervisors of Chesterfield Township include William J. Hagen (served from 1922–1933); Adolph Veryser (1933–1953), a member of the People's Party; Keith Bovenschen (1953–1958); Carl A. Brandenburg (1958–1967); Joseph Weisenberger (1967–1968); Matthew A. Wagner (1968–1976); Otis Dean Smith (1976–1977); Rodger Knight (1977), who was appointed by the governor for the interim period; James Pollard (1977–1992); Ray Richards (1992–1995); James Pollard (1995–1996); James Tharp (1996–2000); Jim Ellis (2000–2008); and Michael Lovelock (2008–present). (Courtesy of Trinity Archives.)

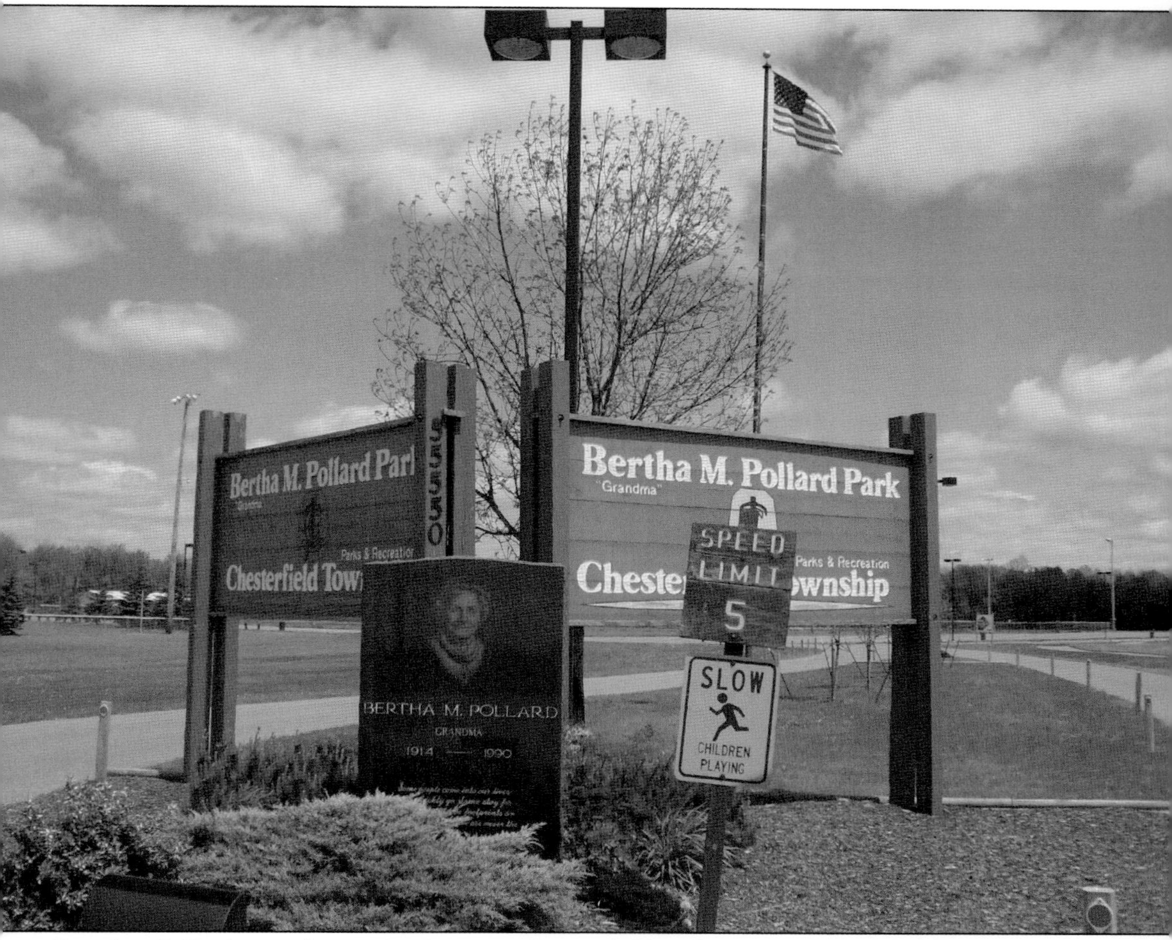

Grandma Pollard was a famous fundraiser in Chesterfield in the 1960s and has a park with sports fields named in her honor. Her son Jim Pollard was the township supervisor from 1977 until 1992 and then again in 1995 and 1996. (Courtesy of Trinity Archives.)

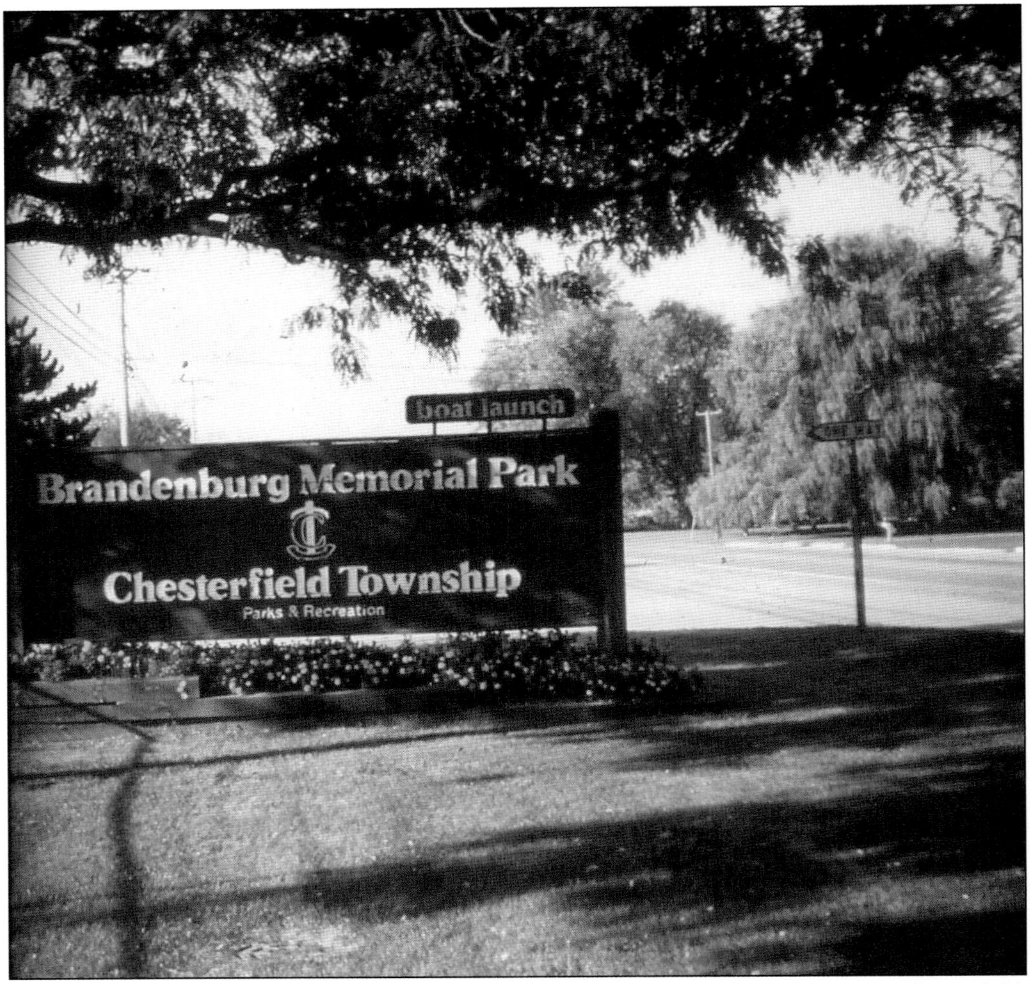

Brandenburg Park, located on a site of one of the early Native American reservations in Chesterfield, boasts boating facilities and was named for Carl Brandenburg, who was township supervisor from 1958 to 1967. (Courtesy of Trinity Archives.)

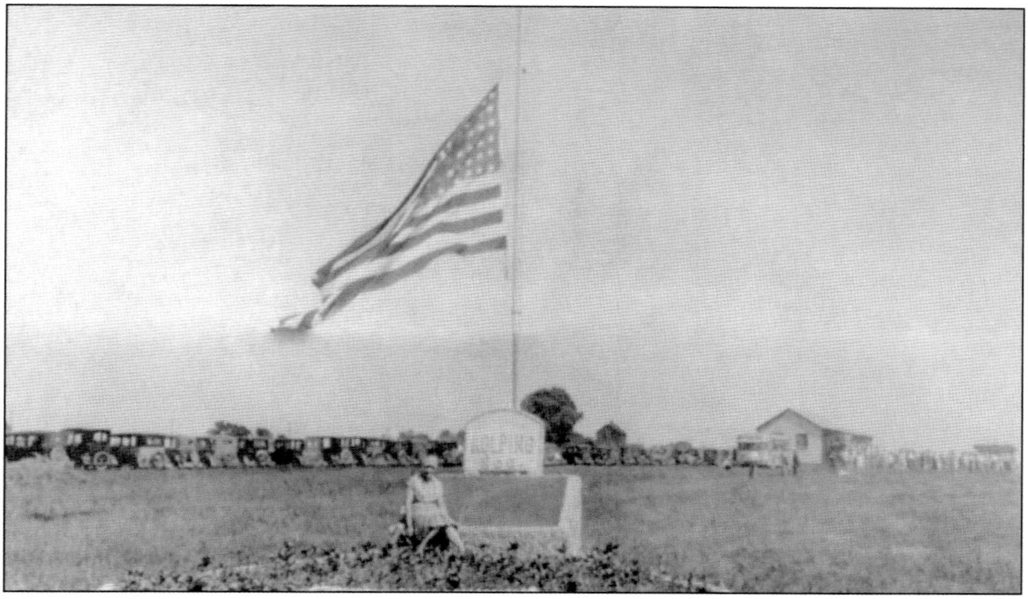

In 1926, the Kolping Society, a German religious group, established a chapter in Detroit, and in 1932 it constructed a chapel in Kolping Park, located on six acres near the Au Vase River on Sugarbush Road. Both images are of the park prior to the building of the chapel.

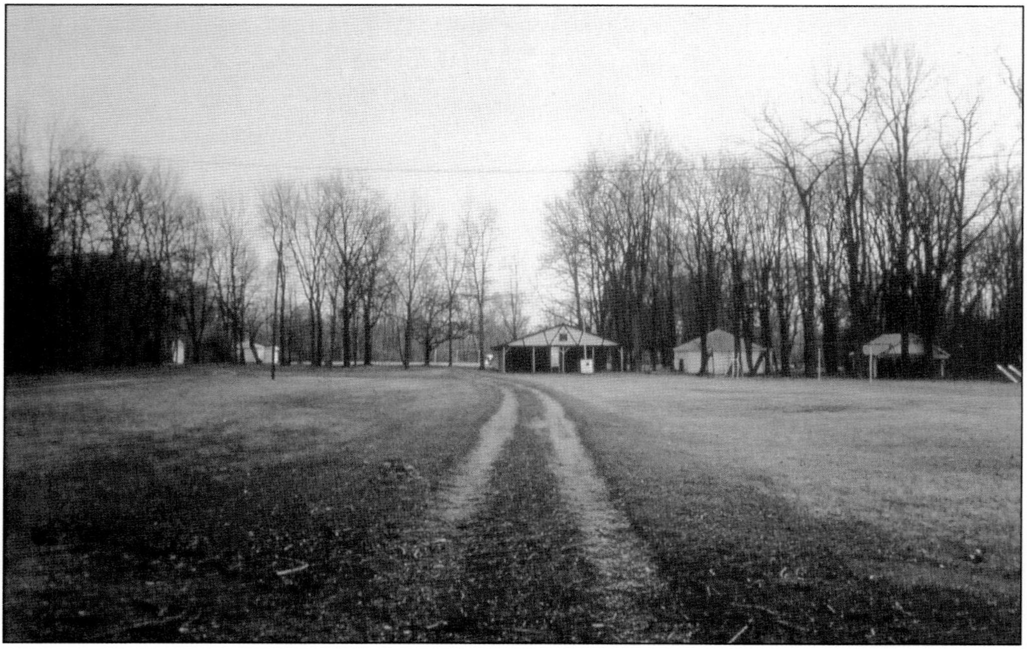

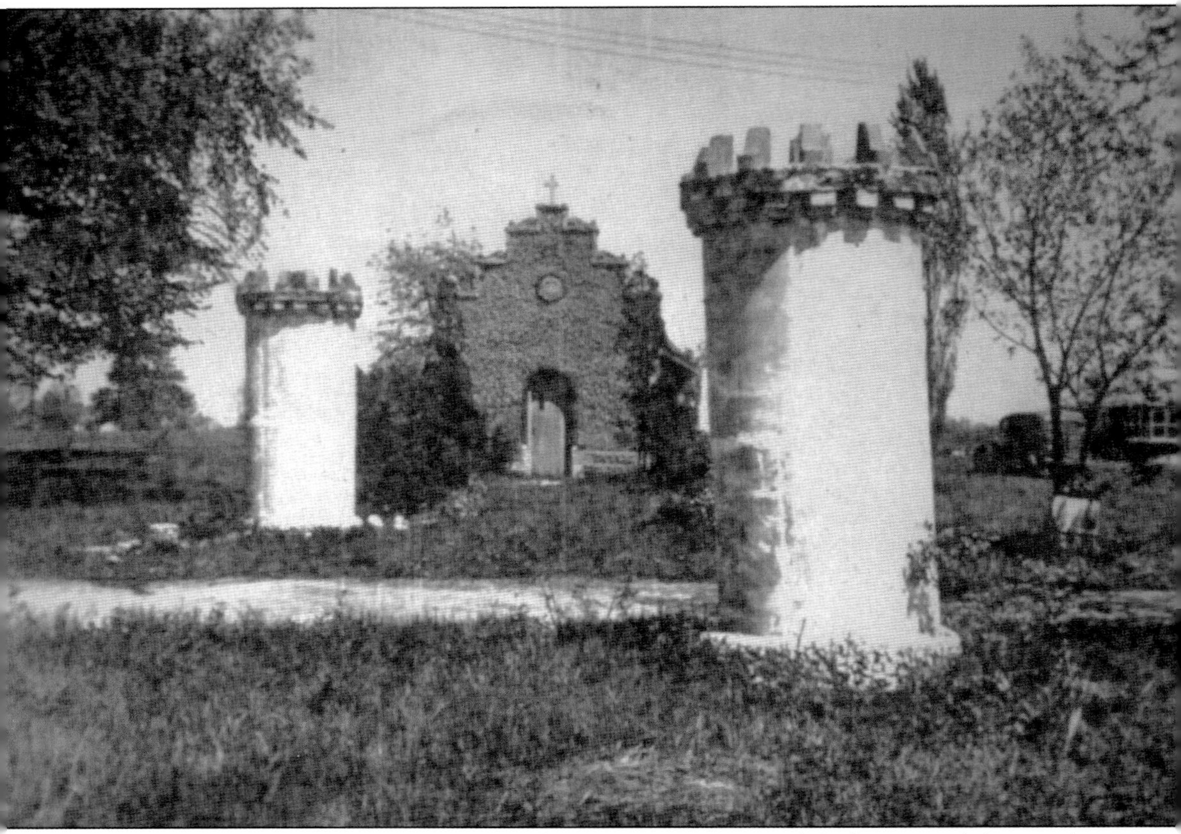

The chapel is constructed of coral, marble, granite, stones, and shells received from Kolping societies, churches, and missions located all over the world. Father Wuest, president of the Detroit Kolping branch, was in charge of the construction and personally placed many of the pieces, including a stone from the Holy Land.

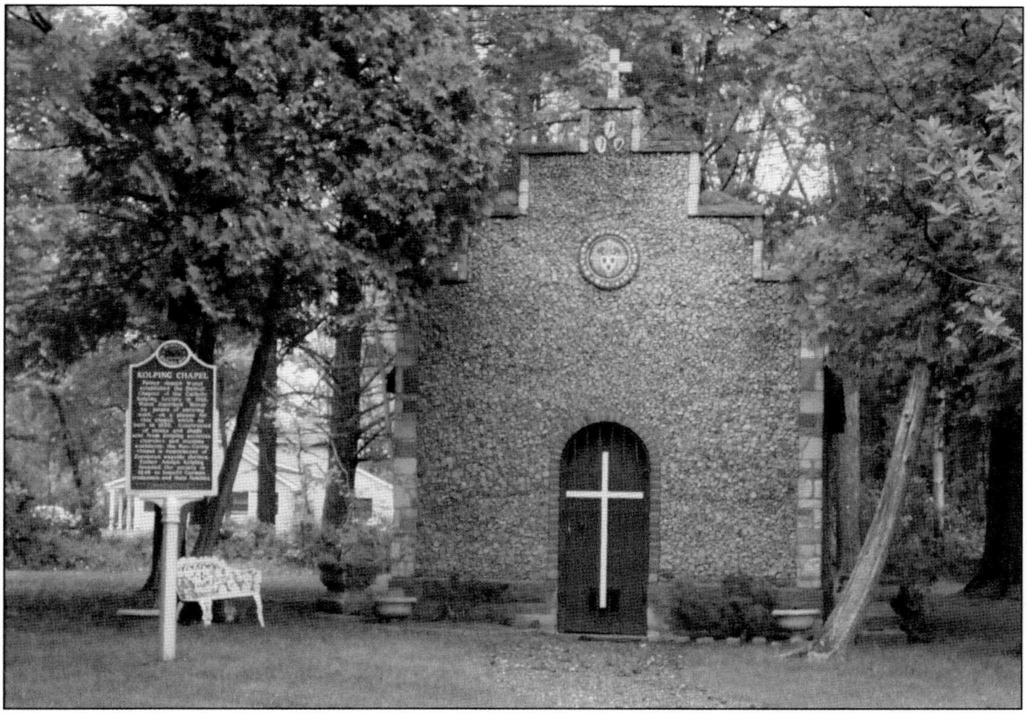

Kolping Park is seen above as it has appeared since the 1980s. On October 24, 1997, a state historical marker was erected on the site, as seen below. It is also listed on the National and State Registers of Historical Places. In addition to the chapel, Kolping Park also offers a pavilion, dance hall, rifle range, picnic shelter, parade grounds, playground, soccer field, and parking lot, all contained within a 19-acre parcel of land. As a privately owned park, it is often rented out for events such as Oktoberfest. (Above, courtesy of the Trinity Archives; below, Bob Mack.)

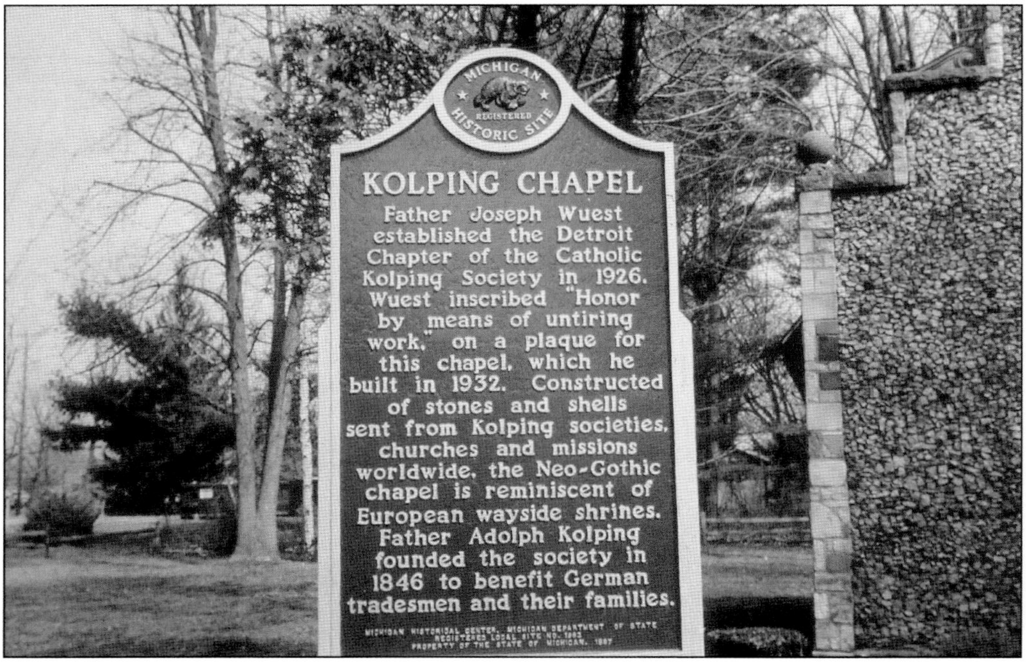

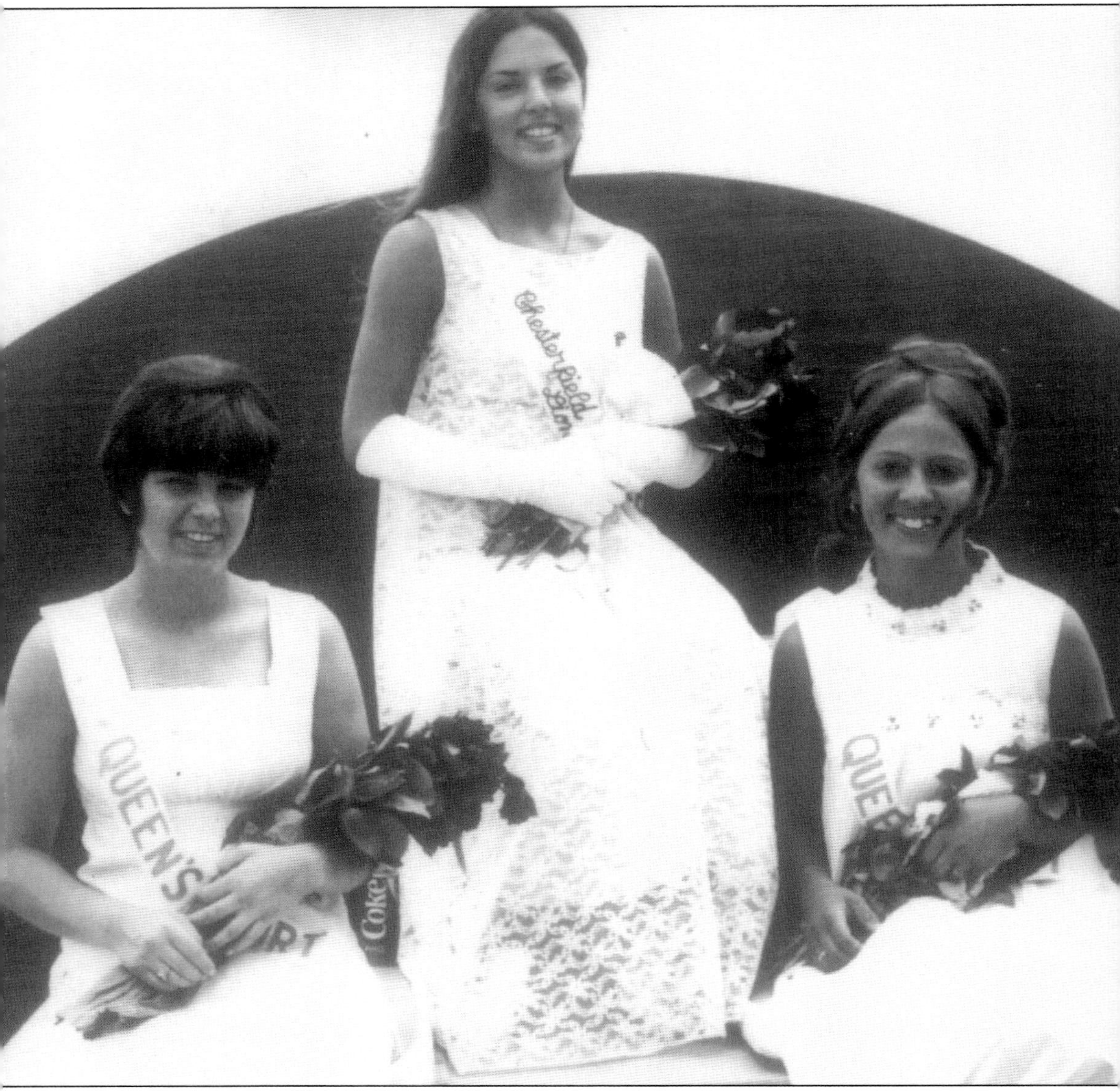

In 1970, Jacalyn Hortos (center) was crowned the first queen of Chesterfield Township by the Chesterfield Lions. Her court included Doris Carpenter (left) and Linda Mae Aiuto (right). Although Chesterfield had no local carnival, the queen and her court would ride in the various parades of surrounding communities like New Baltimore and Richmond. (Courtesy of Mary Hortos.)

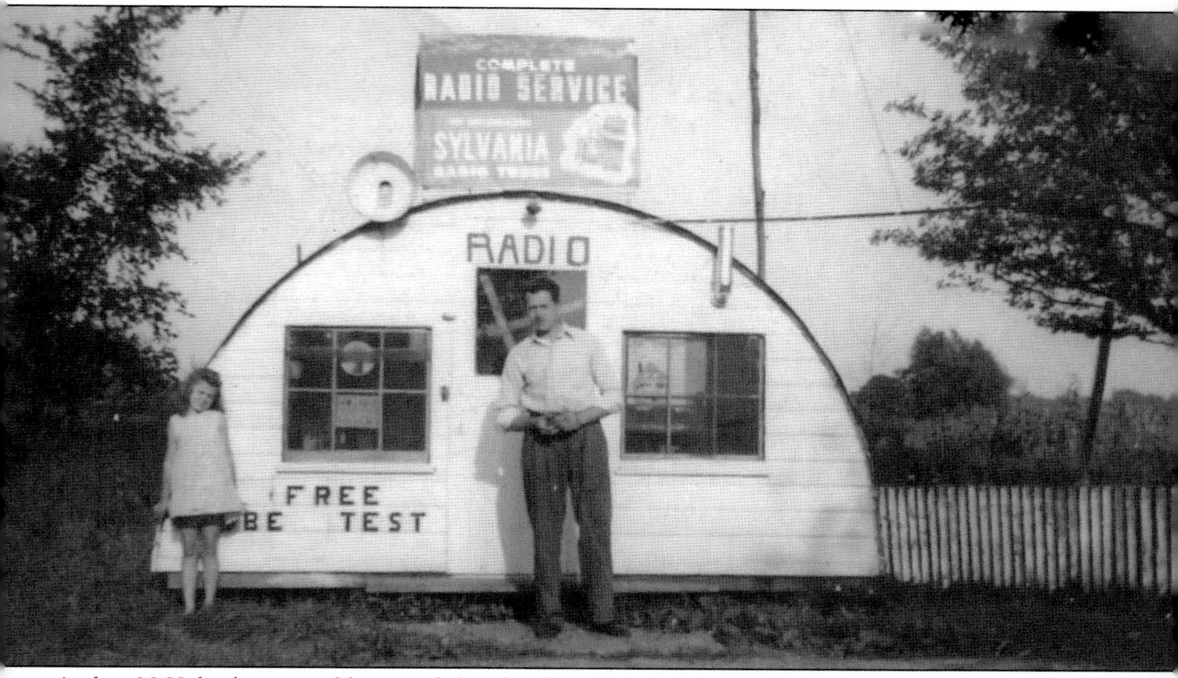

Arthur V. Kaherl, pictured here with his daughter Deanna outside his radio shop on Sass Road near Callens Road, moved to Chesterfield in 1941. He built his house, garage, and business structure and would repair radios, toasters, and any other electrical kitchen appliance. Later on, he expanded his repairs to televisions. Besides having his shop constantly filled with repair jobs, he painted and created renowned miniature scenes. (Courtesy of Deanna Kaherl Wolschon.)

Bibliography

Furton, George. *Can't Keep My Feet on the Ground: Life's Memories.* Chesterfield, MI: Chesterfield Township Historical Society, 1998.

Gonyeau, Richard. "Tales of Yesteryear" series. *Anchor Bay Beacon*, the *Bay Voice* (newspapers), 1980–1996.

Leeson, M.A. *History of Macomb County, Michigan.* Chicago: Leeson, 1882.

Pall, Karl Mark. "Amazing History of Macomb County." Mt. Clemens: Macomb County Historical Commission Local History Spotlight Archive, 2007. www.macombhistory.org.

Romig, Walter. *Michigan Place Names.* Detroit: Wayne State University Press, 1986.

Rynearson, Elton James, Jr., Dr. *The History of the Anchor Bay School System.* 1973.

Skinner, Grace C. and Elmer L. *History Stories of New Baltimore, 1845–1951.* Port Huron, MI: 1961.

Trinity, Bernard. *Many Yesterdays.* Dublin, OH: Trinity Enterprises, 1986.

INDEX